Mastering Evidence

Mastering Evidence

Ronald W. Eades
Louis D. Brandeis School of Law
University of Louisville

Carolina Academic Press
Durham, North Carolina

Library of Congress Cataloging in Publication Data

Eades, Ronald W.
Mastering evidence / by Ronald W. Eades.
    p. cm. -- (Mastering series)
Includes bibliographical references and index.
ISBN-13: 978-1-59460-261-0 (alk. paper)
ISBN-10: 1-59460-261-1 (alk. paper)
1. Evidence (Law)--United States. I. Title. II. Series.

KF8935.E15 2008
347.73'6--dc22   2007043830

Carolina Academic Press
700 Kent Street
Durham, NC 27701
Telephone (919) 489-7486
Fax (919) 493-5668
www.cap-press.com

Printed in the United States of America

Contents

Series Editor's Foreword

The Carolina Academic Press Mastering Series is designed to provide you with a tool that will enable you to easily and efficiently "master" the substance and content of law school courses. Throughout the series, the focus is on quality writing that makes legal concepts understandable. As a result, the series is designed to be easy to read and is not unduly cluttered with footnotes or cites to secondary sources.

In order to facilitate student mastery of topics, the Mastering Series includes a number of pedagogical features designed to improve learning and retention. At the beginning of each chapter, you will find a "Roadmap" that tells you about the chapter and provides you with a sense of the material that you will cover. A "Checkpoint" at the end of each chapter encourages you to stop and review the key concepts, reiterating what you have learned. Throughout the book, key terms are explained and emphasized. Finally, a "Master Checklist" at the end of each book reinforces what you have learned and helps you identify any areas that need review or further study.

We hope that you will enjoying studying with, and learning from, the Mastering Series.

Russell L. Weaver
Professor of Law & Distinguished University Scholar
University of Louisville, Louis D. Brandeis School of Law

Preface

This book is intended to be a companion work to a basic course in evidence. Students will ordinarily be assigned a case book or problem book and a copy of the Federal Rules of Evidence as required texts for a course. This work should provide a nice supplemental reading to help the student understand those other class materials.

Since it is assumed that most students will have a copy of the Federal Rules of Evidence, this book encourages those students to keep that copy of the Federal Rules close at hand while studying. Nothing can surpass the importance of a close reading and re-reading of those Federal Rules. When a student is reading and studying this work, a copy of the Federal Rules of Evidence should be open. This book will cite and discuss the Federal Rules of Evidence. It will not attempt, however, to give the full text of the rules. The student needs to review the full text when reading each section. This work will, however, cite to the correct rule in order to make it easy for the student to find the appropriate rule.

With all of the mention of the Federal Rules of Evidence, a student may wonder about state rules of evidence. This book will comment on the state rules of evidence when appropriate. It will, however, primarily be a book about the Federal Rules of Evidence. Since there are 50 state jurisdictions applying state rules of evidence, making general states about those principles is difficult. In addition, most faculty members teach evidence as a Federal Rules of Evidence course. Finally, the Federal Rules of Evidence are the primary source for bar examinations questions nationwide. For all of those reasons, this work will be concerned with the Federal Rules of Evidence. State rules of evidence will be noted, however, where they offer interesting alternative methods of dealing with problems.

Ronald W. Eades
Professor of Law
Louis D. Brandeis School of Law
University of Louisville
Louisville, Kentucky

Mastering Evidence

Chapter 1

Roles of the Court, Judge, Jury, and Attorneys in Light of Rules of Evidence

---

Roles Roadmap

- Learn the specific stages of a trial.
- When are the federal rules of evidence applicable?
- The methods of making and meeting objections are specified in the Federal Rules of Evidence.

A. Introduction

The rules of evidence had a long history as a traditional common law topic. The intricate rules concerning the admissibility of evidence were developed by court decisions. Although the codification movement in the United States began in the 1800's, it would not be until the 1900's that a major, codified version of the rules of evidence would exist. In the 1970's the Uniform Rules of Evidence and, more importantly, the Federal Rules of Evidence appeared. The adoption of the Federal Rules of Evidence in 1975 changed the nature of the subject.

The study and use of evidence principles no longer start with the case. It is now necessary to start with the rule and analyze the problem from the language of that rule. All cases in Federal Court are, of course, governed by the Federal Rules of Evidence. Many states have also adopted rules of evidence that are patterned after the Federal Rules of Evidence. For a student beginning a study of evidence, the place to focus the work is on the Federal Rules.

This book will provide a discussion of the Federal Rules of Evidence. There will be some discussion of traditional common law rules, but those will be in the nature of illustration only. They will be offered only where it is felt to be helpful to understand the current modern trend. Since the book will focus on the Federal Rules of Evidence, it is assumed that the student will have a copy of the Federal Rules of Evidence close at hand. Since most publishers offer some available source for the rules, the rules will not be provided in their entirety in this work. The book will make reference to the applicable rules throughout. The appropriate Federal Rule will be noted with the title of sections of this book where they will be discussed. In addition, particular language of some rules will be quoted in the text. It is suggested that students using this book should keep their copy of the rule book open for easy reference while studying.

B. Stages of the Trial

Throughout the rules of evidence, is may be possible to offer testimony at some stage, but not others. Some of the rules themselves, for example, state that the accused in a criminal case may introduce some particular types of evidence and the prosecution can rebut that evidence. In order to understand how those rules operate, it is necessary to understand the stages of the trial. Although each jurisdiction and some local courts have their own procedures for conducting the trial, the typical patterns for a trial may be outlined and explained. The methods and practices for the organization of a trial are not found in the Federal Rules of Evidence. These techniques are matters of local custom and practice. There are minor differences between civil and criminal cases, but the basic order of presentation for a trial is as follows:

1. Impaneling the Jury

The rules of evidence are usually pictured as having the most importance in jury trials. Most non-lawyers have heard of Grand Juries and jury trials, but may not have a good idea of the difference. Grand Juries are those bodies that are formed to investigate activities and return indictments in criminal matters. They are called "Grand" only because of their size. Grand Juries are usually composed of around 21 members or more. The jury in a jury trial is called a Petite Jury. It is smaller. Criminal cases traditionally had 12 members of the jury but now may have 6. Civil cases may have 6 to 12. In either type of case, the court will usually require the selection of alternate jurors in case someone on the jury must be excused during the course of the trial.

In a jury trial, the court will supply a group of people from which the jury is chosen. This group of people is frequently referred to as the jury pool. Before selecting the members of that jury from the broader jury pool, the attorneys in the case are allowed to ask questions of the prospective jurors. This stage of the trial is called *voir dire*. The *voir dire* allows the attorneys to determine whether prospective jurors may have conflicts of interest, predetermined views or other reasons they should not serve. After being given the opportunity to ask these questions, the attorneys are allowed to challenge jurors. Challenges to jurors come in two types. An attorney may challenge a juror for "cause." This type of challenge would be based on some clear problem with bias, conflict or interest the juror would have in the outcome of the case. When the attorney informs the trial judge that the party wishes to challenge a particular juror for cause, the trial judge will rule on that challenge. Attorneys may have an unlimited number of challenges for cause. As a practical matter, however, it is difficult to convince the trial judge to dismiss a juror for cause. In addition to challenges for cause, attorney's have "peremptory" challenges. In every case the attorney's will have a set number of peremptory challenges that they may use to exclude jurors from the trial. There does not need to be any reason stated for excluding such jurors while using these challenges. Once the attorneys have completed their *voir dire* and their challenges, the remaining jurors become the jury panel for the case.

2. Opening Statements

After the jury is selected and receives initial comments from the judge, the attorneys give their opening statements. Traditionally the plaintiff (in a civil case) or prosecutor (in a criminal case) goes first and the defense attorney goes second. It is routinely said that the statements made by the attorney's during opening statements are not evidence and are not intended to argue the case. It is expected that the attorneys will explain or outline what they hope to prove during the course of the trial. Frequently the attorneys will give their theory of the case and explain what witnesses will be called.

It is interesting to note that the plaintiff (civil case) and prosecutor (criminal case) get to go first. In most cases the plaintiff or prosecutor has the burden of proof. Burden of proof is discussed later in this text, but can be summarized fairly simply. The plaintiff or prosecutor must convince the jury that their side of the case is correct. In some ways, it may be stated that the plaintiff or prosecutor has the burden to change the *status quo*. The defendant in a civil or criminal case would like for things to stay just as they are. The plaintiff or prosecutor is seeking to force the change. Since the plaintiff and prosecutor have that heavy burden, the procedure of the case is to let them go first and last. It is said that the party with the burden of proof is allowed to open and close.

3. Plaintiff's (Civil Case) or Prosecution's (Criminal Case) Case in Chief

The "case in chief" is the primary portion of the trial. This is the period in which the parties to the litigation get to put on the evidence that the jury will hear and consider. As the period in which the parties are introducing all of their evidence, it is also the stage where the rules of evidence are most important. Again, whether it is a civil case or criminal case, the party with the burden of proof goes first.

Ordinarily at this stage of the trial the trial judge will ask the plaintiff or prosecutor if they are ready to proceed. The attorney will then "call their first witness." The witness will proceed to the chair made available for witness and, thus, "take the stand." Before testifying, the witness will be asked to take an oath.

Once that preliminary matter is completed, the plaintiff or prosecuting attorney who called the witness to the stand will ask that witness questions. This stage of the witness's testimony is called direct examination. The attorney will seek to draw out all of the evidence that the witness has been called to give.

After the plaintiff or prosecutor is finished with the direct examination, the opposing counsel, defendant, will be allowed to ask questions. This is where that party is allowed to cross examine the witness. This period of cross examination is used to seek to impeach the witness and make him or her appear less credible to the jury.

After cross examination is completed, this first witness may not be finished. The attorney who called the witness, the plaintiff or prosecutor, may feel that certain things were raised on cross examination that need to be explored further. If so, the plaintiff or prosecutor may ask additional questions during a period that is called re-direct examination. It is important to note that the courts assume that the only questions that will be asked at this point are about matters raised on cross examination.

After the re-direct, the witness may still not be finished. If the opposing counsel, defendant, believes that matters were raised on re-direct that need additional coverage, the defense counsel may ask additional questions. These questions are considered to be re-cross examination and are intended to cover only those matters raised on re-direct.

It is possible that the plaintiff or prosecuting attorney could claim that additional matters were raised on re-cross examination and demand the right to again ask more re-direct. If so, the defense attorney would probably seek to ask even more re-cross examination. It is unlikely, however, that this will happen or that the court would allow it. The typical case has the witness being questioned on direct, cross, re-direct and re-cross. The witness is then excused from the trial.

It is at this point that the plaintiff or prosecutor will call his or her second witness. The process described above for the first witness will be repeated with this second witness. In fact, the process will be repeated for each witness that the plaintiff or prosecutor wishes to call. After the plaintiff or prosecutor finishes calling all of his or her witnesses the plaintiff's or prosecutor's case in chief is over. Traditionally the plaintiff or prosecutor would announce to the court that they "rest." It is then time for the defendant's case in chief.

4. Defendant's Case in Chief

This portion of the trial is almost identical to the other party's case in chief. This is the time that the defendant has for putting on all of the evidence for his or her case. The process will run just as it did for the plaintiff or prosecutor.

The defense attorney will call his or her first witness. After that witness has taken the oath, the defense attorney will begin to ask questions. This asking of questions by the defense attorney of their own witness is the direct examination of this witness. After the defense attorney has finished asking questions on direct, the plaintiff's attorney or prosecutor can ask this witness questions on cross examination. Again, just as during the plaintiff's or prosecutor's case in chief, this is the time for this party to try to attack the credibility of the witness. When the cross examination is completed, the defense attorney may ask questions on re-direct to cover items that were raised on cross examination. When re-direct is concluded, the opposing attorney has the opportunity for re-cross examination for items raised on re-direct.

When the attorneys have completed questioning that first witness, the defense attorney will then call his or her second witness and the question process will proceed in the same manner. The defense attorney will continue to call witnesses until he or she has concluded call all of the witnesses in defense of the case. At this point, the defense attorney may announce that the defense "rests."

At this stage of the trial, the major portion of the evidence has been introduced and the trial is just about completed. There are, however, several more steps that will occur.

5. Rebuttal

Although most of the evidence has been introduced by this stage of the trial, a few more witnesses may be called. If the plaintiff's attorney or prosecutor feels that matters were raised during the Defendant's case in chief that were not adequately covered during the plaintiff's or prosecutor's case in chief, then the plaintiff or prosecutor may call another witness. This witness is a "rebuttal" witness. The witness would be questioned on direct and cross examination in the same manner as in the cases in chief.

It is important to note that this stage of the trial is only to respond to evidence raised during the defendant's case in chief. A good example of the use of such a witness could occur in a simple tort, negligence case. During the plaintiff's case in chief, the plaintiff's attorney will try to prove that the defendant was negligent. During the defendant's case in chief, the defense attorney will offer evidence showing that the defendant was not negligent. In addition, the defense attorney might offer evidence tending to show that the plaintiff was also negligent in an attempt to prove comparative fault. Since comparative fault is a defense that the defendant must plead and prove, then it is appropriate that it be raised for the first time in the defendant's case in chief. After the defendant finished the defense case in chief, the plaintiff might want to call several witnesses in rebuttal to disprove the facts concerning comparative fault. The plaintiff, however, should not be allowed to offer more evidence on the issue of the defendant's fault. That evidence should have been introduced during the plaintiff's case in chief.

6. Sur-rebuttal

Since the plaintiff or prosecutor has the opportunity to call a rebuttal witness, the defendant may feel it necessary to call additional witnesses to respond to the evidence offered during rebuttal. If the court allows the defendant this opportunity, the witness is testifying in "sur-rebuttal." The direct and cross examination would be conducted in the same manner as other witnesses.

It should be kept in mind that rebuttal and sur-rebuttal witnesses are not the usual practice. Most of the evidence is introduced in the parties' cases in chief. Trial court judges will seek to limit the calling of additional witnesses after the close of those cases in chief.

7. Closing Statements

After all of the witnesses have had an opportunity to testify, it is time to turn the case over to the jury for decision. This process has a couple of steps. This outline notes that the closing statements are given before the instructions to the jury. That particular order is subject to local court rules. Many jurisdictions do have closing statements before the jury instructions are given by the trial judge. Others, however, have the trial judge give the instructions before the closing statements. Attorneys typically prefer to give the closing statements after the instructions. That allows the attorneys to fashion some of their remarks based upon the instructions.

Once it is time for the closing statements, the trial court will tell the attorneys how much time they have to "argue" the case. In most jurisdictions the plaintiff or prosecutor will go first with the closing argument, but have the option to reserve some time to make some concluding remarks after the defendant's closing statement. Recall the earlier discussion about the policy of allowing the party with the burden of proof to open and close. Since the plaintiff or prosecutor will typically have the ultimate burden of proof in the case, that party is allowed to begin the trial and have the last word.

Closing statements, just like opening statements, are not to be considered evidence in the case. These statements are arguments by the attorneys as to whether the facts and elements of claims and defenses have been proven. Closing statements are frequently discussed in courses on trial practice and tactics, but have no real guidelines in the rules of evidence.

8. Instructions to the Jury

Before the jury is allowed to decide the case, the court must instruct the jury on the law. This occurs during the jury instruction period. The trial judge is not expected to prepare all of the jury instructions alone. The attorneys in the case may be preparing proposed jury instructions throughout the trial and will submit them at the time specified by the court. The trial judge will then consider all of the proposed jury instructions, select those that are appropriate and correct, possibly add some additional ones of his or her own, and then read them to the jury. Most jurisdictions will also allow the trial judge to give a written copy of the jury instructions to the jury in order to allow the jury to take that copy to the jury deliberation room.

Typically, before the jury is taken back to the jury deliberation room, they will be told that they should select a foreman of the jury as their first act once they begin the deliberations. They will also be given a copy of the instructions. This copy will also contain a form that is to record the jury verdict in the case.

9. Jury Deliberations

Deliberations in the jury room are, to a large extent, secret. Individual jurors do not have to reveal what occurred. Attorneys may frequently ask jurors in major cases in order to determine what was persuasive and what hurt the case.

If the jury follows the court's instruction, the first task will be to select a foreman. The role of the foreman is to act as chair of the meeting and to fill out the jury verdict form. The jury may conduct its discussion and voting in any manner deemed appropriate by the jurors. When the jury has reached a verdict, they notify the court that they are ready.

Once a verdict has been reached, the jury returns to the court room and announces that verdict in open court. Announcing the verdict is usually done by the jury foreman. In most jurisdictions, attorneys are allowed to "poll" the jurors. This is a process where the trial judge asks each juror if the verdict that was announced was also his or her individual verdict.

10. Motions

Motions are noted here but may, in fact, occur at any time during the course of the trial. Frequently, for example, attorneys will make before trial motions, called motions *in limine,* in order to seek evidentiary rulings before the trial starts. These may be, for example, motions to suppress certain types of evidence.

In addition, throughout the trial, defense attorneys may make motions to dismiss the case. They frequently make such motions at the close of the plaintiff's or prosecutor's case in chief, at the close of all of the evidence and at the time the jury is sent out to deliberate. The losing party to the case may also make motions for a judgment notwithstanding the verdict after the jury returns.

Motions may also occur during the presentation of evidence. Attorneys may make motions to strike evidence that has been admitted.

11. Entry of Judgment on Jury Verdict

Once the jury has returned a verdict, the judge must enter a judgment on that jury verdict. This will usually not occur immediately. As noted above, attorneys in the case may want to make several motions concerning the outcome of the case. Local or jurisdictional rules of procedure will ordinarily specify when and how the judgment is to be entered.

12. Appeals

Appeals to judgments are not covered in the rules of evidence. That process is part of the rules of civil procedure. The parties to the case will have to decide whether sufficient error has occurred during the trial in order to have some hope for success on appeal. An important practical matter should be noted here. Errors made by the trial court on matters of evidence rarely provide sufficient basis for reversal on appeal. The rules of evidence suggest that only "substantial error" can provide a basis to set aside a jury verdict. Appellate courts rarely find that. Trial attorneys tend to recognize that evidence issues need to be won or lost at the trial level. Getting them corrected with an appeal is difficult.

13. Summary of Trial

In order to provide a quick outline of the stages of the trial, the following is a list of those stages by name only. It may be useful to mark this page of the text in order to make quick reference during the course. As the discussion of the rules of evidence suggests that certain items may be entered at particular times, this outline may prove helpful.

A. Impaneling the Jury
  1. *voir dire*
  2. Challenges
B. Opening Statements
  1. Plaintiff or Prosecutor
  2. Defendant
C. Plaintiff's (Civil Case) or Prosecution's (Criminal Case) Case in Chief—each witness will be subject to:
  1. Direct examination
  2. Cross examination
  3. Re-direct
  4. Re-cross
D. Defendant's Case in Chief—each witness will be subject to:
  1. Direct examination
  2. Cross examination
  3. Re-direct
  4. Re-cross
E. Rebuttal—each witness will be subject to:
  1. Direct examination
  2. Cross examination
  3. Re-direct
  4. Re-cross
F. Sur-rebuttal—each witness will be subject to:

      1. Direct examination

      2. Cross examination

      3. Re-direct

      4. Re-cross

  G. Closing Statements

      1. Plaintiff or Prosecutor

      2. Defendant

      3. Plaintiff or Prosecutor if time reserved

  H. Instructions to the Jury

  I. Jury Deliberations

  J. Motions

  K. Entry of judgment on jury verdict

  L. Appeals

C. Purpose and Application of the Rules of Evidence (Fed. Rules 101, 102)

1. Federal Courts (Fed. Rules 1101)

Prior to 1975, the rules of evidence in federal court were the result of the common law process. Appellate courts would create, reform, change and develop the rules of evidence over time and as cases with evidence issues arose before them. The original bases to these rules traced a history back to common law rules developed in England. There had been pressure, dating back to the codification movement in the United States in the 1800s, to create a codified set of rules of evidence. The federal courts did not adopt such a set of codified rules until 1975.

The Federal Rules of Evidence clearly state the purpose of the rules in one of the early sections. "These rules shall be construed to secure fairness in administration, elimination of unjustifiable delay, and promotion of growth and development of the law of evidence to the end that the truth may be ascertained and proceedings justly determined." Fed. R. Evid. 102.

The more difficult early issues for students of evidence are: When are the Federal Rules of Evidence to be used and when are state rules of evidence to be used? The Federal Rules of Evidence have two sections which help answer that question. First, the rules state that the rules are to be used in "courts in the United States." Fed. R. Evid. 101. This, of course, suggests that the rules are applicable in all federal courts. The rules, however, add more detail in Rule 1101. That rule indicates that the rules are applicable in almost all cases appearing in federal court. There are some specific exclusions that include such things as grand juries, sentencing, granting probation and extradition. As should be obvious by that list, the exclusions are few in number and do not include the usual trial in Federal District Court. If a student has a specific type of proceeding that they wish to consider, a close reading of Rule 1101 will reveal whether it is excluded from operation of the Federal Rules of Evidence.

A question that many students will have is whether the Federal Rules of Evidence apply in cases in Federal District Court when the case is in that court on diversity jurisdiction. The federal courts have a long history of seeking to determine when to apply federal law and when to apply state law in cases. The rich tradition of this issue is found, of course, in *Swift v. Tyson,* and *Erie R.R. v. Thompkins.* The specific details of those cases are beyond the scope of this work, and more properly belong in a course and text on Civil Procedure or Federal Jurisdiction. A brief discussion of those issues, however, is necessary.

When cases are in federal court on federal question jurisdiction, there is no issue of what law applies. Those are federal cases, in federal court and federal law applies. When, however, cases are in federal court on diversity jurisdictions, the issue is harder. Those are cases that could have been brought in state court and state law would have applied. To be consistent with the concept of federalism and to avoid forum shopping by parties, the federal law has adopted a simple principle. When in federal court on diversity jurisdiction, the appropriate state law will apply.

The difficulty with applying state law, however, is the idea that the *appropriate* state law will apply. This has routinely meant that *substantive* state law will apply. When cases are in federal court, even when they are there by diversity jurisdiction, and the substantive state law will control the decision, the procedural law of the federal courts is used. Students will recall that in courses on Civil Procedure, the Federal Rules of Civil Procedure apply to all cases in federal court even when the case is there on diversity jurisdiction.

The Federal Rules of Evidence operate in the same manner as the Federal Rules of Civil Procedure. The Federal Rules of Evidence apply to all cases in federal court regardless of the basis of jurisdiction.

There is a small difficulty with that analysis. When the Federal Rules of Evidence were being debated, there was a concern that some of the rules of evidence were more substantive than procedural. Such critics felt that those types of issues should be governed by state law when a case was in federal court due to diversity jurisdictions. The Federal Rules of Evidence handle those issues by operation of the rules themselves. There are three places in the Federal Rules of Evidence that the rules specify that the court is to use state law of evidence. Where a case is in federal court and state law will supply the substantive rule of decision in the case, the federal court is to use state law dealing with Burdens of Proof (Fed. R. Evid. 302); Privileges (Fed. R. Evid. 501); and Competency of Witnesses (Fed. R. Evid. 601). Those specific issues will be discussed more fully in the chapters that follow and deal with those sections. It is sufficient right now to note that the Federal Rules of Evidence are always used in federal court cases regardless of the basis of jurisdiction. If a state rule of evidence is to apply, the appropriate Federal Rule of Evidence will so direct.

2. State Courts

The rules of evidence in state courts are, of course, determined by state law. Since there are 50 different state court jurisdictions, it is not always possible to make general statements regarding the nature of evidence law in the states. Here, and throughout this book, attempts will be made to make such general statements about the state law of evidence where it is appropriate.

The federal courts used a system of common law developed rules of evidence for almost 200 years before adopting a codified set of evidence rules. Some states still use a system of common law developed rules. Others states, many as a result of the leadership shown by the federal courts, have adopted codified sets of evidence rules. Care, however, must be used in making assumptions about state rules of evidence.

States that use common law developed rules, may or may not being referring to the Federal Rules of Evidence as a persuasive statement of the most modern thinking on evidence. Those states may be applying rules that are very similar to the Federal Rules. Some states that have adopted codified sets of rules may have fashioned them in a manner that look identical to the Federal Rules. The state of Kentucky, for example, has a set of state rules that bear a close resemblance to the Federal Rules of Evidence. Even though a state may use the Federal Rules of Evidence as a guide, there may be important distinctions and differences. It will require a close reading of the state rule and a comparison with the Federal Rule of Evidence to determine whether it is the same or different. Finally, some states have adopted codified sets of rules that, on first glance, do not appear to be anything like the Federal Rules of Evidence. The state of California, for example, has such a set of evidence rules. A close reading of the California Evidence Code, however, reveals that some of the rules are very similar to the Federal Rules of Evidence.

In short, there is probably only one thing that can be said when comparing state rules of Evidence to the Federal Rules of Evidence. If the nature of a state rule is important, great care should be exercised in reading the law from that state to determine the nature of that rule. It is important to note, however, that the Federal Rules of Evidence are having a great persuasive impact on the rules of evidence in the 50 states. Many appellate judges and attorneys appearing before them find it useful to cite to the Federal Rules of Evidence and cases interpreting those rules as the most modern thinking on evidence law. The Federal Rules of Evidence will probably continue to be a powerful force in controlling the rules of evidence across the nation.

3. Application in Bench Trials and Administrative Hearings

Although neither the Federal Rules of Evidence nor most state rules make a specific mention of bench trials and administrative hearings, some interesting trends have developed in those areas. The strict reading and application of the rules of evidence have usually been limited to cases tried before juries. The assumption has been that lay jurors are most subject to bias and prejudice and need to be protected from inappropriate evidence. The appellate courts have been inclined to feel that trial judges sitting without a jury or administrative law judges can hear all types of otherwise inadmissible evidence and still reach a just result. It has routinely been stated, for example, that the strict rules of evidence do not apply in administrative hearings. The actual practice and the future of the law of evidence may not be as simple as that traditional statement would imply.

A "bench trial" is when a trial judge is conducting the trial without a jury. The judge will act as finder of both law and fact. Appellate courts will usually not reverse a trial judge that admits evidence that could have been excluded. The appellate court will reason that the judge knew what types of evidence to rely on when making a final decision. If, however, that trial judge excludes evidence that should have been admitted, the appellate court may feel compelled to reverse the decision. The appellate court will be confronted with the fact that the trial judge did not consider evidence that should have been considered. With this obvious difference of treatment, trial judges use a practical approach to the problem. Many trial judges when sitting on a bench trial will allow all evidence to be admitted. That same judge will then be very careful in writing a final opinion to only state reliance on the most obviously admissible evidence. That practice will make reversal impossible.

When an administrative law judge is hearing a matter, the "ALJ" will ordinarily assume that the rules of evidence do not apply. There are sufficient cases that state that principle that it appears to be well decided.

There are changes occurring in this area. First, many state administrative procedure acts are starting to require the application of some rules of evidence to administrative hearings. In addition, even while stating the old rule that "rules of evidence do not apply to administrative hearings," some appellate courts are starting to require the application of some basic rules of evidence to such hearings. In short, administrative procedure is in a period of transition. Old cases still say that the rules of evidence do not apply. At the same time, some specific statutes and appellate decisions are applying some rules. The future will probably require practitioners in the administrative arenas to be more conscious of the rules of evidence.

D. Making and Meeting Objections (Fed. Rules 103, 104)

1. General Issues on Objections

Even most non-lawyers are familiar with the idea of standing up in the courtroom and saying, "Objection, your honor." Most television and movie court dramas use that image as a regular, recurring, and important part of the story. The portrayal of making and meeting objections has lead to misconceptions about the use and purpose of the objection. Although some objections are made as a result of a sudden decision to object, many are planned out well in advance. Attorneys preparing the case should know what their opponent must prove and what evidence is available. Well prepared attorneys will know when the opponent will be attempting to use questionable evidence to prove an important point. Such preparation allows the attorney to be well prepared to object and state a correct reason. In addition, attorneys will know what they have to prove for their own case. They'll also be aware of when they will be using questionable evidence and should be prepared to respond to opponents' objections. With such preparation, many objections will come as no surprise. Of course, there are times when something arises during the course of the trial that the attorney must make a sudden decision to object.

The objection actually serves several purposes. For the attorney making the objection, the major purpose is to prevent inadmissible, damaging evidence from being presented to the jury. In addition to that, however, the objection provides a benefit to the trial judge. The objection notifies the trial judge that inadmissible evidence is being offered and provides an opportunity to prevent error from entering the trial. From a trial efficiency standpoint, the major purpose of the objection is to make sure that the trial of the case is conducted and decided using only appropriate evidence. When that is done, there is no need for appeals, reversals and retrial. Courts have routinely said that when an attorney fails to property object, any objection to the inadmissible evidence is waived. It is important, therefore, to understand "when" and "how" the objection must be made.

2. Specific Objections

a. Role of Attorneys (Fed. Rule 103)

The primary role on making sure that only appropriate evidence enters the trial is in the hands of the attorneys in the case. As noted above, the failure to properly object will be grounds to declare that any objection to the inadmissible evidence is waived. When the attorney makes a proper objection, it is said that the error is preserved for appeal. The Federal Rules of Evidence indicate when and how the objection must be made.

In terms of "when," the rule indicates that the objection, or motion to strike the evidence, must be "timely." Fed. R. Evid. 103(a)(1). The idea of timely is fairly easy to explain. The objection should come after the objectionable question has been asked and before the answer has been given. If there was nothing about the question that suggested that it was objectionable, the attorney may wait for the answer. If the answer then appears inadmissible, the attorney may move to strike the answer. The requirement of timeliness places a high burden on the attorney making the objection. That attorney cannot wait to see what the answer is and then object. The objection must be made as soon as the question suggests that inadmissible evidence is being sought. This requirement of timeliness is frequently referred to as the contemporaneous objection rule.

The rules also explain how the objection is to be made. The rule indicates that the attorney is to object and state the "specific grounds of objection." Fed. R. Evid. 103(a)(1). The use of the term "specific" is important to the rule. An objection will not be valid by just stating "objection." That would not inform the trial judge of the reason for the objection. In addition, adding a general reason would not be sufficient. For example, and attorney that objected by saying, "Objection, your honor. That evidence is irrelevant," would not have made a valid objection. An objection based merely on "relevancy" would not specifically inform the trial judge of the reason for the objection. If the attorney felt the answer would be irrelevant, the attorney would have to add the specific reason for the irrelevancy. An appropriate objection might be something like, "Objection, your honor. That evidence is irrelevant in that it seeks to prove the character of the defendant in this case." The rule does provide that the specific reason does not have to be given if "the specific ground is ...

apparent from the context." Fed. R. Evid. 103(a)(1). Practicing attorneys, however, should not rely on that portion of the rule. In making the objection initially, the attorney should try to state the specific reason. If the attorney failed to make a specific objection, there could then be a claim on appeal that the specific grounds were apparent from the context.

Although the rule does not provide for a response to an objection, most trial judges will allow the opposing attorney, the one seeking to introduce the evidence, to respond to the objection. This response would attempt to show why the evidence should be admissible. The trial judge would then rule on whether the evidence will be allowed. The details of the judge's rule in this process, is discussed in the next subsection. If the judge overrules the objection and allows the evidence to be admitted, that ends the issue with that objection. If, however, the trial judge sustains the objections and will not allow the jury to hear it, additional steps may be taken.

The attorney that was trying to introduce evidence but was prevented from doing so by the objection will also want to preserve the record for appeal. The attorney seeking to present the evidence needs to have the evidence appear in the record in order to allow the appellate court to review it. This evidence will not be heard or seen by the jury, but will be part of the written record available to appellate courts. In order to get the excluded evidence into the written record, the attorney must make and "offer of proof." The rule indicates that the offer of proof is completed when the "substance of the evidence was made known to the court by offer or was apparent from the context within which the questions were asked." Fed. R. Evid. 103(a)(2). Although the rule suggests that the attorney may rely upon the possibility that the original question would have suggested the content sufficiently to meet the offer of proof requirement, practicing attorneys should not rely upon that. Practicing attorneys should make the evidence know to the court. The offer of proof may be accomplished in several ways. One method is for the trial judge to excuse the jury from the courtroom and then have the witness answer the questions for the written record. This would provide the most detailed offer of proof. Some state jurisdictions refer to this as an "avowal." A quicker method, and therefore one preferred by trial judges, is to have the attorney just state the nature of the expected evidence for the written record.

Several additional problems must be noted with the making of the offer of proof. The rules allow the trial judge to make additions to the record in order to assist the appellate court. That may include explaining the evidence, making statements or asking the attorney to present the offer of proof in the full question and answer format. Fed. R. Evid. 103(b). In addition, the trial judge must try to conduct the hearing so that the jury does not hear inadmissible evidence. This would suggest that the trial judge needs to make sure that offers of proof are conducted out of the hearing of the jury. Fed. R. Evid. 103(c).

Once the offer of proof is completed, the case should continue with the introduction of other evidence. There was a time when there was an additional step to the making and meeting objection technique. Courts once required that when an attorney was dissatisfied with the final ruling on an objection, the attorney had to notify the trial judge that he or she was taking "exception" to the ruling. That would be accomplished by the attorney merely stating, "Your honor, I take exception to that ruling." That practice is no longer necessary, nor is it appropriate.

In addition, an attorney may be faced with the issue of seeing the same or similar objectionable evidence offered numerous times. The portions of the rule already discussed would suggest that the attorney must renew the objection every time the same or similar evidence is offered. Although a practitioner may wish to renew the objection, the rules suggest that it is not necessary. Once a trial judge has made a definitive ruling, the attorney need not renew an objection or offer of proof. Fed. R. Evid. 103(a)(2). This problem arises in the most serious form when attorneys seek to have rulings on evidence decided before the case even comes to trial. The attorney may seek a motion *in limine* in order to determine whether evidence will be used. The attorney may need to know the answer to that question in order to make final preparations on trial tactics. The rule noted above seems to suggest that once the ruling is made, the attorney can rely upon it. The practical problem is that the trial court does not have to make a ruling at the pre-trial stage. The trial judge may postpone ruling on the issue until it is offered in the context of the trial.

As suggested earlier, the proper making and meeting of objections is necessary in order to preserve any error for appeal. It must also be noted that not every evidentiary error will be grounds for a reversal. Practicing attorneys realize that there are probably many evidentiary mistakes in a trial, but appellate courts are not likely to reverse a case because of them. In order for an evidentiary mistake to lead to reversible error, it must be a serious mistake. The rules state that such error will not be predicated upon an evidentiary ruling "unless a substantial right of the party is affected." Fed. R. Evid. 103(a).

Finally, although the rules do provide the fairly strict method of making and meeting objections, the rules also provide for an exception. There are times when the evidentiary mistake is so serious, that it can be considered reversible error even though the proper steps were not taken to exclude it. The rules provide for taking notice of "Plain Error." "Nothing in this rule precludes taking notice of plain errors affecting substantial rights although they were not brought o the attention of the court." Fed. R. Evid. 103(d).

b. Role of Trial Judge (Fed. Rule 104)

As suggested above, the primary role to make sure that appropriate evidence is admitted in the trial and that inappropriate evidence is excluded is on the attorneys in the case. They must make proper objections and offers of proof. Once those objections or offers of proof are made, the trial judge has a decision making role in admitting and excluding evidence.

The rules make it clear that it is the role of the trial judge to make decisions on the admissibility of evidence. It is frequently stated in law school that judges decide questions of law and juries decide questions of fact. That statement, however, is too simplistic. There are many questions of law that require a preliminary decision on a question of fact. Many evidence rulings, for example, will require the trial judge to hear some facts before deciding whether the evidence should be admitted. The rules indicated that the judge must decide the issues as concerns "qualification of a person to be a witness, the existence of a privilege, or the admissibility of evidence." Fed. R. Evid. 104(a).

When determining the evidence issues, the trial judge is not bound by the rules of evidence. The only exception to that is that the trial judge is bound by the rules of privilege. Fed. R. Evid. 104(a). What this allows is that when the trial judge is expected to make a ruling on evidence, the trial judge may consider any evidence, even otherwise inadmissible evidence, before making the decision. The only type of evidence that the judge may not hear is privileged information.

The exception that keeps the judge from hearing privileged information when making evidentiary rulings has led to some problems. Imagine, for example, that an attorney was seeking to get a witness to reveal information. The witness could claim that it was subject to attorney-client privilege. The trial judge would be required to determine whether there was sufficient attorney-client relationship in order to bring the privilege into play. The witness could claim that was privileged also. The rule would suggest that the trial judge would not be allowed to hear the privileged information in order to determine if it was privileged. Obviously such a rule cannot exist. That would allow parties to claim privilege for all information and the trial courts could not rule on it. It has been stated that the privilege may be broken a little in order to allow the judge to determine if a privilege actually exists. In short, although the rule indicates that the trial judge shall not hear privileged information, a judge may require the release of some of the information in order to properly rule whether a privilege actually exists.

There is a narrow exception to the rule that the trial judge determines admissibility of evidence. When the admissibility of evidence is being challenged as not being relevant and the relevancy is conditioned upon the existence of some external fact, the trial judge may admit the evidence subject to introduction of sufficient other evidence of the facts that would support the admissibility. Fed. R. Evid. 104(b). Relevance will be discussed later, but basically means that the evidence tends to prove or disprove a fact in issue. Sometimes, it is necessary to link together a chain of facts in order to show that one fact actually proves the existence of a fact in issue. Where, for example, someone in a civil case remains silent when they are accused of owing some money, that silence is relevant to the fact that they probably owe it. (That is called the tacit admission rule.) The silence is only relevant to owing the money if the silent witness heard someone accuse them of owing it. Under those facts, the issue of whether the witness heard the accusation is the conditional fact that must be found before the evidence of silence is relevant. Using this rule, the court could admit the evidence of silence upon finding that the witness heard the accusation or upon the condition that such evidence would be forthcoming.

In making decisions on the admissibility of evidence, the trial judge must try to keep inadmissible evidence away from the jury. Fed. R. Evid. 104(c). The Rules specifically require that hearings on the admissibility of confessions in a criminal case must be conducted away from the jury. Other preliminary matters may be conducted as the interests of justice requires.

The rules also have another specific provision for testimony by a criminal accused. When a witness testifies that witness is opened up to general cross examination. Where, however, a criminal accused testifies only to a preliminary matter, that does not open up that witness to general cross examination.

Finally, it is important to note the distinctive roles of the judge and jury. It is not as simple as the judge deciding questions of law while the jury decides questions of fact. There is a simple point that must be made on the issue of deciding admissibility. The trial judge has the responsibility to determine whether evidence is admissible. Once the trial judge determines that the evidence is admissible, however, it is up to the jurors to determine what evidence they shall or shall not believe. It is frequently stated that the judge determines admissibility, while the jury determines the weight and credibility of the evidence. Fed. R. Evid. 104(e).

3. Commonly Heard Objections

The rules of evidence contain sections that give rise to technical objections during the course of the trial. Those will, of course, be discussed in detail throughout this text. Outside of those technical objections, however, one may

frequently hear objections that do not seem to be covered by the rules themselves. These commonly heard objections may have arisen as a matter of common law or local court rule practice. They are frequently heard, but have very
little solid substantive law supporting them. The rules provide that the trial
judge rules on evidence, Fed. R. Evid. 104, and that the trial judge controls
the trial, Fed. R. Evid. 611. That is sufficient authority for the trial judge to
rule on these objections.

The list that follows in not intended to be exhaustive. It is offered to show
examples of objections that may be heard during the course of a trial. Once
out in practice, these, and others will become part of the tools of the trade of
the practicing attorney.

One such frequently heard objection that is not appropriate is that evidence
is either "irrelevant" or "immaterial." Although the concepts of relevancy and
materiality have long histories in the law of evidence, objections based upon
those terms alone are inadequate. As noted earlier, objections must be based
on specific grounds. "Relevant" and "material" are terms that are much too
general to form the basis of a valid objection.

a. Leading

Leading questions are noted in the Federal Rules of Evidence. The use and
misuse of leading questions will be discussed in the chapter on Witnesses, Testimony and Credibility. Since the objection based on leading seems to be heard
so often, it is worth noting here also. Leading questions may be used for some
narrow purposes, but are generally inappropriate. The appropriate use will be
noted in that later chapter. This discussion is intended to note the nature of a
leading question. A leading question is one that suggests the answer. The attorney posing the question is, in fact, suggesting to the witness what the answer should be.

b. Argumentative

In some ways, a question that is argumentative is similar to one that is leading. Here, the attorney is seeking to present his or her own view by arguing
with the witness. Such a tactic is not appropriate. The attorney is to seek evidence, not offer his or her own testimony.

c. Asked and Answered

This objection would be used where the opposing attorney continues to ask
the same question while hoping to get a different answer. This may be seen as
a specific example of being argumentative.

E. Limited Admissibility and Remainder of Writings (Fed. Rules 105, 106)

In the general rules dealing with the admissibility of evidence and the roles of the attorneys and judges in that procedure, there are a few more minor issues that must be noted.

First, when evidence is challenged, it may be viewed as admissible for some purposes or against some parties while not admissible for other purposes or against other parties. A trial judge may be confronted, for example, with evidence of a prior crime of a party that is not admissible to prove that the party has probably committed another similar crime for which he or she is now charged. It may be admissible; however, if that party decides to testify and the evidence is offered to show that the party is not a credible witness. Evidence that a party has been convicted of perjury in the past would be admissible to challenge his or her credibility as a witness but not admissible to prove that he or she committed a bank robbery for which they are now charged. Under the rules, the court may admit such evidence but shall give the jury an instruction that limits the jury to the proper use of the evidence. Fed. R. Evid. 105.

Practitioners wonder about the use of such limiting instructions. When evidence is admissible for some purposes but not others, it is usually a complex, difficult issue to understand. Some worry that the jurors will not be able to understand the limiting instruction and will use such evidence in any way they wish. Such concerns, however, do not automatically cause the evidence to be excluded. If an attorney feels that the evidence is too damaging, even with the limiting instruction, the attorney can seek to have it excluded. The objection would be based upon the idea that even though the evidence should be admitted, the danger of unfair prejudice is too great. This type of issue is dealt with in Fed. R. Evid. 403 and will be discussed in the chapter that discusses that rule.

In addition, there are times when a party may seek to introduce parts of a written document as being important to his or her case. The opposing party may feel that the admitted evidence was taken out of context and when considered in light of the entire document, different conclusions would be reached. The rules provide that the opposing party may introduce other parts of a writing or a recorded statement when it ought to be considered with parts already introduced. Fed. R. Evid. 106.

Checkpoints

- The party with the burden of proof has the right to open and close the trial. For the specific parts of the trial, review section b.13 above.

- The rules of evidence are applicable in all cases in federal court, even those based on diversity jurisdiction. If reference is to be made to state rules of evidence, the Federal Rules of Evidence will so direct.

- The most rigid application of the rules of evidence will occur in jury trials. Less focus on the rules will be made in bench trials. Further reduced focus on the rules of evidence will occur in administrative hearings.

- The attorney making an objection must make a timely objection and state the specific reason for the objection in order to preserve the record for appeal.

- The attorney seeking to introduce the evidence must make an "offer of proof" in order to preserve the record for appeal.

Chapter 2

Judicial Notice (201)

Judicial Notice Roadmap

- Distinguish between adjudicative facts and legislative facts.
- Determine what type of facts of which a court may take judicial notice.
- Determine when a court may take judicial notice.

A. Introduction

It is usually assumed that all evidence in a case must be presented through witnesses. Whether those witnesses are giving testimony or introducing documents, that assumption is usually true. Most of the evidence that the jury will be expected to rely upon is presented by witnesses. There are facts, however, that do not need proof in order for the jury to consider them.

Some facts are so well know or so well documented that an attorney that needs to prove that fact does not need to introduce evidence of that fact through a witness. An attorney may ask the trial judge to instruct the jury that such facts are known to exist. If the judge is willing to so instruct the jury, the jury will take those facts as true and there is no need for proof. When this occurs, the party seeking such an instruction is relieved of the burden of proof on that fact. This process is called "Judicial Notice," and is recognized by the Federal Rules of Evidence. Fed. R. Evid. 201.

Since the application of judicial notice will relieve a party of proving an important fact, the process is one that has substantial detail and complexity. The rules indicate the nature of the facts that may be subject to judicial notice and the process that is to be used in taking judicial notice.

B. Legislative Facts and Adjudicative Facts (201(a))

The first important step in using judicial notice is determining the nature of the facts that may be "noticed." The first step in reaching that determination is not clearly stated in the rules, but found by reasoning from the language of the rules. The rules state that "This rule governs only judicial notice of adjudicative facts." Fed. R. Evid. 201(a). That statement provides the language from which substantial complexity must be inferred.

Careful reading of the rest of the rule that covers judicial notice reveals that the rule is a rule of exclusion or limitation. The terms of the rule limit and restrict the type of facts of which a court may take judicial notice. In analyzing the rule, a reader could assume that, but for the rule, all facts could be judicially noticed. Using the rule, therefore, the rule limits the types of facts that may be noticed.

Since the rule indicates that it only covers "adjudicative facts," the limitation on judicial notice of facts only applies to adjudicative facts. The rule limits and restricts the courts ability to take judicial notice of adjudicative facts. If, however, there are other kinds of facts in the case, the rule would not limit judicial notice of those other types of facts. Since there are no other rules dealing with judicial notice, the only limitation on judicial notice is a limit on adjudicative facts. Any other types of facts can be judicially noticed without any limits. That raises, of course, the question of whether there are any other types of facts.

The only other type of facts that can arise in a trial are what are known as "legislative facts." Since the rule does not limit judicial notice of any facts except adjudicative facts, then legislative facts may be judicially noticed without limit. In short, the trial judge may only judicially notice adjudicative facts under the strict and limiting terms of Fed. R. Evid. 201. That same trial judge, however, may judicially notice any legislative facts without any limitations. The difference between adjudicative and legislative facts must be determined.

Adjudicative facts are merely the facts that must be proven in the case. Easy examples of adjudicative facts can be seen. In a traffic accident tort case the plaintiff may be seeking to prove that the traffic light was red when the defendant's car went through it. The fact of the light being red is an adjudicative fact. In a contract case the plaintiff may be trying to prove that the nuts and bolts that the defendant shipped were not of the 5/16 inch size required by the contract. Whether those nuts and bolts were 5/16 inch or 1/4 inch would be an adjudicative fact. In a criminal case the prosecutor may be trying to prove that the finger prints found on the murder weapon were those of the defendant. Whether those finger prints belonged to the defendant would be an adjudicative fact.

All of the above examples are clearly adjudicative facts. In most of those examples the fact is probably one of the most critical facts in the case. Adjudicative facts may be less critical. In the traffic accident example, the color of the traffic light will probably be determinative of the outcome of the litigation. If that light was red when the defendant's car when through it, then the defendant will probably be found liable. When a witness testifies that the light was red, the credibility of that witness will be challenged. The defense attorney may claim that the weather, rain, and fog were so bad that the witness could not have seen the color of the light. The weather conditions also become adjudicative facts. They are part of the facts of the case that are sought to be proven.

Those adjudicative facts must ordinarily be proven by the party seeking to carry the burden on that fact. Fed. R. Evid. 201 does allow judicial notice of such facts, but only under the limitations and restricts in the rule. Those limits will be discussed below.

Since legislative facts are not limited by Fed. R. Evid. 201 and may be judicially noticed without limit, it is important to be able to distinguish legislative facts from the adjudicative facts. Legislative facts are fundamentally different from adjudicative facts. Where adjudicative facts are the facts that make up the case, legislative facts are the background facts that are used to form the reasoning for a legal conclusion. Legislative facts are those facts that trial judges used to determine the appropriate rule of law to apply. They are also those facts that legislators used to formulate legislation.

Since legislative facts are those facts which make up the reasoning to support legal theories, examples of such facts may also be shown. In a basic torts class, the course studies the landmark decision of *U.S. v. Carrol Towing Company*. In that case, Judge Learned Hand discussed how a judge should decide whether there is a duty to prevent a risk. Judge Hand indicated that a judge would have to balance the burden to prevent the risk against the probability an injury would occur times the seriousness of that injury should it occur. This classic example of a risk/utility analysis was even reduced to the formula B<LP. When Judge Hand is discussing the burdens and risks, he is discussing facts. A trial judge and ultimately an appellate judge would have to decide whether there was a substantial risk of injury and what would be the burden to prevent it. The judge could decide that the probability of an accident happening was 1 in 10 while the burden to prevent that accident would have been $10. Once the injury occurred, the plaintiff suffered $1 Million in damages.

Based upon that logic, the judge may determine that the defendant had a duty to use reasonable care. The judge would be deciding the facts that the probability was 1 in 10 and that the burden to prevent the accident was only $10. All of those, however, are legislative facts. The judge is deciding and using those facts as part of the legal reasoning to reach a decision of law in the case. Since this is an example of a judge using legislative facts, the judge may judicially notice those facts without any limit. There is no requirement of proof of those facts.

Another classic example of legislative fact use is in the "Brandeis Brief." Prior to being appointed to the United States Supreme Court, Louis D. Brandeis was a practicing attorney. He handled such matters as seeking to uphold the validity of legislation that limited the number of hours a week that employees could be forced to work. In briefing and arguing his cases before the appellate courts and the United States Supreme Court, he would include substantial socially important facts in the brief. These facts would indicate the extent of harm that extended work hours would cause employees. These facts were legislative facts. There were not facts used to show that some particular employee was hurt. They were instead used to justify the validity of the legislation. The facts were being used to prove that the legislation had a valid purpose. The use to support the legal reasoning behind the legislation and not seeking to prove the issues in a particular case makes the facts legislative. Since the facts that the future Justice Brandeis was using were legislative facts they could be judicially noticed by the appellate court without any limitation. There was no requirement that the facts be proven by witnesses under oath.

Possibly the easiest example of legislative facts is one well known to law students after the initial class in legal research. In researching legislation, attorneys must frequently seek to find the legislative history of a statute. This history may tell the attorney the background and reasoning of the legislation. This legislative history is legislative facts. Attorneys may supply that history to the trial judge or appellate judge without limitation. The judge may consider that history without requiring that the attorney prove that history with witnesses. In fact, that history is usually recited in a brief.

This distinction between adjudicative facts and legislative facts again brings to mind the simple statement given to law students early in law school. Students are frequently told that juries determine questions of fact and judges determine questions of law. That is too simple. Although judges must determine questions of law, those judges must frequently review facts as part of the legal reasoning to reach a decision of law. Those facts that go to support that legal decision are the legislative facts. Judges may review, notice, and decide such facts without any limitation or restrict. The facts that are supplied to the jury in order to reach a decision in a case, however, are the adjudicative facts. Those, ordinarily, must be proven though a witness. With the limitations to be discussed in the rest of this chapter, however, those facts may be judicially noticed by the judge.

C. Facts That Can Be Noticed (201(b))

As already discussed above, not all facts can be judicially noticed. First, legislative facts can be noticed without limitation. Adjudicative facts may be noticed, but there are limitations. Fed. R. Evid. 201(b) provides the guidelines for determining when such adjudicative facts may be judicially noticed.

The purpose of judicial notice could be one of efficiency. When facts are so well known or just not subject to dispute, there is something to be gained by not requiring the attorneys in the case to prove the fact. If the judge will merely instruct the jury that the fact is known to exist, time and effort could be saved. Of course, the attorneys in the case could accomplish this same result by agreeing that the fact is known to exist. The procedure known as stipulations allows the parties to "stipulate" that certain facts exist. Once a fact is stipulated, the attorneys do not have to prove it. Simple examples of stipulations may be seen. When a complaint if filed, the plaintiff will identify the name and address of the defendant in the complaint. Frequently, the defendant, in the answer, will stipulate that the name and address is correct. Judicial notice, therefore, arises in an interesting setting. One party will claim that a fact is so well known or not subject to dispute that it should be judicially noticed. The other party, however, is unwilling to stipulate that the fact is true. This will force the judge to determine whether the fact is appropriate for judicial notice or whether it must be proven by witnesses.

The primary basis for judicial notice, therefore, is that the fact at issue is not subject to reasonable dispute. This concept of "not subject to reasonable dispute" is the overriding requirement before a fact may be judicially noticed. Fed. R. Evid. 201(b). The rules further elaborate on the concept and give two forms that may be used to determine whether a fact meets the test of "not subject to reasonable dispute."

The first basis that may be used for a fact to be found not subject to reasonable dispute is that the fact is "generally known within the territorial jurisdiction of the trial court." Fed. R. Evid. 201(b) (1). It is important to read that language closely. The rule requires that the fact by *generally known* within the jurisdiction of the trial court. It is not sufficient if the judge or attorneys know the fact to be true. The fact must be *generally known* within the territorial jurisdiction of the trial court. It could easily be seen that in the jurisdictions of the trial courts for New York City, it is *generally known* that Macy's Department Store is located at Herald Square. If for some reason that location of Macy's Department Store was a fact to be proven, the trial judge could take judicial notice of that location. If, however, the fact that a delightful little bar happens to be located just down 35th Street was a fact at issue, the trial judge could not take judicial notice of the location of that bar. Even if the judge and attorneys both knew of the location of that bar and had frequented it often, the judge could not take judicial notice of its location. The location might be known to the judge, but it would not be *generally known*. Using those examples, it should be easy to imagine the types of facts that fit this form. In every community, there are facts that are so well known that no one disputes them. Such facts are generally known in the community and would be accepted. Those types of facts are the type that are "generally known within the territorial jurisdiction of the trial court" and may be judicially noticed.

The second form of facts that meet the requirement of not subject to reasonable dispute is a little more complex. The rule provides that a fact is not subject to reasonable dispute if it is "capable of accurate and ready determination by resort to sources show accuracy cannot reasonable be questioned." Fed. R. Evid. 201(b)(2). This form of determining that evidence is appropriate for judicial notice may give greater problems. Courts may be find it difficult to determine what types of sources cannot be questioned. It could be seen, for example, that the times of sunrise or sunset could be critical in litigation. Surely the reports of the National Weather Service on those times would be adequate to convince the judge to take judicial notice.

In summary, only those facts that are not subject to reasonable dispute are appropriate for judicial notice. Where there is dispute as to the facts, the parties must seek to prove the facts with witnesses and then let the jury decide whether the facts are true.

D. Procedural Concerns
(201(c), (d), (e), (f) & (g))

Once it has been determined that an adjudicative fact is appropriate for judicial notice, there are several procedural issues that must be examined. Again, it is important to note that these limitations apply only to adjudicative facts. A judge may take judicial notice of a legislative fact without restriction or limitation. That includes the procedural issues. Although there are procedural limitations on taking judicial notice of adjudicative facts, a judge may take judicial notice of legislative facts at any time and in any manner. In addition, the judge may use the legislative fact in any manner. The limitations or restrictions imposed procedurally only apply to judicial notice of adjudicative facts.

The first issue is whether the judge has any discretion in taking judicial notice. It is clear that the court "may take judicial notice , whether requested or not." Fed. R. Evid. 201(c). This allows the court to have discretion in taking judicial notice whether any of the parties make such a request. The court can use this flexible practice to save time and make the development of cases much easier for the litigants. The court does not need to wait for a special request or motion, but may decide that a judicial notice fact exists.

There are times when the court must take judicial notice. The court "shall take judicial notice if requested by a party and supplied with the necessary information." Fed. R. Evid. 201(d). This portion of the rule removes discretion from the court. If a party requests that judicial notice be taken of a fact and supplies the type of information that indicates that the fact is generally known or capable of accurate and ready determination, then the court must take notice of that fact.

Looking at those two features of the rule concerning judicial notice, it is clear that there is a broad opportunity for the court to take judicial notice. The court may take judicial notice where requested or not. The court must take judicial notice and supplied with appropriate information. It is important to note, however, that even when the court takes judicial notice without request, the court must still be certain that the facts are ones which are generally known or subject to accurate and ready determination.

The taking of judicial notice dispenses with the necessity of proving the facts that are noticed. Because of this, the taking of judicial notice may, at times, allow the introduction of facts to the jury that an opposing counsel finds to be harmful to his or her case. It is important to provide an opportunity to argue against the taking of judicial notice. The federal rules of evidence, Fed. R. Evid. 201(e), specifically allow for the "opportunity to be heard." The rule provides for a "timely" opportunity to be heard as to the taking of judicial notice and the facts to be noticed. If the opportunity did not arise before the taking of the notice, it must be allowed after the taking of the notice. This rule, therefore, allows opposing counsel to dispute the propriety of taking notice in the particular case and the nature of the facts actually being noticed.

Since much of the rule speaks of the "court" taking judicial notice, the question may arise as to when may the court take judicial notice. The rules make it clear, Fed. R. Evid. 201(f), that judicial notice "may be taken at any stage of the proceeding." This allows any court to take judicial notice at any time.

Although it is routinely assumed that trial courts would be the logical place for the taking of judicial notice, appellate courts may also and frequently do, take judicial notice. It should be recalled that a court may take judicial notice whether or not it is requested. When matched with the timing rule, this means that any court may take judicial notice at any time whether or not there has been a request. Again, if the court is seeking to take judicial notice of adjudicative facts, it is important to make sure that the facts are generally known or subject to accurate and ready determination. If, of course, the facts are legislative facts, any court may take judicial notice of those legislative facts at any time without limit.

The final procedural problem with judicial notice is the method that the judicially noticed fact is actually entered into the case. If the trial judge is sitting as both decider of law and finder of fact, there will be no jury. The trial judge can just make a finding of fact for the judicially noticed fact. If the judicial notice occurs at the appellate level, the appellate judge writing the opinion may just note the fact in the opinion. The most difficult problem arises, of course, when there is a jury trial.

The federal rules explain how judicial notice is to occur in a jury trial. Fed. R. Evid. 201(g). If the action is a civil case, "the court shall instruct the jury to accept as conclusive any fact judicially noticed." Jury instructions are given at the end of the trial before the jury goes out to decide the case. The jury instruction is the opportunity for the judge to explain the law to the jury. This is an excellent opportunity for the trial judge to inform the jury that a fact shall be accepted as conclusive. The trial judge does not, however, have to wait until the final jury instructions. If the fact to be noticed is raised at an earlier time in the case, the trial judge may instruct the jury at that time to accept the fact as conclusive.

The use of judicial notice in criminal cases raises possible constitutional issues. As discussed in the section on burdens of proof, the prosecution in a criminal case must prove all elements of the case beyond a reasonable doubt. It could be imagined that the prosecution could request the judicial notice of a fact that made up an element of a crime. If the trial judge judicially noticed such a fact and instructed the jury to accept it as conclusive, that would relieve the prosecution of the burden of proving that fact and raise the constitutional issue. Fed. R. Evid. 201(g) avoids that problem by stating that "In a criminal case, the court shall instruct the jury that it may, but is not required to, accept as conclusive any fact judicially noticed." This allows the jury to treat the instruction as a fact they can consider, but may disregard.

The distinction between civil and criminal cases must be clearly understood. When the trial judge judicially notices a fact in a civil case, the jury must accept the fact as conclusive. When, however, the trial judge judicially notices a fact in a criminal case, the jury may, but is not required to, accept the fact as conclusive.

Again, it is important to remember that the limitations made on judicial notice only apply to adjudicative facts. When the court is taking judicial notice of legislative facts, there are no limits.

E. Jury's Knowledge

The previous sections discussed the idea that a judge, at any stage of the trial, may judicially notice that a fact is conclusive without requiring proof by the attorneys. It is not usually accepted that a jury may do the same thing on their own. Jurors are usually instructed that they must decide a case on the facts that are presented in evidence. Jurors should not be deciding cases on what they personally believe to be the facts of the matter. It is a common practice of trial lawyers to use the opportunity of voir dire to determine whether any prospective juror believes he or she has special knowledge of the matter to be litigated. If a juror believes that, that juror is usually not allowed to serve on the case. The goal of the trial judge and the attorneys is to impanel a jury that has no special knowledge of the matters to be tried and then for that jury to decide the case on the facts offered into evidence.

Once that general principle is stated, however, it must be admitted that the trial judge and the attorneys expect the jurors to come to the trial with a basic understanding of their community and the world around them. It has frequently been stated throughout the history of jury trials that, "The jury acts as the conscience of the community." Jurors must use their understanding about people, truth telling, common sense, logic, and the community to determine who to believe and which stories appear credible. If jurors were to enter the case with brains that were completely clean slates while waiting for judges and attorneys to write on the slate, the trial system would fail. All trials would take too long. There is, therefore, a natural tension that exists in every trial. Jurors are expected to use their common sense and community understanding to weigh and determine what facts to believe. Those jurors are not to bring new facts into the trial that have not been introduced through the formal witness process.

This issue is discussed, but it is rarely litigated. The discussions that occur in the jury room are considered confidential. It is rare for the parties or the court to gain information or insight into what could be jury misconduct. If a juror suggests facts that were not introduced into evidence, it is likely that no one outside of the other jurors will ever know it. As such, these issues are rarely litigated.

The issue does tend to arise when it becomes obvious that the jurors have run their own experiments on exhibits. An exhibit may be returned to the courtroom in a substantially different condition than it was originally seen. That could prompt the judge or the attorneys to question that condition. In such cases, the courts have not expressed a clear rule. Courts are inclined to say that jurors may inspect and review exhibits closely. They may not run new or different experiments on the exhibits. It is obvious that determining whether it was merely a "close inspection" or a "new experiment" is very difficult. As suggested, this is an issue that has been discussed by writers, but is rarely raised. It is unlikely that the ordinary practitioner will see it arise in a whole career. The federal rules of evidence do not provide a specific rule on this problem.

F. Jury View

One additional fact gathering issue that needs to be discussed in this context is the jury view. This is another practice that is becoming rarer and does not have a specific federal rule of evidence to offer guidance. The procedure for a jury view is to have the jury go to the physical location of the events being described in the litigation and actually view that location. The purpose behind such a procedure is to allow the jury to get a better idea of physical location and be better able to understand the testimony that will be offered. The jury is not to listen to comments made while on the jury view and the facts observed on the view are not considered evidence. It is assumed that the view will just provide a framework for understanding testimony.

The problem, of course, is that jury views lead to appeals. Whichever side loses the litigation will appeal and claim that inadmissible or inappropriate comments were made to the jury during the view. In addition, jury views are expensive. The court must transport the jury and court employees to the location for the view. This also results in an inefficient use of court time. The case must be postponed while the jury is out viewing the location. Because of the expense, delay, and opportunity for error, jury views are rarely conducted.

The most common type of case were jury views are still conducted are eminent domain cases. Where a state or federal agency is condemning property for public use, jury trials are permitted. In many such eminent domain cases, courts may still allow jury views. This allows the jury to go to the location of the property being condemned and look at it before the trial is concluded.

Checkpoints

- Adjudicative facts are facts that are a part of the case and usually to be determined by the jury.

- Legislative facts are those facts that form the underlying basis to legal rules.

- Courts can take judicial notice of legislative facts without limit.

- Judicial notice of adjudicative facts is limited.

- Courts may take judicial notice of adjudicative facts when they are not subject to dispute.

- Facts not subject to dispute are those that are generally known in the territorial district of the court or capable of determination from sources that cannot be questioned.

- Courts may take judicial notice at any stage of the proceeding.

Chapter 3

Burdens of Proof and Presumptions (301, 302)

Burdens of Proof and Presumptions Roadmap

- Learn the burdens of proof for civil cases and criminal cases.
- Understand the impact that presumptions have on civil and criminal cases.

A. Introduction

Burden of proof is a phrase that is frequently heard in law school. From the first day of class, students hear faculty members stating that one or the other parties has the burden of proof. This concept is expressed in many different ways. It may be said that a party "must plead and prove," "has the risk of non-persuasion," "has the burden of going forward," "has the burden of production," or some other similar phrase. In fact, by stating that something is an element of the plaintiff's case or an affirmative defense also implies the existence of the burden of proof.

Although this concept of burden of proof is frequently mentioned in other classes, it is rarely explained in any class except evidence. It may be one of the most important concepts in the law. For the practicing attorney, meeting a burden of proof is necessary in every case or the case will be lost. It is, therefore, critical in every case.

The basic use of the concept of burden of proof is not difficult to understand. In every trial, someone will win and someone will lose. Trials always conclude with a winner and loser. There are no "ties" in litigation. The law must be arranged to make sure that litigation ends with a winner and a loser. The concept of burden of proof acts as something of a tie breaker. The party that has the burden of proof must produce more convincing evidence then the opposing party. It is possible to imagine the situation where the plaintiff and defendant have each produced their evidence. To use the appropriate

37

terms, both the plaintiff and defendant have completed their cases in chief and are preparing for closing arguments. The case was close and the evidence is evenly balanced. If the case was to be submitted to the jury, the jury would have to declare that they would not know how to decide the case. The facts were so balanced that the jury would want to call the case a tie. This is where the burden of proof has the strongest impact. If the plaintiff had the burden of proof, which they usually do, then the plaintiff would have to lose that case. If a party has the burden of proof and fails to meet it, then the party with the burden of proof loses.

Since the burden of proof rules can mean the difference in winning or losing litigation, they are important. The burden of proof rules are also complex. Courts have developed rules that identify which party has the burden of proof and what that burden actually is. To complicate the matter, the rules are different for civil and criminal cases. In addition, the law has created another set of rules to help the party with the burden of proof meet that burden. These aids to meeting the burden of proof are called presumptions.

In order to understand this area of the law, it is necessary to study the burdens of proof and the presumptions together. In addition, it is important to distinguish the differences between the civil and criminal rules. The following material will accomplish that. The text will start with civil cases and discuss burdens of proof and presumptions. The material will then go to criminal cases and again discuss burdens of proof and presumptions.

B. Civil Cases

1. Burdens of Proof

One of the first problems that must be understood is that there are actually two burdens of proof in every case. The first is called the burden of going forward or sometimes referred to as the burden of production. The second is called the burden of persuasion. Both of these must be met in every case. Ordinarily the plaintiff will have both burdens of proof for the major elements of the claim. The defendant may ordinarily have both burdens of proof for affirmative defenses. That is not the issue to be discussed in this book. The question of who has the burden of proof in any one case is actually a matter of substantive law and is discussed in the substantive law course. This text will try to point out what impact on the case those burdens of proof have. For matters of convenience this text will assume the plaintiff has the burden of proof. It is important, however, to carefully review the substantive law in any particular case to determine who has the burden of proof on specific issues. There is also one additional general matter to note. In reviewing the Federal Rules of Evidence, it is clear that there is no specific rule that deals with the burdens of proof. The law concerning the burdens of proof has been developed by the courts.

a. Burden of Production

To begin the discussion, the first burden must be understood. This first burden, called the burden of going forward or the burden of production, requires that the party with the burden must produce sufficient evidence to even get the case to the jury. (For convenience, this burden will be called the burden of production throughout the rest of this text.) Not every plaintiff is entitled to get a jury decision regardless of the amount of evidence available to support the case. In a course on civil procedure, the options of having a case dismissed by motions for summary judgment or motions to dismiss were discussed. Those motions allow the trial judge to end the case if there is insufficient law or facts to support the outcome that a plaintiff would seek. The law concerning the burden of production allows the same outcome. After hearing some of the evidence, the trial judge may be asked to determine whether the plaintiff has produced sufficient evidence to have met this burden of production. If the burden of production has not been met, then the case will be dismissed.

The procedural device that is used to test whether the burden of production has been met is the motion for summary judgment. A common example is easy to visualize. The jury has been chosen, plaintiff and defendant in a case have made their opening statements and plaintiff has completed calling all of the witnesses for the plaintiff's case in chief. At this point, the defendant may move for directed verdict. (The defendant may also wait until the close of all the proof and make the motion just before the case is submitted to the jury.) The underlying meaning of the motion is the defendant claims that the plaintiff has not produced sufficient evidence to support the allegations that were made in the complaint. To state it another way, the plaintiff has not produced evidence of the elements of the claim. The defendant is asking the trial judge to direct a verdict in the defendant's behalf. Since the plaintiff had the burden of production of that evidence, the trial judge must determine whether sufficient evidence was presented.

At one time, courts used what may be called the "scintilla rule" for the burden of production. Although a few courts may still use that rule, it would be an extreme minority of jurisdictions. The "scintilla rule" held that if the plaintiff produced any evidence of each element of the claim that was sufficient to go to the jury. Even a mere "scintilla" of evidence was sufficient to meet the burden of production. Obviously that rule would have allowed almost all cases to go to the jury. Even cases with very little evidence would not be dismissed. Most jurisdictions have moved away from that rule.

The majority rule, and the one used in the Federal Courts, is referred to as the "substantial evidence" rule. The party with the burden of production must produce substantial evidence of every element of the claim in order to have met the burden. The phrase, "substantial evidence," is vague and difficult to apply. Courts have developed a test to determine whether the current standard has been met.

When a party makes a motion for directed verdict, the courts routinely use a two part test. First, the court should consider all of the evidence in the light most favorable to the non-moving party. This means that the trial judge will think about all the evidence that has been produced. Of that evidence, the trial judge must consider it and any inferences or presumptions that may have been raised by it. Before making a decision, the trial judge should think about that evidence in a way that is most favorable to the non-moving party. As suggested above, the non-moving party is usually the plaintiff.

The second step of the test is that the judge should not grant the motion unless the judge determines that reasonable minds could not differ with the motion. The law is set up to allow jurors to decide civil cases. The law also assumes that jurors are "reasonable people." The test that states that the motion should not be granted unless reasonable minds could not differ with the motion is merely asking the judge to determine whether the "reasonable" jurors would have to decide in favor of the party making the motion. If that is true, then the judge should grant the motion. If, however, reasonable jurors could, based on the evidence heard, decide in favor of the non-moving party, then the judge should not grant the motion. This will allow the judge to send the case to the jury and let those jurors decide the case.

This second step is frequently stated in a different way. It will be discussed further below, but the burden of persuasion in a civil case is that the jury is to find for the plaintiff if it is found that the plaintiff proved the case by a preponderance of the evidence. To begin to relate that back to the burden of production, the jury could only find for the plaintiff if reasonable jurors could find for the plaintiff by a preponderance of the evidence. That language is sometimes used to state the second part of the burden of production test. After the trial judge considers all the evidence in the light most favorable to the non-moving party, the trial judge will grant the motion for directed verdict if the trial judge finds that reasonable jurors could not find for the non-moving party by a preponderance of the evidence.

That additional explanation will also help explain one additional point. Jurors will ultimately have to find for the plaintiff by a preponderance of the evidence. If, at the close of the case, the evidence is so equally balanced that the jury cannot find the preponderance, then the jury must find for the defendant. Keep in mind, there are no "ties" in a jury trial. One party wins and the other loses. The party with the burdens of proof must offer more convincing evidence than the other. As such, if the evidence is even, the party with the burdens of proof loses. The trial judge must consider that same point when ruling on a motion for directed verdict. In order to deny the motion, the trial judge has to be able to decide that reasonable jurors would find for the plaintiff by a preponderance of the evidence. If the trial judge decides that the evidence is evenly balanced, then the party with the burden of proof must lose.

As noted above, this discussion has assumed that the plaintiff had the burden of production. There are, of course, times that the defendant might have the burden of production on some affirmative defenses. Where that is true, the plaintiff may try to take advantage of a motion for directed verdict in order to have an affirmative defense dismissed from the case and not submitted to the jury. The plaintiff could wait until the defendant had presented the entire defense proof and then move for the directed verdict. The trial judge would use the same two step test. The judge would consider all of the evidence in the light most favorable to the non-moving party. Here, that would be the defendant. Then decide where reasonable people would differ from the motion.

If the party with the burden of production does not meet that burden, that party loses by directed verdict. If, however, the trial judge determines that sufficient evidence was presented to meet that burden, the case is ready to go to the jury. The jury is allowed to ultimately decide the case. The question of when is there sufficient evidence for the jury to find in a party's favor is the question that concerns the second burden of proof.

b. Burden of Persuasion

The second burden of proof is the burden of persuasion. It is, in fact, the one that most non-lawyers think about when they consider the idea of burden of proof. Unfortunately for attorneys that try civil cases, most non-lawyers think of the criminal burden of proof when they think of it at all. Most people who serve on juries are, of course, non-lawyers. If they have any knowledge of trials it is knowledge gained from watching television or movie trials. Those entertainment events are usually criminal trials and often are not accurate productions. One item that is frequently raised in the entertainment trial is that the burden of proof is to prove the case "beyond a reasonable doubt." That is, in fact, the burden of persuasion for criminal trials and will be discussed below. It is not, however, the burden of persuasion in civil trials. Plaintiff's lawyers in civil trials are sometimes concerned that jurors expect them to prove the case "beyond a reasonable doubt." That is not the requirement.

The usually burden of persuasion in a civil case is that the plaintiff has to prove every element of the claim by a "preponderance of the evidence." This means that in order to win the trial, once it goes to the jury, the party with the burden of proof must prove the elements of the claim by a preponderance of the evidence. Since a failure to offer sufficient proof will result in the party with the burden of persuasion losing the case, it is sometimes referred to as a "risk of non-persuasion." It is useful to note that the defendant may have the burden of persuasion on elements of affirmative defenses by a "preponderance of the evidence."

Most jurisdictions agree that the burden of persuasion in a civil case is "preponderance of the evidence," but there is some disagreement as to how that concept is to be explained to the jury. Practitioners must consult local law to determine how the trial judge will instruct the jury on the definition of that burden.

There are some general things that can be said about the burden. Jurisdictions agree that the concept is not solely concerned with the number of witnesses. A party does not meet the preponderance burden by bringing on more witnesses than the opponent. Numbers alone do not create a "preponderance." A preponderance of the evidence is a mixture of the number and the quality of the witnesses offered. That can be easily seen when it is considered that a party may bring numerous witnesses who are just not believable. Some jurisdictions have sought to explain further what preponderance means. It has been suggested that it means things like a greater weight of the evidence, a greater probability of the evidence, more likely than not or even a "little more than half." At least one jurisdiction, Kentucky, has indicated that the jury is not to be told that the burden is a preponderance nor is the concept to be explained.

Although the "preponderance of the evidence" standard is the usual burden of persuasion, there is one additional standard that has been used. Courts have stated that for some issues in a civil case, the party with the burden of proof may have to prove the case by "clear and convincing" evidence. This has been stated, for example, as the burden of proof for defamation cases and is routinely stated as the burden for proving fraud. The easiest way to think of clear and convincing is that it is a greater standard of proof than preponderance, but less than the burden of beyond a reasonable doubt that is used in criminal cases. Again, it is important to research the substantive law to determine when that burden of persuasion is to be used for particular issues.

2. Presumptions

Once it is clear that a particular party has the burden of proof, it is necessary then to consider the nature of presumptions. As a simple explanation, presumptions are merely procedural tools that assist a party with a burden of proof to meet that burden. In fact, one of the difficult things about presumptions is that they must be defined in terms of how they meet burdens of proof. It is also troubling that presumptions must be distinguished from inferences. Each of those has a different procedural effect. Some background information is probably necessary to understand the concept. Before proceeding, however, one additional point must be noted. This text is designed to discuss the impact that presumptions and inferences have on the case. In order to find out the nature of particular presumptions, it is again necessary to consider the substantive law in particular areas. Each area of substantive law has developed presumptions that pertain specifically to that area.

Ordinarily a plaintiff in a case has the burden of production of the evidence. If, for example, the plaintiff in a civil case cannot offer evidence on one of the elements of a claim, the plaintiff must lose. In fact, the defendant will probably make a motion for directed verdict and the judge would have to grant it. The discussion of the burden of production that appears earlier in this chapter details how that would happen. The plaintiff has the burden of production. If the plaintiff fails to product substantial evidence of every element of the claim, the trial judge would direct a verdict for the defendant.

In offering evidence to meet that burden of production, a party does not have to offer direct, eye witness testimony on every element. Indirect or circumstantial evidence may be used for elements of a claim or defense. An easy example may be seen where an automobile accident happens in an area where there is a 35 mph speed zone. After the accident experts measure the tire skid marks and are will to testify from those marks that one of the automobiles was going at least 50 mph. No one is offering direct, eye witness testimony that the automobile was going 50. The evidence by the experts, however, allows the jury to consider that the automobile may have been going 50.

Evidence of circumstances that tend to prove an element of the claim is considered relevant evidence. It is sufficiently strong to allow it to be admitted into evidence. A trial judge may consider it when a motion for directed verdict is made.

Some circumstances are so strong as to be given greater procedural impact in the case. Such examples are referred to as inferences. In most jurisdictions, for example, the tort doctrine of res ipsa loquitur is an inference. A plaintiff in a negligence case must prove duty, breach, injury and causal connection. If the plaintiff does not have evidence of breach, the plaintiff would lose by a directed verdict. As noted above, the plaintiff has the burden of production on those issues. Failure to offer substantial evidence of an element of the claim would result in a directed verdict for the defendant. Res ipsa loquitur is an inference that assists the plaintiff in proving breach. Although the plaintiff may not have direct evidence of breach, if the plaintiff can prove that the accident that happened was not the type of thing that ordinarily occurs in the absence of negligence and the defendant had the exclusive custody or control over the instrumentality of the injury, then the doctrine of res ipsa loquitur will act as an inference of breach. As an "inference," the circumstantial evidence that the plaintiff proved will be sufficient to meet the plaintiff's burden of production, get the plaintiff past the motion for directed verdict and allow the case to go to the jury. Once the case gets to the jury, the jury may consider that evidence the way it would consider any other evidence, but the plaintiff will still be required to prove the whole case by a preponderance of the evidence.

The doctrine of res ipsa loquitur is, however, especially helpful to this discussion. Although most jurisdictions consider it an inference, a few jurisdictions give it a stronger effect. Some jurisdictions treat it like a presumption. Using the doctrine of res ipsa loquitur, therefore, can also explain the usual operation of a presumption in a civil case.

The usual operation of a presumption in a civil case has been called the Thayer-Wigmore-Bursting Bubble theory. This doctrine creates a form of rebuttal presumption. It is the rule adopted in Fed. R. Evid. 301 for use in federal court. This doctrine indicates that when a party with the burden of production on an issue offers evidence that gives rise to a presumption, that presumption not only meets the burden of production and gets the party past the directed verdict, the presumption shifts the burden of production to the other party. The other party must meet or rebut the presumption or that other party will lose on that issue by a directed verdict. To rebut the presumption, the party must offer the same level of substantial evidence that the first party had to produce to meet the burden of production.

The difficulty occurs when the other party meets and rebuts the presumption. The best explanation is that the presumption itself disappears and the original circumstantial evidence is treated like an inference. That means that the original party is still allowed to take the case to the jury, but gets no additional benefit from once having created the presumption. This effect is what has given the presumption the name of "bursting bubble." Once the rebuttal evidence comes into the case, the presumption bubble bursts and the evidence goes to being an inference.

It is possible to use the idea of res ipsa loquitur in jurisdictions that call it a presumption as an example. Imagine that a person is walking along a street when a flour barrel flies out of a warehouse window and hits the pedestrian. The pedestrian, now plaintiff, sues the owner of the warehouse. The plaintiff cannot prove the breach of the duty to show why the barrel came out of the window. Without such evidence, the plaintiff has failed to meet the burden of production on the issue of breach and should lose by directed verdict. If, however, the plaintiff proves that barrels do not usually fly out of windows in the absence of negligence and the owner had exclusive custody or control over the barrel, then the doctrine of res ipsa loquitur is created. In jurisdictions that use this as a presumption, the court would find that the plaintiff met the burden of production on the issue of breach, and, in fact, the burden of production on breach would be shifted to the defendant. If the defendant offered no rebuttal evidence of breach, the plaintiff would received a directed verdict on that issue. Of course, the issues of injury and causation would still have to go to the jury. If, however, the defendant offered rebuttal evidence of breach, the conditions would change. The defendant might offer evidence, for example, of usual maintenance records, time cards of faithful employees, and the fact that on the day of the accident a band of masked marauders broke into the warehouse and began to throw barrels out of windows. This evidence would tend to rebut the presumption. As such, the presumption would disappear and become an inference. That would mean that the case would go to the jury, the plaintiff would have the burden of persuasion on all elements of the case, including breach, but that the jury would consider all of the evidence that had been produced. In a true "bursting bubble" jurisdiction, the jury would not be told that a presumption once existed.

There is a minority rule in the use of presumptions. This rule is referred to as the Morgan rule. The Morgan rule sees the importance of presumptions as having a stronger effect than the "bursting bubble" theory. In the Morgan rule, the presumption, once created, does not just shift the burden of production. The presumption shifts the burden of persuasion. As such, once a presumption is created, the opposing party must present evidence of rebuttal to the jury by a preponderance.

Although the Morgan rule is not specially adopted by Rule 301 of the Federal Rules of Evidence, it must still be considered when dealing with the Federal Rules. Rule 302 of the Federal Rules of Evidence is one of three places in the Federal Rules where litigants must, at times, make reference to state law.

Rule 302 indicates that when state law will supply the rule of decision in a case in federal court, then state law must also supply the rule for effect of a presumption. An example of this can be easily seen. State law supplies the rule of decision in diversity cases tried in federal court. In such a case, if a presumption arises, the litigants must look to the effect of presumptions in the state that is supplying the rule of decision. Although the federal courts use the "bursting bubble" theory for most cases, if that state law supplying the rule of decision uses the Morgan theory, then the federal court, under rule 302, must use the Morgan theory.

Again, it is important to note that this discussion only deals with the effect of presumptions. Substantive law materials will provide specific presumptions that deal with those areas of the law. This text noted the res ipsa loquitur doctrine that is common in torts. In family law, one finds such presumptions as seven years absence is presumption of death or a marriage is presumed to continue until terminated by divorce or death. To find other presumptions it is necessary to research the substantive area.

C. Criminal Cases

1. Burdens of Proof

Just as was noted in civil cases, there are two burdens of proof in criminal cases. There is the burden of production and the burden of persuasion. Of critical importance in criminal cases, however, is that the Constitution of the United States has been interpreted as protecting the rights of the criminal accused and insuring that the proper burdens of proof are used. Usually, the prosecution will have the burden of production and the burden of persuasion on every element of the crime. It would violate the Constitution to shift either burden of proof to the defendant. There are no specific rules in the Federal Rules of Evidence that deal with the burdens of proof in a criminal case.

It is easy to see the reasoning behind such decisions. First, it is recognized that under basic concepts of due process, the prosecution must prove every element of the crime. Secondly, those accused of crimes have the right to remain silent. If the law imposed a burden to disprove elements of a crime, the defendant could be forced to speak. Seeing those two simple principles, it is clear that the prosecution will have the burdens of proof.

That, of course, raises the issue of whether the defendant can have any burdens of proof in a criminal cases. The constitutional decisions indicate that the prosecution must have the burden of proof on *every element of the crime.*

That leaves open the possibility that the defendant could have the burden of proof on items that are not elements of the crime. It is possible, for example, for the law to create affirmative defenses and then place the burden of proof on the defendant. Self defense, for example, is an affirmative defense for which the defendant can have the burden of proof. When seeking to use self defense, the defendant is admitting that the act occurred, but is claiming there is an excuse. It could arise in a homicide. The prosecution would have the burden to prove every element of the crime of homicide, while leaving elements of self defense on the defendant. In such defenses, that is defenses that admit the existence of the act but offer an excuse, the defendant can have the burden of production and the burden of persuasion.

There are other kinds of claims that the defendant may offer that are different. A defendant, for example, may claim that he or she could not have committed the crime, because he or she was somewhere else. This may be referred to as an alibi. Jurisdictions may require that the defendant have the burden to raise the issue much like a burden of production, but the ultimate burden of persuasion of proving the elements of the crime remain on the prosecution. This issue remains one of great concern in criminal cases. Those concerned about the rights of criminal accused worry that states will use legislation to circumvent the intent of the principle. The concern is that states will change the definitions of crimes in order to remove elements from the actual legislative definition. The legislation could then place such elements as affirmative defenses and require defendants to prove the negative of such elements. The federal courts continue to review such cases.

a. Burden of Production

The burden of production, or sometimes called the burden of going forward, is on the prosecution in a criminal case. This burden of production operates in a manner that is very similar to the burden of production in civil cases. The prosecution must plead and prove sufficient facts to convince the trial judge that the case should go to the jury.

This burden is tested when the defendant in a criminal case makes a motion for a directed verdict of acquittal. It can arise, for example, when the prosecution has completed presentation of all of the evidence in the prosecution's case in chief. Before the defendant begins to put on proof, that defendant might move for the directed verdict of acquittal. In the alternative, the defendant might wait until the end of the trial and make the motion just before the case is submitted to the jury. The defendant's motion for directed verdict of acquittal is making the claim that the prosecution has failed to introduce sufficient evidence of every element of the crime in order to get the case to the jury.

Once the motion has been made, the trial judge must consider whether there is sufficient evidence to give the case to the jury. The test is similar, but not exactly the same as the test for reviewing the burden of production in civil cases. The primary reason that the tests are different is that the ultimate burden of persuasion is different in civil and criminal cases. As noted in the section on civil cases, the burden of persuasion in such cases is by a preponderance of the evidence. In criminal cases, the burden of persuasion is beyond a reasonable doubt. It is clear that the burden of persuasion is much greater in criminal cases. It would not be appropriate to send a case to the jury in a criminal case unless reasonable jurors could find the defendant guilty beyond a reasonable doubt. For that reason, the burden of production standard is also higher in criminal cases then in civil cases.

Much like civil cases, however, there is a two-step approach to testing the burden of production. The first step is the same as in civil cases. When the trial judge is reviewing a motion for directed verdict of acquittal, the trial judge is to consider all of the evidence in the light most favorable to the non-moving party. The moving party will always be the defendant, and the non-moving party will always be the prosecution. Since the prosecution will always, as required by the United States Constitution, have the burden to prove the case beyond a reasonable doubt, the prosecution cannot get a directed verdict of guilty. When the trial judge is considering all of the evidence in the light most favorable to the non-moving party, that means that the judge is considering the evidence in the light most favorable to the prosecution.

After considering all of the evidence in the light most favorable to the prosecution, the trial judge must determine whether the evidence is sufficient to go to the jury. Because of the higher burden of persuasion, it is obvious that criminal cases cannot use a "scintilla" rule. There must be more than a scintilla of evidence concerning every element of the crime. Defendants have sought to place a very high standard on the burden of product for prosecutions. The defendants would like the trial judge to grant the motion for directed verdict of acquittal unless the evidence is so strong that it would exclude every possible hypothesis except for the hypothesis of guilt. In short, defendants would like to receive a directed verdict of acquittal unless the evidence is so strong that the jury must return a verdict of guilty. The courts have not been inclined to require such a strong burden of production. The current theory is that the evidence must be sufficient to exclude every "reasonable" hypothesis except the hypothesis of guilt. That would indicate that if there were "reasonable" hypothesis that could be raised from the evidence that indicated the defendant was not guilty, then the trial judge should direct a verdict of acquittal. If, however, the only hypothesis of non-guilt were unreasonable, then the case should go to the jury. One way of stating this test has been to ask whether "reasonable jurors could find the defendant guilty beyond a reasonable doubt?" If the answer to that question is yes, then the case should go to the jury for determination. If, however, reasonable jurors could not find the defendant guilty beyond a reasonable doubt, then the trial judge should grant the motion for directed verdict of acquittal.

b. Burden of Persuasion

Once the trial judge has determined that the prosecution has met the burden of production, the case will go to the jury. The jury will be instructed on the burden of persuasion. The criminal case burden of persuasion may be one of the best known "rules" in law. The prosecution must prove every element of the crime "beyond a reasonable doubt." Not only is that the universally recognized and constitutionally mandated burden of persuasion in criminal cases, it is also required that the jury be instructed on that burden. The courts have been protective of that phrase "beyond a reasonable doubt." At times, trial courts have tried to further explain the meaning of the phrase "beyond a reasonable doubt." That has not lead to much success. Appellate courts have routinely overturned convictions because attempts to further explain "beyond a reasonable doubt" have either been over or under inclusive. Many jurisdictions merely instruct the jury on the simple phrase itself.

Trial practitioners of civil cases sometimes worry about the confusion that may exist in the minds of jurors. Since most television and movie court room dramas concern criminal cases, the burden of proof that most non-lawyers hear is the "beyond a reasonable doubt" standard. It is feared that non-lawyers assume that standard is the burden of proof in all trials. Plaintiffs' lawyers in civil trials worry that the jury will be expecting them to put on a case that removes all reasonable doubt. When comparing the "beyond a reasonable doubt" standard to the true civil standard of "preponderance of the evidence," it is clear that the civil standard is substantially less. Plaintiffs in civil cases do not have to produce as much evidence as their counterparts in the criminal cases. This issue has not been adequately covered in appellate decisions, but does remain a lingering concern among the plaintiffs' civil trial bar.

2. Presumptions

As discussed in the material on civil cases, presumptions are designed to assist the party with the burden of proof with meeting that burden. It was also

stated earlier that a true presumption could actually shift the burden of production and, in some states, shift the burden of persuasion in a case. Since
the U.S. Constitution requires that the prosecution prove every element of the
crime beyond a reasonable doubt, it would seem difficult to create a true presumption for criminal cases. If such a true presumption were created for criminal cases, the prosecution could raise the presumption and require the defendant to rebut the presumption or suffer a directed verdict of guilty. Since
the Constitutional requirements would prohibit that, it would seem that a true
presumption cannot exist in criminal cases. Although that sounds like a good
approximation of the rule, it is necessary to examine the actual details of the
problem. It is important to note that the Federal Rules of Evidence, rules 301
and 302, deal specifically with presumptions in civil cases. There are no specific rules in the Federal Rules of Evidence that deal with presumptions in
criminal cases.

Criminal cases may frequently mention the idea of presumptions in such
cases. The United States Supreme Court has faced the issue of the conflict between allowing presumptions to assist the prosecution and the need to uphold
the defendant's constitutional rights. The leading case of *County Court of Ul-
ster v. Allen*, 442 U.S. 140 (1979) explained the issue.

It is recognized that the proof of some basic facts may lead reasonable
minds to believe other facts exist. A criminal defendant may claim that he or
she did not "intend" to kill someone, but surely if they shot that person with
a gun, a reasonable person would have figured out that death was likely. Intent may be a difficult issue to prove when the defendant continues to say, "I
didn't mean to do it." Courts are likely to state that a defendant is assumed to
have intended the natural and probable consequences of his or her act. This
is beginning to sound like the courts are applying a presumption in a criminal case.

As a first step in approving such language, it is necessary for the courts to
find that there is a "rational connection" between the proven, basic facts and
the facts that the court wants to assume exists. From the example above, that
connection appears to be met. When someone shoots another person with a
gun, it appears rational to assume that the shooter intended to kill or, at least,
seriously harm the person being shot. The court would approve such assumption. The difficult issue, however, is what procedural affect should that
assumption have on the case.

The Supreme Court stated that if the assumption is to be used for a "permissive presumption" then the rational connection could be tested by looking
at the specific facts of the case. In other words, the court should test the rational connection between the proven facts and the assumed facts as it applies

to the case at hand. If the rational connection if found, then the court can use it as a "permissive presumption."

It is important, however, to understand what the Supreme Court meant by the term "permissive presumption." The Court meant that the jury could consider such evidence as proving the assumed fact, but was not required to accept such evidence. It appears, therefore, that the term "permissive presumption" is actually the device that the above text refers to as an inference. This "permissive presumption" will get the prosecution past a directed verdict and allow the case to go to the jury. It does not, however, shift any burdens of proof.

The Supreme Court did, however, recognize that there may be times when a court would want to use a "mandatory presumption." Such a "mandatory presumption" would require the jury to find the assumed fact unless it was rebutted by the defendant. This is the device that is described in the above text as a true rebuttable presumption. In order to use such a device in criminal cases, the Supreme Court articulated a stronger test. First, the basic facts must give rise to a belief in the assumed facts beyond a reasonable doubt. Second, the connection between the basic fact and the assumed fact is not to be tested by the actual facts of the case. The Court held that the connection is to be tested "on its face." That would mean that the connection between the basic facts and the assumed facts would have to be true for all possible sets of circumstances.

In reviewing the Supreme Court decision on criminal presumptions a practical answer seems to emerge. Although the Court has indicated that a true presumption may exist, the test is so difficult to meet, it is unlikely that any will be approved. The test to approve "permissive presumptions" is easier to meet. It is more likely, therefore, that inferences will exist in criminal cases.

Checkpoints

- Civil and criminal cases have two burdens of proof. They each have a burden of going forward and a burden of persuasion.

- The burden of going forward in a civil case is tested by a motion for directed verdict. When the motion is made the trial judge must consider all the evidence in the light most favorable to the non-moving party and ask whether reasonable jurors could find for the non-moving party by a preponderance of the evidence.

- The burden of persuasion in a civil case is usually stated as a preponderance of the evidence.

- Some issues in a civil case may use a clear and convincing standard as the burden of persuasion.
- The burden of going forward with the evidence in a criminal case is tested by a motion for directed verdict of acquittal. The judge will consider the evidence in the light most favorable to the defendant and ask whether reasonable jurors could find the defendant guilty beyond a reasonable doubt.
- The burden of persuasion in a criminal case is that the prosecution must prove every element of the crime beyond a reasonable doubt.
- Inferences in a civil case will get the plaintiff past a directed verdict, but still leave the burden of persuasion on the plaintiff.
- Presumptions in a civil case will get the plaintiff past a directed verdict and shift the burden of going forward with the evidence to the defendant. If the defendant fails to offer evidence in rebuttal, then the plaintiff is entitled to a directed verdict on the issue. If the defendant does offer rebuttal evidence, the presumption disappears, falls back to being an inference and the issue goes to the jury.
- Inferences and presumptions should work the same way in criminal cases. In order for an inference to be valid in a criminal case, there must be a rational connection between the proven fact and the inferred fact. The rational connection will be tested as applied to the circumstances of the case. In order for a presumption to be valid there must be a rational connection between the proven fact and the presumed fact, but the connection will be tested on the face of the presumption. That means that the connection must exist for all possible facts.

Chapter 4

Relevance

A. Introduction

The concept of relevance may be one of the most important issues to address in the whole subject area of evidence. Many text books and text writers begin the analysis of evidence principles by starting with relevance. Regardless of any other rules of evidence that may be in issue, in order for items of proof to be admitted in a trial, those items must first be relevant. Once it is determined that an item of proof is relevant, there may be other rules of evidence that exclude it from the trial. It must in the first instance, however, be found to be relevant. As a corollary to that idea, evidence that is not relevant is not admissible. Regardless of how important an item of proof appears to the parties, lawyers or judge, if that item of proof is not relevant it is not admissible.

It might be possible to develop a few "rules of thumb" in light of those above assumptions.

First, evidence that is not relevant is not admissible.

Second, evidence that is relevant is admissible unless there is some other rule that excludes it.

Although those two "rules of thumb" may set the general tone of a relevance discussion, they are too simplistic. They do, however, introduce the topic of relevance and give some guidance as to the primary issues to resolve.

The following material will discuss several primary issues. It is necessary first to determine the meaning or definition of relevant evidence. That definition will provide the initial rules to determine whether evidence is admissible. After the definition is determined, it is necessary to review the general rules that control the admissibility of relevant evidence. Finally, through the course of years of common law decisions, several particularized rules of relevance have developed to deal with specific fact issues. Those special rules must also be discussed.

It is important to note, that the Federal Rules of Evidence have a whole Article devoted to the issue of relevance. Rules 401 through 415 are the Federal Rules of Evidence Relevance rules.

B. General Requirement of Relevance (401, 402, 403)

1. The Basic Rule (402)

The initial rule of relevance is found in Federal Rule of Evidence 402. The rule basically repeats the little "rules of thumb" mentioned above. Relevant evidence is admissible unless there is some other rule that excludes it. In addition, evidence that is not relevant is not admissible.

2. The Definition (401)

That simple statement of rule leaves questions unanswered. It is, of course, necessary to determine the meaning of "relevant evidence." In order to find the definition of relevance, reference to Federal Rule of Evidence 401 is necessary. That rule explains that relevant evidence is any evidence that makes a fact of consequence in a case more probable or less probable than it would have been without introduction of the evidence. It is still necessary to break that definition down into smaller parts.

A relevance issue arises when an attorney for a party seeks to introduce evidence. The opposing party may object claiming such proof is "not relevant." The evidence that the proposing attorney wants to offer must make a fact of consequence more or less probable. The concept of a fact of consequence is the first problem area.

Before the adoption of the Federal Rules of evidence, courts use to talk about the concept of "materiality." Evidence had to be relevant and material. Material was the concept included the idea that evidence offered in the case must relate to something important. The Federal Rules of Evidence got rid of the separate concept of materiality and merged it into the word relevance. The phrase, "fact of consequence," is the phrase that replaced the word "materiality." Evidence that is relevant must make a fact of consequence more or less probable. In short, evidence that is offered must have something to do with important issues in the case. The easiest examples of "facts of consequence" are the elements of claims, defenses or crimes. In a negligence case, for example, it is necessary to prove duty, breach, injury and causation. Those four elements would be "facts of consequence." The common law crime of burglary required proof of breaking and entering into the dwelling house of another at night with the intent to commit a felony. All of those elements would be facts of consequence.

In the initial discussion of relevance, therefore, it is necessary to determine what the facts of consequence are. Evidence is only relevant if it relates to the facts of consequence. It might be said that this is an identity problem. The lawyers and judge must identify the facts of consequence in order to determine whether the evidence offered is actually related to such facts. It is, again, important to note that modern lawyers using the Federal Rules of Evidence do not use the term materiality. The phrase "facts of consequence" has replaced the word materiality.

The second step to determine if evidence is relevant is to see if it makes a fact of consequence more or less probable. This can be seen as a logic problem. Does the introduction of one fact tend to suggest that another fact may exist? In order for the first fact to be admissible, there must be the suggestion that another fact exists. The suggestion must be strong enough for the court to find that the proof of the first fact makes the existence of the second fact "more probably or less probable." In other words, the proof of the first fact must create a probability that the second fact either does or does not exist. (Keep in mind that the second fact that the court is concerned about is a "fact of consequence.")

Putting the two concepts together, it seems that the idea of relevance raises two problems. It has an identity and a logic problem. The courts must first identify the fact of consequence that is sought to be proven and then check to see if the evidence offered does, in logic, tend to make that fact of consequence more or less probable.

3. A General Exclusion (403)

It was noted earlier that not all relevant evidence is admissible. Relevant evidence is only admissible if it is not excluded by other rules. Federal Rule of

Evidence 403 provides the first and most general rule of exclusion for relevant evidence. This exclusion is accomplished by way of a balancing test. Evidence that is relevant may be excluded if the probative value of the evidence is "substantially outweighed by dangers of unfair prejudice, confusion of issues, or misleading the jury, or by considerations of undue delay, waste of time, or needless presentation of cumulative evidence." Fed. R. Evid. 403. This general exclusion creates several problems.

It is clear that the use of this rule is usually vested in the sound discretion of the trial judge. Attorneys will frequently seek to have evidence excluded on the basis of this principle and the trial judge must make the decision.

The rule is broadly stated and appears to apply to any issues of evidence. Whatever the circumstances of the evidence issue, an attorney seeking to exclude the evidence may usually add this argument to the grounds for exclusion. Just as an example, although evidence might be found to be admissible under an exception to a hearsay rule, the opposing counsel may argue that it should be excluded under this rule.

It is important to note that the evidence is excluded only if the danger of prejudice is due to "unfair" prejudice. A party to the case may feel that evidence being offered will prejudice the jury against him or her. That party may fear the jury will rule against him or her because of the evidence. Frequently, evidence comes into a case that will cause "prejudice" to a party. It is part of the traditional trial practice that one party will lose. This rule is not designed to exclude all prejudicial evidence. It is only designed to exclude evidence that is "unfairly" prejudicial.

As stated above, there is a balancing test in this rule. In determining whether to exclude the evidence, the trial judge must perform the appropriate balance. The evidence is only to be excluded if the trial judge determines that the probative value is "substantially outweighed" by the danger of unfair prejudice. As such, the judge may assume that relevant evidence is to be admitted unless it can be shown that there is this substantial danger of unfair prejudice.

These basic principles of relevance set out the general rules to follow. As noted earlier, several particularized problems arose over a sufficient number of times to allow for the development of additional rules. These additional relevance rules give govern very specific issues.

C. Character for the Purpose of Proving Propensity (404, 405)

1. Types of Character Evidence (404)

It is generally assumed that evidence of a person's general character traits is not admissible as evidence in a trial. Trials are designed to determine what a person did on a particular occasion. In civil trials, the court is not interested in whether a person is generally a good driver, but whether that same person was negligent on a particular day and that negligence caused an accident. In criminal trials, the court is not interested in whether the defendant is generally a good person. The court is interested in whether that defendant committed the particular illegal act for which he or she is charge. The mere fact that a person is a good person or a bad person is not considered to be relevant to whether they did or did not commit an illegal or negligent act. For these reasons, the general rule is that evidence of a person's character traits is not admissible to prove that the person acted in conformity with that character trait. (Fed. R. Evid. 404(a)).

Rule 404 of the Federal Rules of Evidence is the basic rule for character evidence. As noted above, the general rule is that such evidence is not admissible to prove that a person acted in conformity with that character. There are, however, several problems with that rule.

This rule deals specifically with the problem of trying to use such evidence to prove that a plaintiff or defendant acted in conformity with his or her character, and that the "act in conformity" is a "fact of consequence" in the case. That is the type of example that the rule intends to exclude from the trial. There are some other examples of the use of character that may be admissible. In addition, the rule itself allows for exceptional uses of character evidence.

First, it is important to note a type of example that the rule does not exclude because it is not an "act in conformity." There are some types of cases where a party's character is actually in issue in the case. These may be referred to as "character in issue" cases. The easiest example of those may arise in a defamation case. In a defamation case, the plaintiff is seeking to show that his or her reputation has been harmed by the defamatory remarks. In order for the plaintiff to recover damages, it will be important for that plaintiff to prove that he or she had a good reputation and that the reputation was harmed. The defendant may want to prove that the plaintiff had a bad reputation in the first place and suffered no harm. In order to prove this element of "reputation" the parties will seek to introduce evidence of the plaintiff's character.

Another type of character in issue case may arise when an employer has been sued for negligently hiring a driver when it was well known that the driver had a history of bad driving. Such "negligent entrustment" cases are "character in issue." The plaintiff will want to prove the prior bad driving character by the employee in order to show that the employer knew or in the exercise of reasonable care should have known that the employee was a bad driver.

It is easy to see that in both of the "character in issue" examples that are given, the character evidence is not being offered to prove that someone acted in conformity with his or her character on a particular occasion. Instead, the character evidence is being offered to prove a particular "fact of consequence" in the case. Such "character in evidence" is admissible under the Federal Rules of Evidence. A close reading of Fed. R. Evid. 404 does not specifically state that the evidence is admissible. Instead, the rule merely explains that character for the purpose of proving acts in conformity is not admissible. This allows other "relevant" evidence to still be admissible. It allows the admission of "character in issue" by not specifically excluding it.

A second special problem arises when a party may want to introduce evidence of a witness's character for telling the truth or for lying. This type of evidence would not go to prove or disprove an element of a claim or defense, but would be used to try to attack or support the credibility of a witness. Rule 404(a)(3) allows such evidence, but makes it subject to rules 607, 608, and 609. Since the rules themselves rely on rules 607, 608, and 609 to regulate character of a witness evidence, this text will discuss that issue in the chapter dealing with the 600 rules.

In addition to the special problems already noted, the federal rules allow the admission of character evidence in two more exceptional cases. The rules mention "character of the accused" and "character of the victim."

Prior to 2006, there could have been some question as to whether these exceptions were available in civil cases. The rules mentioned character of the "accused" and character of the "victim." It is important to note that civil cases do not have an "accused" or a "victim." It may be popular to use terms like "accused" and "victim" in tort cases, but those terms are appropriate only in criminal cases. This means that the special exceptions for "character of the accused" and "character of the victim" only apply in criminal cases. In 2006, the rules were amended to make it clear that the exceptions only applied in criminal cases. Civil cases are controlled by the general principle stated in the introductory part of rule 404. Evidence of a person's character to prove an act in conformity is not admissible in a civil case.

The rules do allow admission of the "character of accused" in a criminal case. Fed. R. Evid. 404(a)(1) is a narrow or limited rule. The rule allows the accused to offer evidence of a pertinent trait of character of the accused and allows the prosecution to offer evidence to rebut that offered by the accused. In a criminal case, the prosecution presents his or her case first. The prosecution is allowed to offer the prosecution's case in chief before the defendant offers his or her case in chief. Since the prosecution is only allowed to "rebut" character of the accused evidence, the prosecution cannot offer evidence concerning the character of the accused during the prosecution's case in chief. Once the accused begins to offer his or her evidence in chief, however, the accused can offer evidence of his or her character. Obviously, the accused will be offering evidence showing that he or she has "good character." Once the accused has offered such evidence during his or her case in chief, the prosecution may offer evidence of character of the accused during a period of rebuttal witnesses. Obviously, the prosecution will be offering evidence of "bad character."

The rule is somewhat specific about the type of character evidence that may be offered. The character evidence must be concerning a "pertinent" trait of character. This means that the trait of character discussed must be in someway related to the type of crime being charged. If the crime is one of violence, such as assault or homicide, then the trait of character should be peacefulness or violence.

Fed. R. Evid. 404(a)(2) discusses "character of victim." As with the "character of accused" rule, this rule allows the defendant in a criminal case to raise the "character of the victim" and the prosecution to rebut such evidence. The rule allows the accused to offer evidence of a pertinent trait of character of the victim of a crime and the prosecution to rebut the same. This would arise, for example, in a case where the accused was charged with the violent assault or homicide of the victim. The accused might want to raise the defense of self-defense. In raising the defense, the accused might claim that the victim had a known character for violent behavior and the accused was merely defending him or herself. The rule allows the admission of such evidence. Once the accused has introduced such evidence, the prosecution can offer evidence in rebuttal to show that the victim had a peaceful character. The rule also notes that the prosecution can offer rebuttal evidence of character in a homicide case where the accused claims the victim was the first aggressor.

One additional feature of these rules must be noticed. If the accused offers evidence of the character of the victim, the prosecution can use that triggering evidence as a reason to also offer rebuttal concerning the character of the accused. That is the only example where the prosecution can offer evidence concerning the character of the accused before the accused offers evidence concerning his or her character.

Probably the most difficult use of character evidence is specified in rule 404(b). This portion of the rule begins by restating the general principle that the evidence of other "crimes, wrongs or acts" is not admissible to prove that a person acted in conformity. The rule goes on to say, however, that it may be used for other purposes. It may be used to prove "motive, opportunity, intent, preparation, plan, knowledge, identity, or absence of mistake or accident." Fed. R. Evid. 404(b). The rule itself is not limited to criminal cases, but may include civil matters. The opportunity for offering such evidence is rare. Courts seem to allow such evidence primarily in criminal cases. It is admitted when a defendant appears to have a common method of committing a crime and has done so numerous times. In order to use such evidence, the prior acts must have been very similar if not identical to the one under trial. Some courts speak of these events as being so similar as being a "signature" for the crime. The evidence is admitted to prove there is no mistake as to the accused. Using such a theory, it could be seen that the use of the evidence is limited. If, for example, the accused had been involved in several violent acts, that may not be sufficient. If the accused had beaten one person, stabbed another, and then was charged with shooting a third, the evidence of the prior beating and stabbing would not be admissible. Such events would not be similar enough. If, however, the person had a particular mode of committing the crime, the evidence of the identical crimes could be admissible. It must be remembered that Fed. R. Evid. 403 would still be applicable when a court considered this evidence. It would be admitted, but the court would still have to determine if the probative value was substantially outweighed by the danger of unfair prejudice.

2. Method of Proof When Character Evidence Is Admissible (405)

The immediately proceeding section discussed the times when character evidence may be admissible. It did not, however, explain the form that the character evidence had to take. Fed. R. Evid. 405 covers the form that such evidence must take if it is to be admissible. In dealing with character evidence, therefore, an attorney must use both rules 404 and 405. Rule 404 will explain when such character evidence is admissible while rule 405 will explain the form it is to take.

The broadest rule for the form the evidence is to take is in rule 405(a). Under any example where character evidence may be admitted, it may take the form of reputation or opinion. The traditional common law rule would have limited character evidence to reputation only, but the Federal Rules added the option of opinion. This would allow the use of reputation or opinion when the accused wishes to offer evidence of his or her own character or the character of the victim. It would allow the use of reputation or opinion when the prosecution wishes to offer rebuttal evidence of the character of the accused or the character of the victim. It also allows the use of reputation or opinion in character in issue cases.

The use of reputation or opinion may be seen in a few easy examples. An accused may want to call a family friend to the witness stand to offer evidence showing the "good character for peacefulness" of the accused. The witness would first be asked about whether he or she had knowledge of such character. The questions and answer might proceed as such:

> Q. How long have you known the accused?
>
> A. I've known the accused for 20 years.
>
> Q. How did you get to know the accused?
>
> A. I live across the street from the family, and have watched the accused grow up.
>
> Q. Did you have any special contact with the family of the accused or the accused?
>
> A. Yes. For several years I coached the neighborhood baseball team and the accused was on my team. In addition, for many summers I hired the accused to cut my yard and tend to my shrubs.
>
> Q. During that same period, did you get to know other people that also knew the accused?
>
> A. Yes. It is a close community. We all know each other. I'm well familiar with the accused and all of our neighbors.

At that point it would be necessary to ask the questions dealing with the character. If the attorney wanted to bring out evidence of the "reputation" for peacefulness, the questions would proceed as such:

> Q. During the years that you knew the accused did you learn of the accused's reputation for peacefulness?
>
> A. Yes, I did.
>
> Q. What is that reputation?
>
> A. The accused has a good reputation for peacefulness.

If the attorney wanted to bring out the witness's opinion on character, the questions would proceed as such:

> Q. During the years that you knew the accused did you form an opinion as to the accused's character for peacefulness?

A. Yes, I did.

Q. What is your opinion?

A. My opinion is that the accused has a good character for peace-fulness.

Once a witness has testified to any matter, that witness is subject to cross examination. The attorney for the other side may ask the witness questions. The cross examination of a character witness may cover the background of how the witness came to the conclusions or the conclusions themselves. Rule 405 provides an additional method of cross examination also. When a witness has testified to character by reputation or opinion, that witness may also be questioned on cross examination about specific instances of conduct. (405(b))

Specific instances of conduct evidence may arise when a character witness has testified that an accused's character for peacefulness is good. The prose-cution may know of examples when the accused acted in a violent manner. There is a danger that allowing that evidence to be introduced will cause con-fusion in the mind of the jury. The jury is only to use that evidence to weigh the credibility of the witness. A jury may decide that a witness who testified that an accused had a character for peacefulness was not telling the truth when it is revealed that the accused had numerous violent episodes. The jury is not to use the evidence to show that the accused was probably violent and there-fore guilty of the crime for which they are being tried.

At common law, there was a difficult issue as to how to phrase the ques-tion concerning specific instances of conduct. Courts once said that the ques-tion had to be phrased as to whether the witness had "heard" of the previous instances of violence and could not be phrased as to whether the witness "knew" of the previous instances of violence. The advisory committee to the Federal Rules has noted that distinction is no longer necessary. The question may be asked as "have you heard" or "did you know." Examples of such ques-tions on cross examination would be as such:

Q. You've testified that in your opinion, the accused has a peace-ful character.

A. That is correct.

Q. Did you know that on June 23, 2001, he beat up the next door neighbor's child?

The question could be phrased as such:

Q. You've testified that in your opinion, the accused has a peace-ful character.

A. That is correct.

Q. Have you heard that on June 23, 2001, he beat up the next door neighbor's child?

One additional example of specific instances of conduct is allowed. Where the character being offered is being offered in a "character in issue" case, the party offering the evidence may use specific instances of conduct. That is, of course, in addition to reputation or opinion.

D. Habit (406)

The issue of whether evidence of habit should be admissible raises a series of questions. Habit is routinely found to be similar to character evidence. The federal rules of evidence, however, indicate that habit evidence is admissible to prove that a party acted in conformity with that habit. It is important, therefore, to first distinguish between habit and character. As noted above, character evidence is admissible only under limited, controlled circumstances, while habit is generally admissible.

Character is usually viewed as the general nature of one's behavior. It may be seen as the total picture of how a person behaves. In some ways, character is the reputation that a person obtains after the community observes all of that person's conduct over a long period of time. Character relates to a broad range of conducts and reflects the nature of responses a person may have to all of those activities. Habit is a narrower personality trait. The law assumes that habit is the regular or routine response that a person will have to a repeated stimulus.

It is probably necessary to consider some examples to understand this difference between character and habit. A witness might want to testify that person A is a careful driver. That would be character evidence and probably not admissible. If, however, that witness wanted to testify that person A went across a particular railroad crossing twice a day, that being on the way to work and the way home, and on every occasion, person A would stop, listen for the train whistle, look both ways, and then proceed, that would be habit. The first statement, the driver is careful, reflects a general conclusion gained from watching the person drive over a variety of different situations. That is character and generally not admissible. Being able to report the regular, repeated conduct that was observed when the driver encountered the railroad crossing on numerous occasions would be evidence of habit. Habit is generally admissible.

Using the above example, it could be imagined that the driver while in his car was struck and killed by a train at the crossing. The family of the driver is suing the railroad claiming that the railroad crossing was unsafe or that the engineer of the train failed to blow the whistle. The railroad company would claim comparative fault on the part of the driver. Since the driver is deceased, there is very little direct evidence bearing on the conduct of the driver. The witness would not be allowed to testify that the driver had the character of being a careful driver. Under Fed. R. Evid. 404, evidence of character is not admissible in a civil case to prove that the person acted in conformity. The witness could testify, however, that he was familiar with the driving of the driver. The witness could say that he had seen the driver approach the railroad crossing on numerous occasions. On all of those occasions the driver had the habit of always stopping, listening for the whistle, looking both ways, and then proceeding. This evidence would be admissible under Fed. R. Evid. 406 as evidence of habit tending to prove that the driver acted in the same manner on the day of the accident.

The issue of habit can arise in a variety of cases in the tort area. It can come up in professional malpractice cases where an injured party seeks to claim a physician failed to use reasonable care while performing a particular procedure. It would not be admissible to claim that the physician was generally careful. It would be admissible, however, to prove that this particular physician always performed the procedure in the same way. That would be admissible to prove that it was probably performed in that manner on the day in question.

Evidence of excessive drinking of alcohol has occasionally raised the issue of habit. Injured parties may have wanted to claim that the opposing party was probably intoxicated at the time of an accident because that party was frequently intoxicated. Courts have usually found such evidence to be attempts to introduce character. The fact that the person is generally known to be a heavy drinker is seen as character evidence. It does not rise to the level of proving a habit of being intoxicate.

In criminal cases, attempts to prove that a person is generally violent are also usually seen as character. Character may be introduced in a very limited manner in criminal cases, but the general nature of being violent is not seen as a habit.

This distinction between character and habit is the most difficult issue with this rule. Cases that have tended to exclude evidence under this rule have usually found that the practice or conduct was not sufficiently uniform or regular to be elevated to the status of habit. The courts in such cases have usually found that the evidence being offered was more of a general statement of the nature of the person's character and was, therefore, inadmissible.

The above discussion of habit assumes that a party is trying to prove the habit or habits of one person. Fed. R. Evid. 406 also allows the introduction of evidence of the routine practices organizations. This permits the admissibility of evidence of the regular customs or habits of such organizations. Again, it is important to distinguish between the general nature of an organization and the regular, routine practice of that organization. If, however, the witness is willing to testify that an organization has a regular, routine practice, that evidence will be admitted as proof that the organization probably acted in the same manner at the time in question.

Evidence of regular practices of organizations may arise in tort or contract cases. When, for example, an organization may be sued for failing to property maintain equipment, evidence of the usually and regular maintenance schedules would be admissible. Such schedules would show the regular practice of the organization and would be evidence that the organization probably followed that schedule with the equipment in question. If there was a case involving the receiving and noting the arrival of goods in a warehouse, the organization may want to offer evidence of the usual practices in noting the arrival of such goods in an effort to show that the goods never arrived. Such evidence would be admissible as the routine practice of the organization.

An issue arises with habit is one with an old history. Some cases in the past have required some corroborating evidence in order to allow the admission of habit or organization practice. It was thought that the evidence of habit alone was not sufficiently strong to allow admission. There should be some support. Fed. R. Evid. 406 specifically rejects this point and allows the admission of habit and organization practice without corroborating evidence.

Another historical issue is whether habit should be admissible when there is eyewitness testimony concerning the same event. Some courts felt that habit evidence was so weak that it should only be admitted if there was no other direct evidence available. Where that rule is followed, the presence of eyewitness testimony would result in the exclusion of the habit evidence. Fed. R. Evid. 406 specifically rejects that rule. Habit evidence is admissible "regardless of the presence of eyewitnesses."

One addition issue may arise with habit evidence. During the discussion of character evidence it was noted that character evidence was admissible in limited circumstances. Once it is determined that character is admissible, Fed. R. Evid. 405 sets out the format that the character evidence must take. Depending on the time and nature of the questioning, character evidence may take the form of reputation, opinion, or specific instances of conduct. The federal rules of evidence do not specify the proper form for habit evidence. In approving rule 406, the House Committee on the Judiciary thought that the form of the evidence should be left up to the trial court to decide on a case-by-case basis. As such, habit may come in as reputation, opinion, or specific instances of conduct. The determination of the proper form will be left to the trial judge.

E. Subsequent Remedial Measures (407)

Fed. R. Evid. 407 deals with a recurring problem in tort law. Once an accident occurs, someone may feel the need to repair the area or the instrumentality of the accident. A person who is injured in that accident, may subsequently decide to bring an action for his or her injuries. If it was the defendant in that action that had made the repairs to the location or instrumentality of the injury, the plaintiff may want to offer evidence of those repairs in an effort to show that the defendant was probably "at fault" in the first instance.

The older cases in this area are best exemplified by railroad crossing accidents. In such cases, an automobile may have been trying to cross a railroad crossing when it was hit by a train. After the accident, the railroad company goes out to the crossing site and makes repairs. In making the repairs, the railroad company may upgrade the crossing; replace the warning devices with newer, brighter lights or more bells and signals. That company may even add a crossing gate where one did not previously exist.

The driver of the automobile then sues the railroad company for injuries suffered during the accident. During the course of the trial, the plaintiff would want to put on evidence of the repair and upgrades made to the crossing. The allegation would be that the evidence of repairs proves that the defendant was negligent in not improving the crossing prior to the accident. Even before the federal rules of evidence, courts would routinely exclude such evidence. The courts had two bases for excluding the evidence.

The first reason for excluding the evidence was that the conduct of the defendant that occurred subsequent to the accident was not relevant to whether the defendant was negligent prior to the accident. The courts would reason that the defendant may have used all due care prior to the accident. After the accident occurred, the defendant, in the exercise of reasonable care may have realized the crossing could be made safer. This analysis would require the exclusion of the evidence since the issue was whether the defendant was negligent before the accident. In addition, even if there was some possible probative value for the evidence, it was outweighed by the real fear of unfair prejudice to the defendant.

The courts would routinely state a second ground for excluding the evidence. There is a public policy that encourages people to continue to upgrade and improve dangerous locations. The courts felt that if railroads, in a trial, would have to face the evidence that the company had improved the crossing, such companies would not make the improvements. The courts felt that by excluding the evidence, the future defendants would be encouraged to continue to make improvements.

The traditional rule, therefore, was simple. In a negligence case, evidence of a subsequent remedial measure could not be introduced into evidence to prove the negligence. The bases of the exclusion were twofold. The evidence was not relevant to negligence and public policy would encourage the exclusion of the evidence. The federal rules of evidence adopted this position.

Even before the adoption of the federal rules, there were exceptions to the rule. The current rule states these exceptions as, "This rule does not require the exclusion of evidence of subsequent measures when offered for another purpose, such as proving ownership, control, or feasibility of precautionary measures, if controverted or impeachment." Fed. R. Evid. 407. The application of these exceptions can also be seen in the railroad crossing cases. The hypothetical could arise in the same manner as stated above. The plaintiff was injured and the defendant railroad company had made repairs and upgrades to the crossing. In this example, however, when the defendant railroad company is sued, they deny that they owned or had control of the crossing. Their defense is not a denial of negligence, but a claim that the plaintiff has sued the wrong person or company. In such a case, the plaintiff could offer the evidence of the repairs and upgrades. The purpose of the evidence would be to show that the defendants either owned or controlled the crossing. The logic of such a relevance argument should be clear. The plaintiff would be claiming that the defendants must have owned or controlled the crossing since they fixed it. The evidence would be admitted for the purpose of proving ownership or control.

The rule also indicates one additional exceptional use of the evidence. If the evidence is offered for the purposes of impeaching a witness, it may be admitted.

As long as the cases dealt with the issue of negligence, the law seemed easy to apply. If the evidence was offered to prove negligence or wrongdoing, it was not admissible. If it was offered for one of the exceptional issues, it was admissible. As the federal courts began to face increased numbers of products liability cases which used strict liability, the rules became harder to apply.

In products liability cases, plaintiffs began to want to introduce evidence of subsequent improvements made to products. The hypothetical example is easy to explain here. The plaintiff would be injured by a product alleged to have been designed defectively. Between the time the plaintiff was injured and the time the case goes to trial, the manufacturer of the product begins to make it using a different and safer design. The plaintiff would want to introduce the evidence of the safer design in order to prove that the product was in a defective condition unreasonably dangerous at the time it left the manufacturer. Courts were split as to how to approach this problem.

Some courts would allow the evidence to be admissible. Those courts reasoned that the evidence in negligence cases had been excluded because it was not relevant to prove the failure to use reasonable care at an earlier time. In strict liability cases, however, the condition of the product and not the conduct of the parties is the issue. The evidence of subsequent re-design of the product would be admissible to show the condition of the product. It would help illustrate that it was possible to make a safer design. Since the conduct of the party was not an issue, and the condition of the product was the sole issue, the evidence was held by some to be admissible.

Other courts excluded the evidence. Those opinions seemed to focus more heavily on the public policy reasons for excluding the evidence. They reasoned that the purpose of the rule was to encourage possible defendants to make repairs and upgrades to dangerous instrumentalities. Those courts thought the same rule should apply to product manufacturers. It would be in the best interest of the public to encourage product manufacturers to continue to improve the safety of products. It was thought that manufacturers might avoid making upgrades if it was known that such evidence of upgrades could be used against the manufacturer. Using that logic, some courts excluded the evidence of subsequent remedial measures in strict liability cases.

In 1997, the issue regarding strict liability in products cases was resolved by an amendment to Fed. R. Evid. 407. Prior to that time, the rule had only excluded evidence of subsequent remedial measures when offered to prove "negligence or culpable conduct." In 1997, the rule was amended to exclude such evidence when offered to prove "negligence, culpable conduct, a defect in a product, a defect in a product's design, or a need for a warning or instruction." The intent of the amendment should be clear.

It is recognized that there are three types of defects which may give rise to strict liability in products cases. The plaintiff may allege a mis-manufacture, a mis-design, or a failure to warn. This amendment to the rule was intended to exclude evidence of subsequent remedial measures in all three types of cases. The language that excludes the evidence to prove a "defect in a product" would apply to mis-manufacture. The language that excludes the evidence when offered for a "defect in a product's design" would apply to mis-design. The language that excludes the evidence when offered for the "need for a warning or instruction" would apply to failure to warn. Although this appears to eliminate any questions, doubts as to the full use of this rule remain.

First, the most likely use of subsequent remedial measures would have been in design defect cases. The most common example of the problem is when a plaintiff is hurt and the manufacturer feels the need to redesign the product. The mis-manufacturer cases do not raise the issue. In those cases, the evidence is clear that the mis-manufactured product has a problem. Plaintiffs would rarely, if ever, need to resort to showing that the manufacturer changed anything. In addition, the failure to warn rarely raised the subsequent remedial measure rule. It has always been clear that manufacturers could make different warnings. The fact that they changed the warning after the fact is rarely used. Because of these realities, there was no great need to deal with mis-manufacture and failure to warn with this rule.

Second, the rule still leaves an exception that may apply. The rule indicates that the evidence might be admissible to prove "feasibility of precautionary measures." It is recognized that many design defect cases will focus on whether it was possible to design the product in a safer manner. If the defendant denies that a "feasible alternative" is available, but has, in fact, changed the design of the product to make it safer, that evidence may be admissible. The plaintiff would argue that the redesign of the product that occurred subsequent to the injury reflects the "feasibility of precautionary measures." It is interesting to note that some jurisdictions have stated that "feasible alternative" is a required element for the plaintiff to prove in a design defect case. It would seem that the evidence of subsequent remedial measures would always be admissible in such jurisdictions.

There are, however, other conflicting issues arising in tort law that may also have an impact on this evidence problem. In the late 1990's, the American Law Institute issued the final version of the Restatement (Third) of Products Liability. This restatement tends to speak of design defect cases in terms of negligence. The plaintiff must prove that the product was an unreasonable design in light of unreasonable risks. If jurisdictions move design defect cases back to negligence and away from strict liability, the amendment to rule 407 was unnecessary. The initial language of the rule that excluded the evidence where it was offered to prove negligence or culpable conduct would control.

Application of the rule, therefore, may leave a few, small issues in question. It is clear that use of the evidence to prove negligence is not permitted. It may be admissible to prove such things as ownership or control. It is also admissible if it is used to impeach a witness. The rule does state that the evidence is also not to be used to prove the three types of defects in a strict liability products case. The only real question is whether the exception for "feasibility of precautionary measures" will allow the evidence to be admitted in design defect cases. That will require the review by more federal courts in order for a final answer to be reached.

F. Compromises, Offers, Payments and Pleas (408, 409, 410)

1. Compromises (408)

Rule 408 is usually raised in civil cases. It is a well known principle in civil cases that the law encourages settlements. Most civil actions settle before trial and, in the absence of that practice, the courts would be overwhelmed. When a case is filed, the attorneys for the litigants begin thinking about that settlement almost immediately. It is common that the opposing counsels will begin discussion of the possibility of settlement very early. It is clear that if attorneys were allowed to introduce offers of settlement made prior to trial into evidence in the trial, that evidence could be substantially prejudicial to the party who made the offer. The jury might believe that the party would not have made the offer unless he or she believed they had some exposure to liability.

Evidence of offers of compromise or settlement is not, however, relevant to the issues in the case. A party might make an offer of settlement even though he or she believes they have no responsibility in the case. Litigation, with the possibility of extended appeals, is very expensive. A party to litigation may make an economic decision that it is cheaper to pay a small settlement rather than pay the costs associated with lengthy litigation even if that party is ultimately successful in the litigation. The offer of settlement is, therefore, merely a way to reduce costs.

Fed. R. Evid. 408 specifically states that offers of settlement are not admissible. The reasons for that exclusion are as set out above. First, the evidence is not relevant. The evidence of an offer of settlement does not tend to prove or disprove any elements of the case. It is more likely evidence of the fact that the parties do not want to expend substantial funds on litigation. Second, public policy encourages settlement. The public as a whole enjoys substantial savings in court resources by having substantial numbers of civil actions settled. The rule of exclusion protects the discussions among the parties in order to accomplish both of those goals.

In addition to excluding evidence of offers of settlement, it is important to note that the rule also excludes evidence of actually furnishing or accepting a settlement. This type of situation could arise where a plaintiff has sued multiple defendants. Prior to trial, that plaintiff may have settled with some but not all of the defendants. The defendants remaining in the case would want to introduce the prior settlements in order for the jury to know that the plaintiff had already received substantial funds. In addition, the defendants would suggest that the defendants that had already settled were probably the ones responsible for the loss. That evidence is not admissible for the same reasons given for excluding offers of settlement. The evidence of the actual settlements is not relevant to issues in the case. Those settlements merely reflect the desire of some defendants to be finished with the litigation. In addition, public policy would not be served by allowing the evidence of settlements. If the plaintiffs knew they would have to defend against that evidence, they would be less likely to accept settlements from some defendants. By excluding evidence of settlements, multiple defendants become more encouraged to settle. Once one or two defendants settle, the remaining defendants do not want to the only one left in the case.

During the course of settlement negotiations, there are times when the attorneys must discuss the nature of the case. These statements may involve discussing the basic facts from the differing points of view. At common law, it was assumed that such statements made during the course of settlement negotiation, but not a part of the actual settlement offer could be admissible into evidence. Such a rule required that attorneys be very careful as to what was actually said when settlements were discussed. They had to be sure not to make any "admissions" about the case. This, of course, meant that there could be no free and open discussions that would help the case move towards settlement. Fed. R. Evid. 408 changes that rule and now states, "Evidence of conduct or statements made in compromise negotiations is likewise not admissible."

The rule that excludes other statements during made during settlement negotiations does have one requirement. There must actually be a claim in order for the rule to take effect. General admissions made by parties or their attorneys would be admissible except for this rule.

The exclusion of offers of settlement, the settlements themselves and statements made during settlement negotiations does have exceptions. Fed. R. Evid. 408 provides that the evidence may be admissible when "offered for another purpose, such as proving bias or prejudice of a witness, negativing a contention of undue delay, or proving an effort to obstruct a criminal investigation or prosecution." The reasoning underlying the exceptional circumstances is easy to understand. The general exclusion is intended to prevent the offers from being used to prove the validity of a claim. The exceptions allow for "other" uses. Where, for example, a witness may have received a substantial sum of money, that evidence might reflect bias or prejudice of the witness to testify in a particular manner. Where a party has been making offers of settlement, that may reflect that the party has not been delaying the matter. Finally, in one of the few uses of this rule in criminal cases, evidence that someone had sought to "pay off" a prosecution witness would be admissible.

2. Payment of Medical Expenses (409)

Fed. R. Evid. 409 is a companion rule to Fed. R. Evid. 408. Where 408 excludes evidence of offers to compromise generally, 409 deals specifically with one type of compromise. Fed. R. Evid. 409 states that, "Evidence of furnishing or offering or promising to pay medical, hospital, or similar expenses occasioned by an injury is not admissible to prove liability for the injury." The brevity of the rule results in some questions.

The purpose of the rule is similar to the broader rule 408. The evidence of offering to pay medical bills is not relevant. It does not reflect that the person actually believe they owe the costs, but may just be reflective of a desire to end litigation. In addition, public polity encourages settlement.

The drafters of the rules, however, thought there were some differences between general offers of settlement and offers to pay medical bills. Since general offers of settlement would be encouraged by free and open discussions of the nature of the case, statements made during settlement negotiations are excluded as well as the offers. The drafters of the rules did not believe that same need arose when offers were made to pay medical bills. As such, there is no general exclusion for other statements made when an offer to pay medical bills is the evidentiary issue to be decided. The offer to pay the medical bills would be excluded, but the other statements may be admissible as admissions of a party.

This rule is also silent on the possibility of exceptions to the rule. Although there may be times when rule 408 allows the admission of evidence of general offers of settlement, rule 409 does not have a specific list of exceptional circumstances where evidence of offers to pay medical bills would be admissible. A close reading of the rule does suggest the possibility of exceptional circumstances. The rule says that the evidence is not admissible to "prove liability for injury." This would suggest that the rule would allow the admission of the evidence to prove such things as bias or prejudice of a witness.

Rules 408 and 409 must be considered together. Rule 408 is the broad exclusion for statements made during settlement negotiations and the offers of settlement. Rule 409 is the narrow exclusion of offers to pay medical bills alone. Attorneys must be careful to understand the differences that exist in these two rules. It is also clear that such differences form some of the reasons that attorneys generally prevent their own clients from talking to the opposing side during litigation. Non-lawyers may have a tendency to say things that may be admissible under such complex rules.

3. Pleas in Criminal Cases (410)

Rule 410 is similar to rules 408 and 409, but is concerned with attempts to "settle" criminal cases. It is well known that criminal cases are frequently "settled" by the defendant pleading guilty to some crime. As with settlements of civil cases, the fact that a criminal defendant pleads guilty to a crime does not necessarily mean that the defendant actually believes that he or she committed that crime. The defendant may be pleading guilty to a lesser offense in order to reduce the amount of time to be spent in jail. Where the defendant pleads guilty and the guilty plea is accepted by the courts, there is no evidence issue. The guilty plea becomes a final settlement of the case and there is no need for trial.

Once a guilty plea has been accepted possible issues in a civil action may arise. A criminal defendant may also be sued for civil damages that arose from the conduct. If a guilty plea was accepted, that guilty plea may be admissible in a civil action. Such an accepted guilty plea acts like an admission of the party. The difficulties with rule 410 begin when the guilty plea is withdrawn.

Fed. R. Evid. 410 specifically states that when a guilty plea is withdrawn it may not be used as evidence against the person who originally made the plea in either criminal or civil actions. This part of the rule is based on the idea that the offer of a guilty plea does not tend to prove that the person was actually guilty. Informing the jury of that information would likely lead to a conviction without any further proof. The evidence is, therefore, excluded for both relevance and policy reasons.

Another method of resolving a criminal case is for the defendant to enter a plea of "nolo contendere." This plea is basically a statement that the defendant does not admit guilt, but will not contest the entry of judgment against him or herself. Fed. R. Evid. 410 states that a plea of nolo contendere is not admissible in civil or criminal matters against the defendant whether that plea was accepted or withdrawn. This is, of course, different than the plea of guilty. It has been recognized that a plea of nolo contendere is not an admission. It is, in fact, a statement that the defendant does not admit guilt. It is not, therefore, relevant to guilt. In addition, there is a concern that jurors would not understand the nature of the plea and assume it was like a plea of guilt. The law encourages settlement of civil and criminal cases. Although a plea of nolo contendere is not an admission of guilt, it does allow the criminal case to be resolved without the necessity of putting the prosecution to the time and expense of a trial. To allow such evidence to be admitted in the criminal or civil matter, would further inhibit defendants from entering the plea. This portion of the rule, therefore, excludes the plea on both relevance and public policy grounds.

In a manner similar to rules 408 and 409, rule 410 also excludes evidence of statements made during plea negotiations. Such statements are excluded from both criminal and civil trials.

Rule 410 recognizes two exceptions to this rule of exclusion. First, if other statements made during the plea or plea discussion have been introduced into evidence and the statement now sought to be introduced should "in fairness" to be introduced, it is admissible. This example could arise where the defendant introduces statements made during the plea negotiations. The prosecution may want to offer other statements made during that same discussion. The rule excludes evidence offered against the defendant but does not exclude evidence offered by the defendant. Under the general terms of the rule, the evidence offered by the defendant would be admissible, while the statement offered by the prosecution would be excluded. Under the exception, the evidence offered by the prosecution in that instance would be admissible if it should be admitted "in fairness."

The second exception allows the introduction of the evidence in proceedings for "perjury or false statement if the statement was made by the defendant under oath, on the record and in the presence of counsel." This exception is, of course, narrow. It would only arise where the prosecution sought further prosecution of the defendant for the crimes mentioned in the exception.

G. Insurance (411)

Evidence that a party to litigation has or does not have insurance is not admissible to prove negligence or other wrongful conduct. Rule 411, which states that principle, is adopting the uniform rule that is recognized in most jurisdictions. As a part of the relevance rules, the primary reason for the rule should be obvious. The fact that a person has either obtained insurance or not obtained insurance does not tend to prove or disprove that the person acted negligently or wrongfully in a particular instance. There is no indication that the purchase of insurance in anyway reflects just how carefully a person behaves. There is also the danger that evidence of insurance might lead to unfair prejudice in the case. If, for example, a plaintiff in a car wreck case was allowed to introduce evidence that the defendant had insurance, the jury might be inclined to increase the amount of the damages. Rather than basing the damages on the amount of actual injury, the jury might base the damages on the ability of an insurance company to pay it. It is clear that evidence of insurance ought to be excluded for both relevance and policy reasons.

Care must be used when considering the issue in state courts. Modern tort reform advocates have begun to encourage states to allow the introduction of evidence of some types of insurance. Where, for example, a plaintiff has been injured but a substantial portion of the medical bills were paid by a health care insurance company, the jurisdiction may allow the offer of such evidence. That principle is not, theoretically, inconsistent with retaining a rule that excludes evidence of liability insurance. Allowing the proof of health care insurance merely goes to show the jury that the plaintiff did not have to pay the full extent of the damages that are being proven. If evidence of liability insurance was offered, however, the jury might make a decision based on the wrong reasons. That is the reasoning that is convincing some jurisdictions to allow the evidence of health care insurance while retaining a rule that excludes evidence of liability insurance.

Rule 410, as do most of the rules in the 400s, recognizes some exceptions. "Evidence of insurance against liability [is admissible] when offered for another [purpose such as proof of agency, ownership, or control, or bias and prejudice of a witness." Examples of these exceptions should be easy to understand. If a person testified that they did not own nor control the instrumentality of an injury, the fact that person had liability insurance on that instrumentality would be admissible. It would be used to show that the person probably did own or control the instrumentality of the injury. The issue of bias or prejudice would most likely arise where a witness has some strong financial ties to an insurance company. The strong financial ties would tend to indicate a reason to testify favorably for that company.

H. Rape Shield Law (412)

1. Background

Prior to the 1970s, trials for rape could take a particular course. The prosecution would seek to show that the defendant had sexual intercourse with a victim. In cases where the victim was older than the age of consent, the defendant would have the opportunity to plead and prove that the victim consented to the act. Consent to sexual intercourse, of course, is a complete defense to the crime of rape. The defendant could also introduce evidence of the past sexual conduct of the victim in an effort to prove that it was likely that the victim consented. This evidence would be admissible.

The reasoning behind the admission of the past sexual conduct of the victim was that the evidence was relevant to consent. It was believed that people who had engaged in sexual activities in the past would be more likely to consent. This logic was thought to be consistent with the use of character of the victim of a violent attack. The law, Fed. R. Evid. 404, still allows the admission of evidence of the character of a victim of a violent attack as tending to prove the victim was the first aggressor. Because of the admission of the evidence of the past sexual conduct of the victim, rape trials could become lengthy discussion of the victim's past behavior. It would lead some to say that the defendant was actually putting the victim on trial.

In the 1970s, there was a complete reversal of thought in this matter. It was recognized that the mere fact that a person may have consented to sexual acts in the past does not tend to prove that they consented on the particular occasion that is the subject of the trial. In addition, there was the recognition that juries might use the evidence improperly. Jurors might feel that, after listening to a complete discussion of the victims past, the victim was just not entitled to claim rape. Finally, it was also recognized that rape is a crime that goes unreported at a very high rate. There are concerns that victims of rape fear having to confront the issue of the event in open forums. Knowing that the defendant would be able to present evidence discussing the victim in open court, victims may chose not to assist in the prosecution. It was during the 1970's that states began passing legislation that limited and restricted the use of evidence of the victim's past sexual conduct in a rape case. These statutes were referred to as "Rape Shield Laws."

The federal rules of evidence added a "Rape Shield Law" in 1978. It has been amended on a few occasions and now broadly excludes evidence of the past sexual conduct of a victim in civil and criminal cases. It is provided as Fed. R. Evid. 412. In order to make it clear that Rule 412 governs the issue of character of the victim in a rape case and not the broader "character of the victim" in Rule 404, Rule 404 now specifically notes that the general rule is subject to Rule 412.

2. The Basic Rule

The initial provision of rule 412 is that in any civil or criminal proceeding involving sexual misconduct evidence will be excluded if it is "evidence offered to prove that any alleged victim engaged in other sexual behavior [or] evidence offered to prove any alleged victim's sexual predisposition." This would mean that the defendant in action involving sexual misconduct cannot introduce evidence of the past sexual behavior of the victim. The mere fact that the victim had engaged in sexual behavior in the past would not be admissible.

There are, of course, specifically stated exceptions to the rule of exclusion. Those are discussed below. In addition, there are types of evidence that have been determined not to be excluded by the rule. The most commonly discussed example is the existence of prior false allegations or claims of sexual assault. This can arise where the victim makes an allegation of rape against the defendant. The defendant has evidence that the victim has made false allegations of rape against others in the past. This evidence has been held to be admissible. False allegations of rape are not considered sexual conduct of the victim.

3. Exceptions

The federal rules provide specific exceptions for admission of evidence concerning the past sexual behavior of a victim. The exceptions are designed to provide admission where the relevance of that evidence makes is important to the case. In addition, the exceptions insure that if a constitutionally mandated example ever arises, the rule allows admission of that evidence. The rule divides the exceptions into those that are allowed in criminal cases and those that are allowed in civil cases.

In criminal cases there are three specifically stated exceptions that allow the introduction of evidence of the past sexual behavior of the victim in a sexual assault case. They are discussed separately.

The first criminal law exception allows the introduction of "specific instances of behavior by the alleged victim offered to prove that a person other than the accused was the source of semen, injury or other physical evidence." Fed. R. Evid. 412 (b)(1)(A). This type of evidence would be admissible where the prosecution offered evidence of the presence of semen or other injury as tending to show rape or sexual assault. The defendant may deny having committed the act and offer evidence that the victim had engaged in sexual conduct with someone else. The evidence would be relevant to show that the semen or physical injury came from the other person. Due to the nature of this evidence, it would not be automatically admissible. If, for example, the defendant admitted having intercourse with the victim but claimed the act was done with consent, the evidence would not be admissible. The sexual behavior with others is relevant to prove that the person may have had the intercourse with others, but is not relevant to consent. This evidence would, therefore, only be admissible when the defendant is denying any contact with the victim.

The evidence concerning the presence of semen may be used in a different way in more recent cases. When the federal rules of evidence were written, DNA testing was not known. The presence of semen was only evidence of sexual contact and could not be used to prove who was the source of that semen. Today, the presence of semen would raise a completely different issue. Prosecutors would want to test the semen sample DNA against the DNA of any defendant. The evidence of matching or not matching would clearly be admissible as relevant to the identity of the defendant.

The second exception allows the admission of "evidence of specific instances of sexual behavior by the alleged victim with respect to the person accused of the sexual misconduct offered by the accused to prove consent or by the prosecution." Fed. R. Evid. 412(b)(1)(B). This portion of the rule allows the defendant in the case to offer evidence, when relevant, of the defendant and victim having sexual contact on prior occasions as being relevant to consent during the time that is critical to the trial. This rule would allow the admission of statements or comments by the victim of an intent to have intercourse with the defendant as well as actual sexual contact between the victim and defendant.

The third specific exception in criminal cases is for "evidence the exclusion of which would violate the constitutional rights of the defendant." Fed. R. Evid. 412(b)(1)(C). It may be argued that this exception is unnecessary. Clearly the federal rules of evidence are subordinate to the Constitution of the United States. Where evidence is Constitutionally protected, nothing in the rules of evidence can exclude it. The specific exception, however, does avoid even the appearance of Constitutional conflict. Without the exception, a court could be faced with declaring part of the rule unconstitutional. With the exception, such a court can use the clear language of the rule to avoid that conflict. An example, of such a use of the exception can arise where the defendant wishes to cross examine the victim on past sexual behavior. Where such cross examination would reveal a bias or motive to allow, the Constitution may allow such evidence to be offered.

The rules also provide a specific exception for the use of past sexual behavior of the victim evidence in civil cases. The rule allows such evidence if "its probative value substantially outweighs the danger of harm to any victim and of unfair prejudice to any party." This example would most likely arise in sexual harassment cases. The victim would be alleging that the defendant engaged in some sexual harassment or created a hostile work environment. The defendant could offer evidence of the victim's prior sexual behavior in the workplace to show a variety of things. I could be relevant to showing the victim consented to the behavior, the victim assisted in creating the environment, or that the victim did not suffer damages to the extent alleged. The key to the admission of such evidence is that it must be relevant to the case and meet the high balancing test of the exception.

4. Procedure

Rule 412 has a detailed procedural section. Since evidence of past sexual behavior is generally not admissible, but may be admissible under several exceptions, the rule provides for the procedure to following in making the evidentiary decisions. Fed. R. Evid. 412(c). The rule provides for prior notice of an intent to use such evidence and an "in camera" hearing where all parties have the opportunity to be heard.

I. Similar Sex Crimes (413, 414, 415)

As a general rule, evidence of past "bad acts" is not admissible to prove that someone has acted in conformity with that prior conduct. It would not, for example, be appropriate to offer evidence that a defendant in a bank robbery case had engaged in prior bank robberies for the purpose of proving that the defendant probably robbed the bank that is the subject of the criminal action. It would also not be appropriate to prove in a criminal case for homicide that a person had engaged in prior violent acts to show that the person probably committed the homicide. The rules, however, have added some special provisions that allow the introduction of certain specified acts in certain cases. In certain civil and criminal cases, the fact that a defendant has engaged in prior sexual conduct is admissible. The jury will be allowed to use the evidence for "any manner to which it is relevant." Fed. R. Evid. 413(a).

Prior to adoption of Fed. R. Evid. 413, 414, 415, there was an interesting legislative history. The Judicial Conference, the ABA, and most academic text writers strongly opposed the adoption of the rules. Congress, however, passed the rules as part of the Violent Crime Control and Law Enforcement Act of 1994. The rules, therefore, remain controversial.

1. Similar Crimes in Sexual Assault (413)

The first provision that was added allows the admission of evidence of a defendant's prior commission of a sexual assault offense in a criminal case in which the defendant is charged with sexual assault. Fed. R. Evid. 412(a). The rule is broadly stated while leaving open several difficult points.

First, the evidence does not have to show that the prior conduct led to a conviction. In fact, the rule does not even require that the prior conduct was ever reported. The prosecution can bring in evidence that the defendant engaged in conduct which would have been a sexual assault even without proof of that conviction or report.

Second, the types of conduct for which the evidence may apply is broadly stated. The rule itself states that the evidence of "sexual assault" may include those that would have be a crime under federal or state law that involved:

(1) any conduct proscribed by chapter 109A of title 18, United States Code;

(2) contact, without consent, between any part of the defendant's body or an object and the genitals or anus of another person;

(3) contact, without consent, between the genitals or anus of the defendant and any part of another person's body;

(4) deriving sexual pleasure or gratification from the infliction of death, bodily injury, or physical pain on another person; or

(5) an attempt or conspiracy to engage in conduct described in paragraphs (1)-(4). Fed. R. Evid. 413(c).

As can be seen by the language, the rule allow a broad range of past conduct to be admissible.

Third, the rule allows the admission of the evidence for "any matter to which it is relevant." Fed. R. Evid. 413(a). This would appear to allow the jury to hear the evidence while inviting the trial judge to give a limiting instruction on appropriate use. It also, allows, of course, the opposing counsel to argue that rule 403 can be used to exclude the evidence. Although the rule 413 suggests that the evidence has some probative value, the defendant would claim that the probative value is substantially outweighed by the danger of unfair prejudice.

Finally, the rule does have a section that indicates some procedural requirements. If the prosecution is planning on use such evidence, it must make the evidence or a summary of such evidence known to the other side 15 days before the date of trial. "For good cause," the court may allow a later time. Fed. R. Evid. 413(b).

2. Similar Crimes in Child Molestation (414)

Rule 414 operates in a manner very similar to rule 413. Where a defendant is accused of an offense of child molestation, "evidence of the defendant's commission of another offense or offenses of child molestation is admissible." Fed. R. Evid. 414. In fact, it could be argued that rules 413 and 414 are so similar, that rule 414 is unnecessary. There is some overlap. The courts will, therefore, be able to use either rule in some cases, while relying on rule 414 where there may be some gaps in rule 413.

The rule provides several important definitions. First, child means a person under 14 years of age. Fed. R. Evid. 414 (d). Second, "offense of child molestation" includes offenses defined by federal or state law that involve:

(1) any conduct proscribed by chapter 109A of title 18, United States code, that was committed in relation to a child;

(2) any conduct proscribed by chapter 110 of title 18, United States code;

(3) contact between any part of the defendant's body or any object and the genitals or anus of a child;

(4) contact between the genitals or anus of the defendant and any part of the body of a child;

(5) deriving sexual pleasure or gratification from the infliction of death, bodily injury, or physical pain on a child; or

(6) an attempt or conspiracy to engage in conduct described in paragraphs (1)-(5). Fed. R. Evid. 414(d).

As with rule 413, this rule provides procedural requirements for the use of the evidence. If the prosecution intends to use such evidence, that shall be disclosed to the defendant "15 days before the scheduled date of trial or at such later time as the court may allow for good cause." Fed. R. Evid. 414(b).

3. Similar Crimes in Civil Cases (415)

Rule 415 is part of the group of rules that allows evidence of prior sexual conduct of the defendant to be admissible. Where rules 413 and 414 are intended to cover the admissibility of such evidence in criminal cases, rule 415 covers the issue for civil cases. Where a civil case seeks to recover damages for conduct that would have been a sexual assault or child molestation, evidence of a "party's commission of another offense or offenses of sexual assault or child molestation is admissible." Fed. R. Evid. 415(a).

This rule appears to be intended for use in civil actions for battery where the defended touched the plaintiff in a sexual manner. The rule has also been used, however, in cases of sexual harassment in the workplace. The difficulty with that use comes from the nature of sexual harassment cases. In the typical sexual harassment case, the plaintiff is suing the employer and not the actual employee or supervisor who is alleged to have been doing the harassment. Rule 415 provides that "evidence of a party's commission of another offense" is admissible. The defendant employer may claim that the company has not committed other offenses and it would be prejudicial to introduce evidence of another employee or supervisor who may not even be a party to the action. The courts have, however, found such evidence to be admissible.

This rule, as do rules 413 and 414, has a procedural section. Where a party intends to use such evidence, it is necessary to inform the opposing party "15 days before the scheduled date of trial or at such later time as the court may allow for good cause." Fed. R. Evid. 415(c).

Checkpoints

- Relevant evidence is that evidence that tends to make a fact of consequence more or less probable.

- The phrase "fact of consequence" has replaced the older phrase "material."

- Relevant evidence is admissible unless the probative value is substantially outweighed by the danger of unfair prejudice.

- Character evidence is ordinarily not admissible in civil or criminal cases.

- Character evidence may be offered in character in issue cases.

- In criminal cases the defendant may offer evidence of good character and the prosecution may offer evidence to rebut that.

- In criminal cases the defendant may offer character evidence tending to show that victim was the first aggressor and the prosecution may offer character evidence to rebut that.

- When character evidence is admissible, it may take the form of reputation or opinion. specific instances of conduct cannot be offered on direct, but may be inquired about on cross examination.

- Habit evidence is admissible in civil and criminal cases. habit is the regular or routine response to a repeated stimuli.

- Evidence of subsequent remedial measures are not admissible to prove fault or defect in products. it may be offered for other purposes, such as control.

- Offers of compromise, settlement, payments or pleas are not admissible. statements made during such negotiations are also not admissible.

- The existence or non-existence of insurance is not admissible.

- The past sexual conduct of a victim of a rape case is not admissible to show sexual predisposition.

- Past sexual conduct of a victim with the defendant or to show source of semen or injury is admissible.

- In civil or criminal cases, the past sexual conduct of a defendant is admissible in a child molestation case or a case of sexual assault.

Chapter 5

Privileges

Privileges Roadmap

- Understand the purpose of privileges.
- Determine how federal privileges are created.
- Learn the details of several common privileges.

A. Introduction

Privileges are difficult evidentiary concepts to master. The evidence that is sought is usually relevant and, sometimes, critical to the truthful determination of the case. Due to the operation of the privilege, however, it will not be admitted. In fact, the party wanting to introduce the evidence may not even be allowed to know the full extent of the evidence. Where a privilege operates, the witness who has the right to exercise the privilege, cannot be forced to reveal the evidence.

With such a strong prohibition against the admission of such evidence, it is important to understand why the privileges are allowed to exist. Privileges have developed under a variety of situations. Usually, however, they arise where there is a conversation between two people and the law seeks to protect the confidentiality of the relationship between the two people who had the conversation. Most privileges arise when there is a special relationship and the information that is shared is important to the continued existence of that relationship. The relationship between and attorney and the client is a good example. In order for the attorney to fully and appropriately represent the client, the client must be able to tell the attorney all of the facts concerning the nature of the legal problem. If the attorney could be forced to reveal that information, the client would have to be less forthcoming during interviews with the attorney. As such, the attorney would not be able to represent the client. A privilege has developed to allow the client to be completely open to the attorney without the fear that the information would then be offered in court. It is felt that the nature of the attorney client relationship is so important to the continued existence of the legal system that the information must be protected.

As can be seen by that example, the nature of special relationships is one of the most important issues that must be confronted when dealing with privileges. The law has determined that certain relationships must be protected and provides privileges for information exchanged in such relationships.

A second important feature of privileges is the identity of the party who controls the privilege. Usually the law recognizes that the privilege exists to aid a relationship, but it is primarily designed to protect one member of that relationship. In the attorney client relationship, for example, the privilege is actually designed to protect the client. Although the attorney may be the one pressured to reveal the information, it is client who controls the privilege. The client is the one who can waive or refuse to waive the existence of the privilege.

As can be seen by the above discussion, there are two major issues that must be addressed in discussing any privilege. The nature of the relationship that gives rise to the privilege must be understood. It is only under the legally recognized relationships that the privilege can exist. Second, the person who controls the privilege must be identified. In the material that follows, the nature of the privileges, the relationships that give rise to them and the person who controls them will be discussed.

Before, discussing specific privileges, however, it is necessary to view the manner in which privileges are created in federal court. The federal rules of privilege operate in a manner somewhat different than the rest of the rules.

B. General Theory of Privileges (501)

When Congress was considering the federal rules of evidence, there was controversy concerning the rules of privilege. The original suggestion was to include a series of traditionally recognized privileges. The issues that arose seem to come from two conflicting sides. Some felt that privileges that were being enacted should either be reduced or not included. Others felt there were privileges that were not being included that should be added. Congress was unable to resolve this dispute and created a unique approach for the federal rules. The final rule on the use of privileges in the federal courts was to leave the creation and application of privileges to common law development by the courts. The privileges "shall be governed by the principles of the common law as they may be interpreted by the courts of the United States in light of reason and experience." Fed. R. Evid. 501. It is clear from the legislative history and the language of the rule that congress did not intend to abolish privileges.

Congress was clearly not intending to refute any particular privilege. In fact, the language of the rule indicates that privileges are assumed to continue to exist in much the same manner as they did at common law. The rule merely allows the courts to continue to develop the privileges in the same manner that was occurring prior to the adoption of the rules.

In studying privileges in federal court, therefore, there is an added difficulty. The rules do not specifically define the privileges that exist nor the extent of those privileges. Lawyers, judges, and law students are forced to research the nature of privileges using case law. A discussion of the most commonly known privileges in federal and state court will be discussed below.

The rules do note that there may be some other sources of federal law on privileges. The rules do accept that privileges may be created by the "Constitution of the United States or provided by Act of Congress or in rules prescribed by the Supreme Court pursuant to statutory authority." Fed. R. Evid. 501. Where such rules exist, they too shall be applied by the federal courts.

When rule 501 was adopted, a special provision was added for certain types of cases. Just as a reminder, ordinarily the federal rules of evidence apply to all cases in federal court regardless of the nature of the jurisdiction upon which the case is based. That means that the federal rules of evidence apply even if the case is in federal court on diversity jurisdiction. As noted, three special provisions of the federal rules require that the court look to state law in certain circumstances. There are three places in the federal rules of evidence where the rules themselves require the application of state law. For questions of presumptions (Fed. R. Evid. 301); competency (Fed. R. Evid. 601); and privileges (Fed. R. Evid. 501), state will supply the evidence rule when state law must supply the rule of decision. "However, in civil actions and proceedings, with respect to an element of a claim or defense as to which State law supplies the rule of decision, the privilege of a witness, person, government, State, or political subdivision thereof shall be determined in accordance with State law." Fed. R. Evid. 501.

Reviewing this special provision, the application is relatively simple. Where state law supplies the rule of decision to the case, then state law must supply the rule for any claimed privileges. As an example, one may consider cases in federal court on diversity jurisdiction. Under traditional rules, when the case is in federal court on diversity jurisdiction, state law shall apply the rule of decision. In such a case, if a witness claims a privilege, the court must look to the same state law to determine the existence, nature and extent of that privilege.

The federal rule for privileges, therefore, tells the lawyer, judge and student where to look for privileges, but does not provide the details concerning such privileges. If the case is one where state law supplies the rule of decision, the state law will supply the privilege rule. For all other cases in federal court, the courts will develop privileges in a common law method. The following material will discuss the usual rules found with the most commonly encountered privileges.

C. Most Commonly Encountered Privileges

1. Attorney-Client

The attorney-client privilege may be the most common privilege that attorneys must confront. Even if the privilege is not specifically raised in a court proceeding, it is an underlying part of every conversation with every client. Not only is the privilege a part of the evidence law of the United States, it makes up a part of the rules of professional conduct that govern the practice of law. An attorney that breaches an attorney-client privilege may not only cause the client some problems in court, that attorney may be disciplined by the state bar association. Such violations of professional rules of conduct may lead to an attorney losing the right to practice law.

This discussion is not intended to cover the problems of professional responsibility or rules of professional conduct. Students will take courses on professional conduct and the rules of confidentiality are usually extensively covered in such courses. The purpose of this material is to cover the nature of the evidentiary problems that arise with the attorney-client evidentiary privilege.

The underlying purpose of the attorney-client privilege has been justified on the basis of the importance of that relationship to the form of law and justice in the United States. It is recognized that to take full advantage of the justice system, a party to litigation will need the assistance of counsel. While seeking that counsel, the party will further need to fully and truthfully reveal all of the facts that are at issue in the litigation. It is feared that if the attorney could be forced to reveal that information, parties to litigation would have to be less than forthcoming to the attorney. Parties to litigation may even decide to avoid seeking assistance of counsel. The law of attorney-client privilege is designed to make sure that parties to litigation receive the full help that they need without fear of having confidential information revealed.

Although this purpose is widely recognized and supported, there are critics. Some complain that the privilege allows wrongdoers and the guilty to seek assistance while hiding the truth. It has been argued that the privilege prevents the courts from doing justice. This criticism has not been adopted and the privilege remains.

In fact, the privilege may even have some Constitutional justification. In criminal trials, the defendant is Constitutionally entitled to counsel. The privilege is recognized as an important part of criminal defendants getting the assistance they are guaranteed. The right to counsel and the right to avoid self-incrimination would be of little value if the attorney for the defendant could be forced to reveal all that had been learned during the representation of the defendant.

Since the law is willing to protect the important attorney-client confidential communications, it is necessary to determine when that protection will attach. It is not, for example, every casual comment to an attorney that gives rise to the privilege. A person who admits to committing crimes to an attorney while sharing drinks at a cocktail party may find that the attorney can easily be forced to reveal those admissions. Some approach to an attorney-client relationship or, at least, the reasonable believe by the client that such a relationship exists may be necessary to protect the information being revealed.

The basic requirement for the attorney-client privilege to exist, therefore, is the formation of something like an attorney-client relationship. This requirement of an attorney-client relationship includes more than a clearly defined contract to represent. It includes the initial consultation when the attorney is deciding whether to accept the client. It then includes that period where the client reasonably believes there is a relationship. Once the attorney had made it clear that there is no attorney-client relationship, then communications are not protected by the attorney client privilege.

When the client is a single person, identifying whose communications are privileged is easy. Obviously that single person client's communications are protected. When an attorney represents a corporation, the issue is more difficult. The corporation is assumed to be the client. The confusion may arise if a corporate officer or member of the board believes that they too should be part of the privilege. Ordinarily, such individuals are not the client and therefore their communications are not privileged. Such individuals should be warned of such dangers and seek their own counsel if they believe that is necessary.

It should also be noted that even where there is an attorney client privilege, it is only the communications of the client. If a third person speaks to the attorney about the client, that is not privileged.

Who is the "attorney" may also raise some issues. Clearly a licensed attorney that has agreed to represent the client is the one to whom communications are privileged. If a client reasonably believes the person offering representation is an attorney, that is probably sufficient. That is true even if the person claiming to be an attorney is not licensed.

A more common situation is where the attorney has hired additional representatives. Those people may include law clerks, paralegals, or other office staff. Communications between the client and those individuals are also privileged.

The privilege arises only in situations where the attorney has been consulted for the delivery of legal services. That concept, however, is broad. It obviously includes consulting an attorney for the purpose of litigation. It may also include the broad range of legal services such as will drafting, negotiations, and tax advice.

The privilege itself is intended to protect "confidential communications" between the client and the attorney. That definition contains two elements. (1) It only protects "communications." (2) Those communications must be "confidential. The following material will explain those two concepts.

Communications that are to be protected are usually oral or written. A client may, however, communicate information by gestures or acts. While being questioned by the attorney, the client may nod or signal an answer. That would be considered a communication. Conduct, dress, property or other non-communicative items would not be protected.

The communication must also be "confidential." Ordinarily this means that the client intended for the communication to be confidential. When the client is meeting privately with the attorney to discuss a legal matter, it is clearly intended to be confidential. During those conversations, the attorney may have office staff available without losing the confidential nature of the communication. Those individuals are assumed to be representatives of the attorney. The client may also have some people available during the discussion without losing the confidential nature of the communication. People that are representatives of the client, spouse, aides or supporting people may be brought into the conversation without losing the privilege. It is necessary for these people to be there to aid the discussion or to care for the client in order to protect the privilege. If the information is revealed while in the presence of other third parties, the privilege is waived.

Making the information public clearly waives the privilege. If, for example, the client publishes the information to third parties, the privilege is waived. In order for there to be a waiver, however, it is important to determine whether the client intended to release the information. If the information was made public due to the fraud or theft of a third party, or inadvertently but not negligently by the client, the privilege is not waived. The privilege is waived where it appears that the client intended to release the information or it was released due to the failure of the client to use due care to protect it.

One of the difficult problems that has arisen under the attorney-client privilege is whether the identity of the client is privileged. Using all of the discussion, it would seem that the identity of the client was not a confidential communication. It was, instead, something observed by the attorney. If that is true, the identity should not be privileged. There have been cases, however, that have allowed the identity of the client to be privileged. Where the identity of the client is such that it would reveal other confidential information, then it is protected.

Another difficult issue arises when it appears that a client seeks to continue some type of criminal or fraudulent conduct. The privilege obviously covers information about past criminal conduct. When a client is represented by an attorney in a criminal matter concerning past conduct, all confidential communications about that past conduct is privileged. The attorney may not, however, assist the client in continuing criminal or fraudulent conduct. Where, therefore, the client provides information to the attorney that seeks assistance to continue that conduct, the information may be discovered from the attorney. As should be clear, the test is simple. Information provided while the client is continuing criminal or fraudulent conduct and seeks to gain assistance from the attorney for that conduct is not privileged.

The question may also arise as to how long does the privilege continue to exist. The privilege continues after the attorney-client privilege is over. It is also clear that the privilege continues until the death of the client. After the death of the client, the jurisdictions are split on whether the privilege continues. Some allow the privilege to continue beyond death. Some allow the privilege to continue through the administration of the estate. Some end the privilege at death.

The final question for the attorney-client privilege is how to claim the privilege. The right to claim the privilege belongs to the client and not the attorney. It is the client's privilege. It must be claimed at every stage of the proceeding where the information is sought. If the client is called to the stand and asked to reveal the information, the client may decline. If ordered by the court to testify, the client may decide to reveal the information and, thereby, waive the privilege. If the client continues to refuse to testify, the court may hold the client in contempt. At that point it would be necessary to appeal the contempt citation and seek review of the privilege at the appellate level. If the attorney is called to testify, the attorney would need to claim that the information is privileged and refuse to testify. If ordered by the court to testify, the attorney is allowed to reveal the information by the rules of professional conduct. The attorney could, of course, continue to refuse and risk contempt citations. Those too could be reviewed on appeal.

2. Spousal

The spousal or marital privilege is another common privilege. The marital privilege actually has two parts. There is a privilege for a witness to refuse to testify against his or her spouse. There is also a privilege for confidential marital communications. Although there may be times that these two overlap, they are two separate rules.

The underlying reasons for these privileges have been repeated over many years. It is recognized that the marriage relationship is protected by important public policy. It is felt that requiring one spouse to testify against another or requiring a spouse to reveal confidential information will damage the relationship.

The privilege that allows a witness to refuse to testify against his or her own spouse has a long history. At common law, a person was incompetent to testify in a matter involving his or her own spouse. This meant that the person could not testify for or against the spouse. The witness was legally incompetent to take the stand. In the 1930's in the United States, the courts abolished the idea that the spouse was incompetent to testify. The rulings began to allow the witness to testify in behalf of a spouse, but continued to allow the spouse to deny the witness the right to testify against the spouse. Under this theory, there was a privilege, owned by the non-testify spouse that could be exercised to prevent the other spouse from testify. It is easy to see how this privilege would be used in a practical setting. If a person believed their spouse would testify in his or her favor, the person would waive the privilege. If a person believed their spouse would testify against his or her interest, the person would claim the privilege. The routine use of the privilege was criminal cases. A person would be charged with a crime, and that person's spouse would be called as a witness. If the spouse was going to testify favorably to the prosecution, the privilege would be claimed. If the spouse was going to testify favorably to the defendant, the privilege would be waived.

In the 1980s, a shift occurred in this privilege. The United States Supreme Court held, in Trammel v. United States, 445 U.S. 40 (1980), that the privilege belonged to the witness and not to the defendant. This change allowed prosecutors to negotiate with one spouse in order to gain that person's testimony against the other spouse.

This part of the privilege exists where there is a valid marriage in existence at the time of the trial. Even though the events that are at issue in the trial may have occurred prior to marriage, if there is a valid marriage at the time of the trial, the witness spouse may decline to testify. This rule raises the possibility of "sham marriages." Courts may be concerned that a couple engaged in criminal behavior get married for the single purpose of avoiding the possibility of testifying against each other. Courts will require that the marriage be one where the parties intend to live or remain together as husband and wife.

The second major part of the marital privilege is the privilege for confidential communication during the marriage relationship. This privilege applies to civil and criminal cases and allows the exclusion of any confidential communications that occurred during the existence of the marriage relationship. The basis of this privilege is the importance attached to the marriage relationship. It is assumed that partners to a marriage must have the freedom to fully discuss any topic. The privilege is designed to allow such discussions without the fear of one spouse being compelled to reveal the information in court.

This part of the privilege belongs to both spouses. Either spouse may claim the privilege and prevent the other spouse from offering testimony about the privileged information.

The privilege only applies to communications that were made during the course of a valid marriage. Communications that were made prior to or after a marriage are not privilege. A communication that was made during a valid marriage is privileged even if the partners are no longer married at the time the testimony is sought.

This part of the privilege only protects communications. Acts or conduct that may have been observed are not privilege.

The privilege also requires that the communication must have been confidential. If the communication was made in the presence of third persons, it is not privileged.

3. Priest-Penitent

Some jurisdictions still recognize a privilege for confidential communications between a member of the clergy and someone seeking counsel from that member of the clergy. Although traditionally known as a "priest-penitent" privilege, it is expanded to other religious groups. The member of the clergy may be a minister, priest, rabbi or other similar official of a religious organization.

The privilege is designed to protect confidential communications made by a person to the member of the clergy. If the statement is made in the presence of a third person, it is not privileged. The privilege belongs to the person who made the statements and not the member of the clergy.

4. Physician-Patient

The physician-patient privilege did not exist at common law. In reviewing cases, the federal courts have been reluctant to create such a privilege. State courts, however, have created and used the privilege. Since it may arise in federal court where state law supplies the rule of decision, the basic outline of the privilege should be considered.

The underlying theory of the privilege is to provide an opportunity for free and open discussion between a patient and physician. It is assumed that the public policy behind adequate medical treatment for all people is sufficiently strong to allow protection for such information.

The privilege is primarily the result of state statutory law. As such, there is a great diversity of rules that create the privilege. Some concepts, however, are consistent.

The privilege ordinarily belongs to the patient. It is the patient that controls when the privilege may be waived.

Information that is privileged must relate to diagnosis or treatment of the patient. Collateral statements or information gained by the physician during the course of the treatment is not privileged.

The privilege protects more than just statements. Obviously, confidential communications made by the patient to the physician are privilege. In addition, information gained about the patient by the physician by medical tests would also be privileged.

This privilege, more than most, has multiple exceptions though out the jurisdictions. It is important to research closely the law of the specific jurisdiction in order to check for exceptions.

5. Psychotherapist-Patient

It has been thought that a privilege to protect the psychotherapist-patient relationship is more important than a physician-patient relationship. Free and open discussion to a psychotherapist is more critical to treatment than discussion to a physician. This privilege is thought to be necessary to effective treatment. As such, the privilege is recognized in all jurisdictions and the federal courts.

The basic elements of the privilege are similar to others. The privilege belongs to and may be waived by the patient. It attaches to confidential communications that are made to the psychotherapist for purposes of diagnosis or treatment.

It was thought that the privilege should be broader than merely attaching to conversations with a psychiatrist. It also applies to psychologists and social workers.

6. Governmental

There are a variety of privileges that may be classified as governmental privileges. Ordinarily, they will be raised in criminal cases.

The broadest claimed privilege was a claim that government has the right to declare any information privileged. The Courts have not read the privilege that broad. The executive branch of government has a privilege to protect confidential information. The privilege, however, may be defeated by a specific showing of necessity in a criminal case.

The more commonly claimed privilege is in criminal cases when the prosecution seeks to protect the identity of an informant. Where the identify or information is helpful to the defendant or essential for a fair trial, the prosecution must make a decision. The prosecution must reveal the identity, the information, or dismiss the case.

Checkpoints

- Privileges prevent the introduction of evidence that might be otherwise relevant.
- Privileges are designed to protect certain relationships.
- The federal rules of evidence allow the federal courts to create and develop privileges as a matter of common law.
- Attorney-client privileges exist where there is an attorney client relationship. The privilege is controlled by the client.
- Marital or spousal privilege exists and has two parts. The first part allows a spouse to refuse to testify against the other spouse. The second part protects confidential communications that arose during the marital relationship. that portion of the privilege may be raised by either spouse.
- A priest-penitent privilege allows religious leaders to maintain a confidential communication. The privilege is controlled by the penitent.

Chapter 6

Witnesses, Testimony, and Credibility

Witnesses, Testimony, and Credibility Roadmap

- Learn the rules concerning competency.
- Recognize that the federal rules have a requirement concerning the oath.
- Lay witnesses must testify to first hand knowledge.
- Distinguish competency from impeachment.
- Analyze the most common methods of impeachment.
- Pay special attention to impeachment by character and prior crimes.
- Recognize the methods of rehabilitation.
- Determine the methods of control over presentation of evidence during trial.

A. Introduction

The rules contained in Article VI of the federal rules deal generally with the testimony of witnesses. The 600's are a broad set of principles that control the basic parts of every trial. These rules generally apply in both civil and criminal cases. This section covers the competency of witnesses, issues of impeachment, and the form of questions that may be asked.

B. Competency, Oath and Personal Knowledge (601, 602, 603)

Rules 601, 602 and 603 deal with some basic issues of competency. At common law, there were numerous competency rules. The law generated multiple rules that restricted who could testify in a trial. For example, a party to the litigation could not testify. It was assumed that a party would be biased in his or her own behalf and would, therefore, not be sufficiently trustworthy. That rule, of course, has disappeared.

Although jurisdictions allow parties to testify in a case, a vestige of that rule remains in many state jurisdictions. Known as the "Dean Man's Rule," jurisdictions limit the testimony of some parties. Under that rule, a party may not testify to a transaction with a party now deceased. The theory of the rule was that death had silenced one party to the transaction, so the law would silence the other.

The major problem with the "Dead Man's Rule" was determining what was meant by "transaction." Obviously, contracts would be viewed as a transaction. Some states, however, even recognized a tort between two people as a transaction. The rule has led to extensive, troubling litigation in some places.

Even apart from the special rules of competence, many jurisdictions retained rules requiring some evidence of competence of all witnesses. Courts have said that a witness must have been able to observe, recall, and relate the events of which they speak. In addition, a witness must be able to understand the necessity of telling the truth and agree to do so.

The Federal Rules of Evidence, rule 601 appeared to abolish all of the traditional competency rules. The rule states that "Every person is competent to be a witness except as otherwise provided in these rules." Fed. R. Evid. 601. This allows the witness taking the stand to be assumed to be competent. It would be up to the party opposing the evidence to offer some grounds to prevent the testimony. One example of this general rule of competency is that the Federal Courts do not have a "Dead Man's Rule."

Recognizing that many states deal with issues of competency in a different manner and that competency to testify may be a substantive issue, rule 601 makes special allowance for cases where state law would supply the rule of decision. "However, in civil actions and proceedings, with respect to an element of a claim or defense as to which State law supplies the rule of decision, the competency of a witness shall be determined in accordance with State law." Fed. R. Evid. 601. The typical example assumed by the rule would be a case in federal court based on diversity jurisdiction. In such a case, state law would be consulted for the appropriate law for the decision. Under those circumstances, state law of competency would also be consulted to determine the competency of a witness.

Although the federal rules assume every witness to be competent, the rules do provide for some additional requirements before the witness may testify. At common law, competency was based partially on the fact of having observed the event. The federals rules have a similar requirement. The rules make it clear that a witness may not testify to facts unless there is sufficient foundation evidence provided to indicate that the witness knows the facts from "personal knowledge." Fed. R. Evid. 602. Rule 602 states that the foundation evidence "may, but need not, consist of the witness' own testimony." Fed. R. Evid. 602. This would allow the witness to provide evidence about the fact that they observed the event prior to testifying as to what happened. In the alternative, a party could have witnesses testify about who observed the event, and then have that observer testify. Rule 602 also notes that it is only addressing the issue of lay witnesses. Expert witnesses are governed by rule 703.

It was noted earlier that the common law used understanding the oath as an issue of competency. The federal rules assume every witness to be competent, but still retain an oath requirement. Under the federal rules, every witness is "required to declare that the witness will testify truthfully, by oath or affirmation administered in a form calculated to awaken the witness' conscience and impress the witness' mind with the duty to do so." Fed. R. Evid. 603.

There does not appear to be a specific format of oath that is required. It is traditionally thought that witnesses should raise a right hand and place a left hand on the Bible while saying "I do" in response to the question, "Do you solemnly swear the testimony you are about to give is the truth, the whole truth and nothing but the truth?" Due to a great diversity of religious beliefs in the United States, such a traditional format has not been workable with some witnesses. Rather than requiring such rigid adherence to tradition, the courts have enlarged the acceptable format. The courts only require some format that relates to the witness the importance of telling the truth and gets a commitment in response to do so. In this regard, at least, the law seems to favor substance over form.

C. Special Problems with Competency

Although the federal rules assume all witnesses to be competent to testify, there still remain some special issues. This section will attempt to discuss those special problems.

1. Judges (605)

Although a lawyer may never see the issue arise during a whole career, the federal rules do deal with the problem of a judge in a case testifying as a witness in that same case. The federal rule is that it is not appropriate. "The judge presiding at the trial may not testify in that trial as a witness." Fed. R. Evid. 605. The reasons for such a rule should be obvious. A judge could not sit impartially on a case in which that same judge had specific knowledge and had testified. The rules do recognize a difficult problem such a circumstance could cause. If a judge, contrary to the law and rules, did decide to testify, how could an attorney object to that? The rule provides that, "No objection need be made in order to preserve the point." Fed. R. Evid. 605. This allows the attorneys in the case to make the judge's testimony a grounds for appeal without having preserved the error by making an objection.

2. Jurors (606)

As with judges, jurors should not testify in a case on which they sit in judgment. "A member of the jury may not testify as a witness before that jury in the trial of the case in which the juror is sitting." Fed. R. Evid. 606(A). Rule 606 also makes sure that an attorney must be given a chance to object to such a circumstance out of the hearing of the jury. In most cases, that portion of the rule will cover most problems.

Special problems with juror testimony, however, may arise when a juror wants to testify that the decision reached by the jury during deliberation was, in some way, tainted. The traditional rule is that a juror will not be heard to impeach his or her own verdict. This has been interpreted to mean that a juror may not testify about matters that occurred or were discussed during jury deliberations. The reason for such a rule should be obvious. The law wants to protect the free flow of information among jurors. The jurors should have the right to freely discuss the case in secret without fear of having their thoughts disclosed to the public. In addition, cases need to reach a final conclusion. If jurors regularly spoke out about the verdict, no case could be considered final.

Although there are sound reasons to prevent jurors from testifying about the deliberative process, occasions may arise when the contrary is true. If a juror has evidence that the jury deliberation was the subject of fraud, bribery, or some other inappropriate interference, there should be some remedy.

The federal rules of evidence tries to reach a middle ground in this area. The rule generally excludes inquiry into the deliberative process of the jury, but does allow the consideration of evidence "on the question whether extraneous prejudicial information was improperly brought to the jury's attention or whether any outside influence was improperly brought to bear upon any juror." Fed. R. Evid. 606 (b). It is important to note that the rule does not specify the types of interference that will be considered as a basis of overturning a verdict. It is only designed to indicate when such types of evidence may be considered.

3. Interpreters (604)

On additional problem arises in the area of competence. With the diversity of languages used in the United States, not all witnesses will be able to understand and speak English. There are times when a court may need an interpreter. The court may also need such language assistance for witnesses who are hearing impaired. The rules make special provision for interpreters. The interpreter must be qualified as an expert in their area and are subject to the rules concerning oath taking. Fed. R. Evid. 605.

D. General Issues of Impeachment (607)

An important part of the trial is when a witness has finished testify on direct and it is time for opposing counsel to cross examine that witness. The opposing counsel may try to impeach the credibility of that witness. By the use of questions, the opposing counsel will try to show that the witness is not worthy of belief.

The first thing that must be noted is how impeachment differs from attacking competency. As was discussed earlier, some witnesses may be "incompetent" to testify. When a court determines that a witness is not competent, that witness may not testify. If the witness has given evidence before the lack of competency is revealed, then that evidence must be stricken from the record and the jury will be told to disregard it. Attacking credibility by impeachment is different. When a witness is impeached, all of the testimony stays in the record and the jury may consider it. The facts brought out for impeachment will be used merely to try to convince the jury not to believe that witness. In short, therefore, there is a great difference between competency and impeachment. A witness held to be not competent may not testify at all. All witness who testify are subject to impeachment and it is up to the jury to determine who to believe.

The second introductory point to consider is who may impeach a witness. As suggested above, the usual practice is that the impeachment takes place during cross examination. That would mean that an attorney calls the witness and brings out favorable evidence on direct. The attorney for the opposing party is usually the one that tries to impeach the witness on cross examination. In fact, at common law, the attorney that called the witness was prohibited from impeaching the witness. The law assumed that when an attorney called a witness, that attorney was vouching for the credibility of the witness. It would have been inconsistent with that assumption if that same attorney was then allowed to impeach the witness.

The modern law and the federal rules of evidence have changed that practice. Today, any party, even the party calling the witness may impeach or attack the credibility of the witness. (Fed. R. Evid. 607). It is now recognized that attorneys and parties do not have great freedom in who they must call as witnesses. Parties must call the witnesses that are available. This will mean that many witnesses will have some positive things to say about a party, but will also have some negative things to say. There may be times when a party may call a witness and first bring out the positive testimony. It may then be necessary to impeach the witness on other items.

There is one problem area with allowing a party who called a witness to impeach that witness. It has been noted that, at times, a prosecutor in a criminal case may call a witness who they know will not testify in their behalf. In fact, the prosecutor is calling the witness for the sole purpose of introducing evidence that will impeach the witness. Courts have been reluctant to allow the use of such witnesses. Courts have allowed the prosecutor to impeach the credibility of a witness, but only where the initial evidence they received from that witness was a surprise. If a prosecutor believed that witness was going to testify in one manner, but the witness, in fact, testified contrary to that, the prosecutor could impeach the witness.

1. Impeachment by Bias

Bias is a large, vague area of impeachment that is recognized by all courts. The Federal Rules of Evidence do not specifically mention "Bias" in a particular rule. The Advisory Committee Notes recognized that bias would be used, by noting that evidence of bias would not create the type of contradiction that would allow rehabilitation by character evidence. Although the details of rehabilitation is to be covered later, it is important to note that using bias for impeachment was so well recognized that the drafters just assumed, without specifically mentioning, that bias could be used. Cases have generally recognized the use of this technique.

There are many types of bias about which questions may be asked. The possibilities may be limited only by the imagination of the attorney asking the questions. Several typical examples should be noted.

Some friendliness or partiality towards a party can, of course, be brought up. This may arise in numerous ways. A witness may be a family member of some of the parties to the case. Opposing counsel could ask questions to illustrate that fact. The bias is not, of course, limited to family members. The witness may be a friend or even a distant acquaintance. In fact, familiarity with the parties or issues in the case could show some partiality. If such evidence would tend to show some bias, then the attorney may ask about it.

It is also clear that familiarity could lead to hostility. If an attorney felt that the witness had some relationship or familiarity with the case or parties that would create some hostility, that "bias" could be shown through proper questions.

Familiarity or family relationships are not the only issues that may create a bias. An interest in the outcome of the litigation can create bias. A witness that hopes to gain something or fears losing something positive may be questioned about such interest. This "self interest" in the outcome of the litigation would obviously reveal some bias.

One type of "self interest" issue is whether the witness is being paid for preparing testimony. Although it sounds a bit unethical to discuss paying witnesses, it is common. Expert witnesses do not prepare testimony and appear at the trial without being paid. When an attorney hires an expert, the expert expects to receive payment for preparing the background information, doing the necessary research, reaching an opinion, and then appearing at trial to testify. Attorneys, judges and expert witnesses are well aware of that fact. Jurors, however, may be surprised to hear of the payments. Because of the slight misunderstanding that jurors may have about this matter, attorneys may, at times, ask an opposing expert witness about the fee arrangement. This line of questioning is considered appropriate to show the possibility of bias.

Questioning experts about fee arrangements does not occur in every case where experts testify. Since both sides to such cases have probably had to employ experts and both sides have made arrangements to pay those experts, attorneys on both sides may opt to refrain from asking such questions. If one side decided to ask such questions, the other side would also ask the same type of question. The type of case where such questioning might be used, however, is where one side is paying substantially more for the expert testimony then the other side. In such case, the attorney who is paying less for experts will raise the issue when questioning opposing experts. That attorney will know that by the time all of the experts have been questioned, the jurors will have heard how much more the other side is paying. There is then the hope that the higher paid experts look biased.

Other types of self interest may also be raise. The witness may be employed by or was once fired from a job by a party with a witness. The witness may be expecting gifts, bribes, or, in the case of criminal matters, possible favorable treatment from law enforcement organizations. Any of these items may be used to show bias.

The only limitation to the use of bias that can be found in the Federal Rules of Evidence is the manner of control of introduction of such evidence. Fed. R. Evid. 611(a) provides that the court shall control the mode and order of the presentation of evidence. This issue is discussed further in section E, below, but needs consideration with the issue of bias. This portion of the federal rules allows the trial judge to have discretion in allowing questioning concerning the issue of bias. In the absence of "abuse of discretion," the decision to allow or deny the questions will not be reversible.

2. Impeachment by Capacity

In section VI.B. above, the issue of the capacity of a witness to testify was discussed. In that section, it was noted that the traditional common law rules of evidence had a multitude of capacity rules. Witnesses would be prevented from testifying for a variety of reasons. Although the federal rules recognize that everyone is now assumed to be competent to testify under modern concepts of capacity, Fed. R. Evid. 601, there were still vestiges of such capacity and competency issues. Very young children and the mentally ill may still, occasionally, be denied the opportunity to testify.

Frequently, however, under the modern federal rules of evidence, witnesses are usually allowed to testify. This is true, even though the witnesses may be very young or suffering some mental illness. When such witnesses are allowed to testify, opposing counsel is entitled to allow the jury to be informed of such deficiencies.

The lack of capacity about which enquiry may be had is broad. Almost any capacity issue that would address the ability to observe, remember and relate the events at issue may be raised. These may include sensory, memory, or mental.

An easy example of impeachment on capacity is one dealing mental issues. A witness may be mentally ill or lack full mental capacity. This could include elderly witnesses suffering lack of capacity due to disease or condition that reduces memory. Such a lack could lead to the witness not being about to correctly observe events or even being unable to remember events observed. Counsel can bring out this lack of mental capacity.

An additional example would be a very young child. Children may not be able to fully understand events they see and may be unable to fully remember such events. That type of problem is also subject to impeachment.

Although the two above examples may be the most obvious, any lack of capacity that can have an impact on observation, memory or the ability to relate the events is subject to impeachment. If the witness is testifying to events seen or heard, a lack of full capacity in vision or hearing would be appropriate impeachment.

It is also appropriate to enquire of the witness about such issues as substance abuse. A history of alcohol or drug abuse may display that the witness's powers of observation and recall are not reliable. It is appropriate, for example, for the witness to be asked about substance abuse history, especially as it relates to the time of the events about which are being testified.

3. Impeachment by Character (608)

Impeachment by character is different from the impeachment by the lack of capacity that was discussed immediately above. The lack of capacity is appropriate for impeachment because it may show that the witness did not see or was unable to remember the events being reported. Such impeachment appears to go right to the issues raised by the testimony. Impeachment by character is allowed more as an inference. The law allows a witness to be impeached by evidence of bad character for truthfulness because public policy believes that the jury is entitled to know that the witness has a character for not telling the truth.

It should be obvious that general testimony that a witness has a tendency to lie may lead to unfair prejudice. Such general, unsupported statements are easily made and difficult to support. Because of the danger of unfair prejudice, the federal rules have specific rules governing the use of character evidence as it relates to truth telling. Those rules are in Fed. R. Evid. 608.

Before discussing the use of character evidence to attack credibility, it is important to distinguish such use of character evidence from a different topic. In Chapter IV of this work, the use of character evidence to show the propensity to commit an act was discussed. That issue is governed by Fed. R. Evid. 404 and 405. For a review of that material, one should return to Chapter IV. The basic difference between that material and the use of character to challenge credibility may be easily stated. Fed. R. Evid. 404 is designed to deal with the issue of using character evidence to show that a person acted in conformity with his or her character in order to prove that he or she committed a specific act. An examples of such use of character would be attempts to show that a violent person committed a violent act. The use of character in Fed. R. Evid. 608 to attack credibility is used against witnesses. It is used to show that a witness is not worthy of belief. In short, Fed. R. Evid. 404 is used to prove that a person acted in conformity with his or her character on a particular occasion. Fed. R. Evid. 608 is used to prove that person who is testifying is not worth of belief. With that short introduction, the details of Fed. R. Evid. 608 must be examined.

It should first be noted that this allowance for character evidence as it relates to credibility is mentioned, briefly, in the 400 rules. Fed. R. Evid. 404(a)(3) specifically allows the use of character evidence as it relates to "character of a witness." The rule also, however, specifically makes a reference to Fed. R. Evid. 607, 608, & 609 for the details of those principles.

When a witness testifies, that witness is, of course, subject to impeachment. In this area, the witness may be asked on cross examination about specific instances or their general character as it relates to a lack of truthfulness. Fed. R. Evid. 608(b)(1). The witness may be asked, for example, if they lied on academic records or misstated accomplishments on a resume. The rule allows the witness to be asked about such specific instances of conduct on cross examination. (It must be remembered, however, if the conduct was subject to or led to a conviction for crimes, Fed. R. Evid. 608 does not allow admission of such evidence. Fed. R. Evid. 608 makes reference to and requires that Fed. R. Evid. 609 be consulted to determine when such convictions may be raised. That rule is discussed below.) If the witness denies those specific instances of conduct, the attorney asking the question must accept the answer. Fed. R Evid. 608(b) excludes the use of other, extrinsic, evidence to prove the existence of those facts.

Extrinsic evidence of the character of a witness for lack of truthfulness, however, may be offered. After a witness has testified, if opposing counsel wishes to impeach by character, that counsel may call a witness to offer evidence of bad character for truth or veracity. Fed. R. Evid. 608(a)(1) specifically allows the use of such character evidence offered in the form of reputation or opinion. It is, of course, necessary for a witness to offer some foundation evidence before getting ready to testify about the reputation or an opinion concerning another witness's character for lack of truthfulness or veracity.

Upon taking the stand, the attorney wishing to offer the character evidence must ask preliminary questions. It would be necessary to start by showing that the witness on the stand has known the person about whom they are going to speak a sufficient period of time. If the testimony is to be in the form of reputation, the witness must be able to testify that he or she has sufficient knowledge of the appropriate reputation in the community for truth or veracity. If the testimony is to be in the form of opinion, the witness must be able to testify that they have known the person about whom they are offering evidence a sufficient period of time in order to have formed an opinion on truth or veracity.

Short examples of such lines of questioning may be seen.

If the attorney is seeking to use evidence of reputation, the questions would start with how long the witness had lived in the community. The attorney would then ask, Do you know the general reputation of [name of witness] in the community of [name community] for truth and veracity. Hopefully, the witness will say, "Yes, I do." The attorney would then ask, "What is that reputation for truth and veracity." The witness will respond, "It is bad."

If the attorney is seeking to use evidence of opinion of the witness, the initial questions about how long the character witness has known the person would be asked. Then the attorney would ask, "Have you formed an opinion about the character for truthfulness and veracity of [name of witness]? The witness should respond, "Yes, I have." The attorney would then ask, "What is your opinion of the character for truthfulness or veracity of [name of witness.] The witness would respond, "It is bad."

Once the character witness has testified that another witness in the case has a bad character for truthfulness, the character witness is subject to cross examination. The attorney that had called the original witness, the one whose character has been attacked, may want to question the character witness to try to rehabilitate the witness that was attacked. The cross examination may delve into whether the character witness is aware of positive features of the attacked witness's character for truthfulness. As with other forms of character evidence cross examination, the common law was rigid on the format of the question. At common law the question had to ask whether the witness had "heard" of the truthful things the other witness had done and could not ask if the witness "knew" of those things. That distinction no longer applies. The character witness may be asked if she or she "heard" or "knew" of such things.

Once a witness's character for truthfulness has been attacked by any of a variety of techniques, attempts may be made to rehabilitate that witness's character for truthfulness. Fed. R. Evid. 608(a)(2) specifically provides for such rehabilitation. That topic is discussed below in section VI.6, Rehabilitation and Refreshing Memory.

4. Impeachment by Crimes (609)

Impeaching a witness by evidence that the witness has previously been convicted of a crime is a difficult issue. The danger of unfair prejudice is probably greater in this area than any other. Evidence that a party to litigation has committed prior bad acts is, ordinarily, not admissible. As discussed in Chapter IV, above, the fact that someone has done something wrong in the past is not relevant to the fact that they may have done something bad again. Imagine, for example, that a person is on trial in a criminal case for bank robbery. If the prosecution was allowed to prove that the defendant had previously been convicted of bank robbery, the jury may decide to convict the defendant on that evidence alone. The jury may decide that since the defendant had committed other bank robberies, there was a good chance that the defendant had committed the one at issue. The law excludes evidence of such prior bad acts where it is being used to show that someone acted in conformity with the prior act.

Under Fed. R. Evid. 609, however, once a witness takes the stand, certain prior crimes committed by that witness may be brought to the attention of the jury. (It is important to note that this applies to any witness in any type of case. It may be a civil or criminal case. It may be a witness that is a party or merely a witness offering testimony.) Fed. R. Evid. 609 is a complex, detailed rule that requires close scrutiny. It is, however, one of the major reasons that defense attorneys representing defendants in criminal trials do not let the defendant take the witness stand in his or her own behalf. Unfortunately, many criminal defendants have records of prior convictions. If such a defendant does not take the witness stand, the prosecution cannot mention the prior convictions. If the defendant decides to testify on his or her own behalf, the prosecution can then offer the evidence concerning some of the prior convictions. The legal theory is that the evidence of prior convictions is being offered to test the credibility of the person as a witness and show that his or her testimony is not worthy of belief. The evidence of prior convictions is not to be used by the jury to show the probability that the witness/defendant probably committed the same type of crime again. The law is so certain of this distinction that, if the evidence of prior crimes is offered under these circumstances, the defendant/witness would be entitled to an instruction to the jury explaining the proper use of the evidence. Defense attorneys are concerned, however, that jurors may not fully understand the difference and use the evidence for the wrong reasons. It is easier to keep the defendant off the witness stand.

Defense attorneys do find use of the evidence of prior crimes in representing defendants in criminal cases. Unfortunately, many of the witnesses that prosecutors must call to testify in criminal cases are, themselves, people who have committed prior crimes. Once they have testified for the prosecution, defense attorneys can use the evidence that those witnesses have been convicted of some crimes.

Although the rule does not limit the use of such evidence to criminal cases and it clearly can be used in civil cases, such use is rare. The prior conviction of crimes that are appropriate for use as attacks on credibility does not come up as often in civil cases.

A major issue in the use of prior crimes is the nature of prior conviction that may be used. The answer to that question varies among jurisdictions and must be appropriately researched to determine the answer in any particular jurisdiction. A common, simple rule is that evidence of prior felony convictions may be used to impeach credibility, but no other convictions. The federal rules of evidence, however, are more complicated.

Fed. R. Evid. 609 begins by dividing the possible witnesses against which such evidence will be used into two groups. A witness may also be an "accused" in a criminal case, or may merely be a witness in any civil or criminal case. Under Fed. R. Evid. 609(a)(1), if the witness is not the accused in a criminal case then evidence that the witness has been convicted of a crime punishable by death or imprisonment in excess of one year may be used against that witness but subject to Fed. R. Evid. 403. You will need to recall that Fed. R. Evid. 403 provides that evidence may be excluded if the probative value of the evidence is substantially outweighed by the danger of unfair prejudice. Using this rule, once a witness takes the stand to testify on any manner, the opposing counsel may use evidence of prior convictions of crimes where the punishment could have been death or imprisonment in excess of one year. In order to exclude this evidence, the attorney that called the witness would have to convince the trial judge that the danger of unfair prejudice would substantially outweigh the probative value of the evidence as it relates to the credibility of the accused as a witness. As should be obvious, this is a fairly high burden. It would appear that a trial judge would usually find that the probative value of such evidence was not "substantially outweighed" by the danger of undue prejudice

It is interesting to note that the rule is, in some ways, tracking the common law, simple rule. In many jurisdictions, crimes which are punishable by death or imprisonment in excess of one year are felonies. All other crimes are misdemeanors. As such, the federal rule is merely saying that, under this portion of the rule, any felony from any jurisdiction may be used. The reason that the rule does not use the term felony and, instead, talks of crimes punishable by death or imprisonment in excess of one year, is that some state jurisdictions define felonies as crimes punishable be imprisonment in excess of two years. Rather than creating confusion in the rule, the federal rules merely defines precisely what types of crimes may be used in this instance.

For witness who are also the accused in a criminal case, Fed. R. Evid. 609(a)(1) provides a different test. Once a witness/accused is on the stand, the prosecutor may use evidence of prior convictions if the convictions are for crimes punishable by death or imprisonment in excess of one year and the probative value of this evidence outweighs the prejudicial effect. Two things are important to be noticed. First, the type of crimes that may be used against the witness/accused is the same type of crime that may also be used against any witness. Second, the main difference in these two examples is the balancing test that must be used to determine if the evidence of the prior conviction is to be excluded. The test for exclusion when the witness is also the accused in a criminal case is not as heavy a burden for exclusion. Where the witness is also the accused, the prosecutor will need to convince the trial judge that the probative value of the conviction as it relates to the credibility of the accused as a witness is sufficiently strong to outweigh the prejudicial effect to the accused. Although the language of the rule makes it appear that it should be easier to exclude this evidence when the witness is the accused, that usually does not happen. As a practical matter, evidence of most of these crimes are admitted.

Fed. R. Evid. 609(a)(2) has one additional type of criminal conviction that may also be used to impeach the credibility of a witness. This additional rule applies whether the witness is an accused in a criminal case or merely a witness in any case. The rule provides that evidence of a conviction of any crime involving dishonesty or false statement may be used to impeach the witness.

There are several issues in Fed R. Evid. 609(a)(2) that must be addressed. First, the convictions involving dishonesty or false statement may be used regardless of the punishment that such convictions would have carried. Simply stated, this means that even convictions for misdemeanors may be used if the underlying crime was one involving dishonesty or false statement. The second issue is more difficult. Unlike the section dealing with the crimes punishable by death or imprisonment in excess of one year, this section does not specify a balancing test to determine whether the evidence should be excluded for being too great a danger of unfair prejudice. There is something of a split of authority on this issue. Some feel that Fed. R. Evid. 403 applies to all evidence issues in the federal rules of evidence. With any evidence, for which there is no specific balancing test stated, the rule stated in Fed. R. Evid. 403 is to be applied. If this is correct, then the evidence of convictions would be admitted and only excluded if the danger of unfair prejudice substantially outweighed the probative value as it related to the credibility of a witness. Others feel, however, that this is incorrect. The contrary view is that there is no balancing test to be applied. The theory is that the drafters of the federal rules clearly showed that they were able to insert balancing tests where they were wanted. Fed. R. Evid. 609(a)(1) has two very specific balancing test. The absence of a balancing test in Fed. R. Evid. 609(a)(2) indicated that the drafters wanted the evidence of convictions of crimes involving dishonesty or false statement to be admissible without limit. If that position is correct, evidence of convictions of crimes involving dishonesty or false statement is admissible regardless of the extent of the danger of unfair prejudice.

Once it is determined what types of convictions may be used to impeach the credibility of a witness, additional issues must be addressed. It is important, for example, to know the age of the conviction. The federal rules of evidence, Fed. R. Evid. 609(b) has a time limit that may be known informally as the "Ten Year Rule." Under this rule, it is first important to view how the court must determine the "age" of the evidence. The rule indicates that the age of the conviction is to be determined from the date of the conviction or the date of release of the witness from confinement whichever is more recent. For example, if the conviction was 12 years ago, but the witness served 4 years in prison, then the conviction is considered to be only 8 years old.

Once the age is determine, the rule specifies the "ten year" rule. If the conviction or release, whichever is more recent, is greater than ten years old, then the evidence of the conviction may not be used unless the probative value of the evidence substantially outweighs the danger of unfair prejudice. It should be clear that this balancing test is the most onerous in this rule for those seeking to introduce the evidence of a prior conviction. The attorney seeking to use the evidence of the prior conviction would have to convince the trial judge that the probative value of the evidence as it relates to credibility of a witness was so great that is substantially outweighed any danger of unfair prejudice. It seems unlikely that this burden will be met.

If there is a possibility that the court will allow the use of a conviction that stands outside the time period of the "ten year" rule, another issue must be confronted. Fed. R. Evid. 609(b) requires that an attorney seeking to use such evidence must give opposing counsel written notice of such intent and give the opposing counsel an opportunity to be heard on the issue.

Fed. R. Evid. 609 has a few additional sections that deal with special circumstances that may arise when confronted with evidence of prior convictions. The possibility that a person has been pardoned of the crime for which he or she was convicted raises a problem. If the witness received a pardon or other similar procedure based upon the fact of having been rehabilitated and that witness has not been convicted of a subsequent crime punishable by death or imprisonment in excess of one year, then the evidence of the conviction is not admissible. If the witness received a pardon based upon a finding of innocence, then the evidence of conviction is not admissible.

Where the witness was the subject of a juvenile adjudication, additional issues arise. Ordinarily, such evidence of juvenile adjudications is not admissible. The rule does state, however, an exception, "The court may, however, in a criminal case allow evidence of a juvenile adjudication of a witness other than the accused if conviction of the offense would be admissible to attack the credibility of an adult and the court is satisfied that admission in evidence is necessary for a fair determination of the issue of guilt or innocence." Fed. R. Evid. 609(d). The exception has several important features. It may only be used in criminal cases, and then only when the witness is not the accused. Also there appears to be a modified balancing test that requires the trial judge to determine that the evidence of the conviction is necessary to the trial.

An issue may also arise where the witness has been convicted of a crime that is on appeal while the witness is testifying. Fed. R. Evid. 609(e) provides that the fact that the conviction is on appeal does not render the evidence inadmissible. In addition, the evidence that the conviction is on appeal is also admissible.

The method of proving the evidence of prior convictions must also be noted. As mentioned earlier, the extrinsic evidence of prior bad acts is generally not admissible. Fed. R. Evid. 608(b). That rule, however, does allow for extrinsic evidence of prior crimes that are admissible under Fed R. Evid. 609. This allows the attorney seeking to use evidence of prior convictions several opportunities to raise the evidence for the jury. While the witness to be impeached in on the stand, the attorney wanting to raise the prior conviction may do so on cross examination of that witness. The attorney may ask, for example, "Isn't it a fact that you were convicted of [name crime or state 'a felony'] on [state date]? The witness may or may not answer truthfully. If the witness says no, the attorney may call a rebuttal witness who has evidence that the conviction did, in fact, occur. Since evidence of convictions is so easily available, many attorneys will have their own witnesses mention the conviction while on direct examination. Attorneys feel that mentioning it on direct, and not waiting for the other side to bring it up on cross examination, makes the witness appear less likely to be trying to hide something.

5. Collateral Matters

The issue of impeachment by contradiction and the problem of collateral matters are not specifically mentioned in the federal rules of evidence. They are, however, issues that continue to be raised in cases in federal court.

It is obvious that trials are filled with contradictions. The only reason that a case goes to trial is that the opposing parties disagree on the facts. One way that contradictions arise, therefore, is that opposing witnesses tell the story of the events differently. In a civil case dealing with an automobile accident, one side will testify that the traffic light was red while the other side will claim it was green. In a criminal case the prosecution will claim that the defendant committed the crime, while the defense will claim the defendant did not.

This obvious contraction goes to illuminate the facts of the case. The attorneys may also suggest that the opposing side is not worthy of belief since their witnesses saw the event differently. As such, the contradictions in facts are offered as proof in the case and as impeachment. There is no problem in introducing such contradictions.

The problem with raising contradictions arises when the facts being contradicted are not important facts in the case. Imagine, for example, the case of the automobile accident where the witnesses disagree on the color of the traffic light. The color of the traffic light is probably a relevant fact in the case and should be subject to testimony. It should also be subject to cross examination. Imagine further, however, if one of the witnesses happened to mention during direct examination that it was a cool day and, "I was wearing my yellow sweater." Opposing counsel may have a witness who was at the scene and is ready to testify that the sweater was, in fact, brown. The issue is whether the opposing counsel should be allowed to cross examine on the color of the sweater, and furthermore, should the attorney be able to call the other witness to testify that the sweater was, in fact, brown.

That hypothetical about the color of the sweater conveys the problem with impeachment by contradiction and collateral matters. The court will probably allow the attorney to cross examine the witness on the color of the sweater. The attorney, however, is probably stuck with the answers the witness gives on cross. If the attorney seeks to call the other witness to testify the sweater was brown, an objection that the material is collateral will probably be sustained. Under Fed. R. Evid. 403, the trial judge has discretion to exclude evidence based upon undue delay or unfair prejudice. Allowing impeachment on collateral matters would tend to take the trial on a tangent that would waste time and confuse the jury.

The issue of contradiction on collateral matters is rarely simple. The above hypothetical seems obvious. Taking the hypothetical one step further, however, illustrates the difficulty. Once the witness had mentioned the color of the sweater, the opposing attorney may now want to claim that the witness has some color blindness or color confusion. That attorney will claim that the color of the sweater is not a collateral matter, but merely indicates that the witness has a problem with perception. Since the color of the traffic light is a major issue in the case, impeachment on perception would be relevant and critical. Similar instances can arise when what appears to be collateral is also argued to reflect bias, capacity, or some other basic impeachment issue. Again, the trial judge has discretion under Fed. R. Evid. 403, to exclude such evidence.

6. Rehabilitation and Refreshing Memory (608, 612)

Once a witness has been attacked on cross examination and some form of impeachment has been used, the attorney that originally called that witness may wish to try to "rehabilitate" the witness. There are several techniques that are recognized and allowed to try to place the witness in a better light in the minds of the jurors.

The first technique for avoiding the sting of impeachment is the cover the matters before the impeachment occurs. Although there is not a specific federal rule of evidence that deals with this issue, it is allowed. An obvious example may occur when a witness that is being used in a trial has been convicted of a crime which can be raised on cross examination as a form of impeachment. While the witness is testifying on direct, the attorney may ask about the criminal conviction. This gives the witness the opportunity to explain the conviction before the opposing counsel has the opportunity to bring it up and make it appear that someone was trying to hide the conviction.

Other examples of explaining impeachment early can easily be imagined. A witness that is testifying in a trial may have a business or family relationship with a party. Opposing counsel would want to raise this as impeachment by bias. Attorneys would want to explain that relationship during direct in an effort to blunt the power of the cross examination.

Another form of "rehabilitation" is specifically covered in Fed. R. Evid. 608(a)(2). That rule, of course, deals with the use of character evidence for truthfulness or untruthfulness. As discussed earlier, it can be used to impeach a witness by showing bad character for veracity. Fed. R. Evid. 608(a)(2) says, "evidence of truthful character is admissible only after the character of the witness for truthfulness has been attacked by opinion or reputation evidence or otherwise."

It is easier to see the operation of Fed. R. Evid. 608(a)(2) by using examples. Imagine that witness Able has taken the stand to testify in a case. After testifying, opposing counsel calls witness Baker to the stand to say that witness Able has a bad reputation for truthfulness in the community. Witness Baker could also testify that, in witness Baker's own opinion, witness Able was not truthful. At this point, as noted in Fed. R. Evid 608(a)(2), the character for truthfulness of witness Able "has been attacked by opinion or reputation evidence." The attorney that originally called witness Able, can now call witness Charlie to testify that the reputation of witness Able for truthfulness in the community is good. Witness Charlie could also testify that in witness Charlie's opinion witness Able was truthful.

Fed. R. Evid. 608(a)(2), however, is more difficult then that simple example. That simple example follows the specific language of the rule and allows rehabilitation with character evidence of good character for truthfulness after a witness has been attacked by character evidence of bad character for truthfulness. A close reading of the rule indicates that it allows further rehabilitation. The rule states that the evidence of good character for truthfulness may be offered not only when the character for truthfulness has been attacked by character evidence, but it may be rehabilitated when it has been attached by "otherwise." Fed. R. Evid. 608(a)(2). The use of the word otherwise suggests that an attorney can use evidence of good character for truthfulness after a wide range of types of impeachment have occurred. The rule itself does not indicate what the limits of the word "otherwise" are suppose to be. The Advisory Committee Notes from the drafters of the federal rules of evidence do provide some guidance. Obviously, attack by reputation or opinion is specifically stated in the rule and would allow rehabilitation by evidence of good character for truthfulness. The Advisory Committee notes suggest that "evidence of misconduct, including conviction of crime, or of corruption" would also trigger the availability of evidence of good character for truthfulness to rehabilitate the witness. "Evidence of bias or interest does not." Advisory Committee Notes, Fed. R. Evid. 608(a). "Whether evidence in the form of contradiction is an attack upon the character of the witness must depend on the circumstances." Advisory Committee Notes Fed. R. Evid. 608(a).

Although not a true form of rehabilitation, there is another method for assisting a witness that appears to be having trouble remembering events. The rules do specifically allow a witness to refresh his or her memory with notes. Fed. R. Evid. 612. That rule is interesting in that it assumes that a witness may use notes to refresh a memory, and then deals mainly with the problem of allowing the opposing attorney to see the notes

It is not hard to imagine a witness that must testify to a long, complex set of facts. This is especially true of expert witnesses. Such witness may have to describe a series of tests and experiments before ever getting to the opinion that is to be given. In addition, an expert is probably working on more than one case or problem at that time. An expert may have his or her own work to do in addition to several cases for a variety of attorneys. To expect such a witness to get on the witness stand and remember all of the evidence they are to give is not rational. Witnesses, as does the general public in daily life, use notes to help refresh their memory.

The first issue to be discussed, however, is that the notes must be used to refresh memory. If questioned about the matter, the witness must be able to say that he or she has "present memory" and is merely using the notes to refresh that memory. At common law, this technique was called, "Present Recollection (memory) Refreshed." If the witness can testify that he or she has that present memory, then the witness may use the notes to refresh that memory. If the witness is unable or unwilling to testify that he or she has that present memory, additional problems arise. If the witness does not have present memory, then the witness is not testifying from memory. The witness would, instead, be merely reading from a list. The written list, and not the witness's testimony, would be the evidence. When that occurs, a serious hearsay problem arises. The list is probably an out of court statement that is being read into the record in order to prove the truth of the matter stated on the list. That is hearsay, and reading the list would be inadmissible. (Later, in the section on hearsay, there is a discussion about a hearsay exception that may be appropriate for this type of testimony. That exception is called "recorded recollection." Fed. R. Evid. 803(5).) If, however, the witness is able to testify that there is present memory, the witness may testify and use the notes to help refresh that memory. There are no formal requirements to the nature of the notes. The notes can be anything, including pictures, documents, graphs and even items prepared by others.

Fed. R. Evid. 612 does allow opposing counsel to see and review those notes. The rule specifically states that if the notes are used during the trial, opposing counsel is entitled to look at them while the witness is testifying. An example of this is easy to see. An expert witness may take the witness stand while carrying a file folder full of notes and papers. After direct examination, the opposing counsel will ask to see the file before beginning cross examination. The court will order the witness to hand the file to the opposing counsel. (Because of this rule, attorneys usually remind witnesses not to take anything to the witness stand that the witness would prefer the opposing counsel not see.)

Fed. R. Evid. 612(2) also allows the opposing counsel to request seeing any files before the witness testifies. This is permitted only if the court feels it is necessary in the interest of justice.

If the attorney calling the witness feels that there are parts of the file or notes that should not be seen by opposing counsel, that attorney may make a motion to withhold that material. The trial judge can then review the file and release those portions that are appropriate. If the attorney calling the witness refuses to turn over the file or notes, the trial judge may make appropriate rulings. If the case is a criminal case and it is the prosecutor who refuses to turn over the ordered notes, then the trial judge may strike the testimony of the witness or declare a mistrial.

7. Religious Beliefs (610)

The federal rules of evidence removes from consideration the religious beliefs or opinions of witnesses as it would relate the attacks on credibility or attempts to enhance credibility. Parties to litigation could try to use the religious beliefs of a witness for one of two reasons. A party calling a witness may want to show the strong religious beliefs of the witness in order to show the witness is worthy of belief. An opposing party to a witness may want to claim that the witness has weak or no religious beliefs in order to attack the witnesses credibility. Fed. R. Evid. 610 specifically declares that such evidence is not admissible for either purpose.

8. Prior Inconsistent Statements (613)

A powerful form of impeachment is the use of prior inconsistent statements. After a witness has testified on direct, an opposing counsel will have the opportunity to question the witness on cross examination. If the opposing counsel is aware that the witness has talked about the matters of importance on prior occasions, and, on those prior occasions, told the story differently, that opposing counsel will want the jury to hear that evidence. It is believed that the jury will realize that the witness has told the story multiple times and tends to change the story to fit the surroundings. If that impression is given to the jury about a witness, that jury will not believe the witness's testimony. Notice one of the critical features of this form of impeachment. The opposing counsel is seeking to introduce the prior inconsistent statement in order to show that the witness is not worthy of belief. The prior inconsistent statement is not being introduced to try to get the jury to believe that the prior statement is true. If the opposing counsel wanted to introduce the prior statement in order to get the jury to believe the prior statement is true, there would be a serious hearsay problem. The prior statement would probably be an out of court statement that the opposing counsel was introducing to prove the truth of that statement. That is hearsay. (In the later discussion of hearsay, the definition of hearsay will allow the use of some prior statements of witnesses to be offered for the truth of the statement. That is discussed in the material on Fed. R. Evid. 801(d)(1)(A).)

At common law, the use of prior inconsistent statements had a formal foundation requirement. If the opposing counsel wanted to introduce the prior inconsistent statement, certain steps had to be followed. While the witness was on the stand, during cross examination, the opposing counsel had to ask the witness about the "time, place, and persons present" when the prior statement was made. Then the witness had to be confronted with or asked specifically about the inconsistent statement. This would, of course, give the witness the opportunity to explain the matter. After this foundation was laid, the opposing counsel would be free, later in the trial, to call another witness to testify about the inconsistent statement. This, therefore, allowed the opposing counsel to offer extrinsic evidence of the inconsistent statement.

Fed. R. Evid. 613 maintains a general opportunity to respond to a challenge by inconsistent statement, but relaxes the traditional, formal common law rule. Under the federal rules, the opposing counsel may prove the inconsistent statement by extrinsic evidence so long as the witness who is being impeached "is afforded an opportunity" to respond or explain the inconsistency.

Fed. R. Evid. 613(2). This means that the opposing counsel does not have to confront the witness with the statement during cross examination. All the opposing counsel has to do is make sure that the witness is not released from the subpoena that required the witness's attendance. The opposing counsel can, for example, just say, "We have no further questions, but we would like the witness to remain available to be recalled later." Then, when the opposing counsel chooses to introduce the inconsistent statement by another witness, the terms of Fed. R. Evid. 613 have been met.

As a practical matter, many attorneys still continue to lay the traditional foundation that was required by the common law. (It is important to note that some state jurisdictions still require that foundation.) The reasons that attorneys still use the traditional foundation when it is no longer required are many and varied. For some, it is a matter of having learned the traditional foundation as a matter of trial practice. Old habits are hard to break and they continue to try cases the way they have always tried them. For others, it appears that the old foundation works better. After the witness has testified on direct, the opposing counsel uses the inconsistent statement during cross examination to impeach the witness. The jury can take the suggestion to just ignore that witness's testimony since the witness appears to have the tendency to lie. As a part of this theory, some attorneys are just concerned that if they wait too long, the jury may be confused and not realize to what the inconsistent statement relates. Finally, if the old common law foundation requirement is followed, it reduces the opportunity for counter argument. The attorney who called the witness in the first instance cannot be heard to claim that the opportunity to explain the statement was lost.

One further matter is mentioned by the federal rules. If the opposing counsel confronts the witness with the inconsistent statement, there is no requirement to show the witness the statement even if it is in writing. Upon request by the attorney who called the witness, however, the statement must be shown to that attorney. Fed. R. Evid. 613(a).

E. Presentation of Witnesses (611)

Both civil and criminal trials appear to have a formal order and process. In Chapter I, a brief outline or summary of the steps of a trial were listed. The Federal Rules of Evidence place substantial discretion over the order and mode of presentation of the evidence in the hands of the trial judge. Fed. R. Evid. 611 provides for some of the specific rules that grant authority to the trial judge.

1. Control by Judge

As noted, the trial judge has control over the presentation of the evidence. Fed. R. Evid. 611(a) states, "The court shall exercise reasonable control over the mode and order of interrogating witnesses and presenting evidence." This rule is rarely discussed or debated by text writers or in opinions. It just states the basic concept that is inherent in the role of the trial judge to take control of the trial. The rule does go on to state some general principles and purposes of vesting control in the trial judge.

The court should make sure that the questioning is effective for the "ascertainment of the truth." Fed. R. Evid. 611(a)(1). A good example of this principle is the judge's role in deciding whether a witness can answer the questions as a long narrative or will be restricted to short questions and answers. Attorneys will, at times, ask a witness to just tell the jury the story of the events as a long single narrative. Opposing counsel usually objects to this. By having the witness tell a long narrative, the risk of objectionable material being stated in front of the jury is increased. The witness may just state some hearsay, for example, leaving the opposing counsel to object or move to strike after the jury has heard it. The opposing counsel would prefer short questions and answers in order to allow the opportunity to object. Of course, not even the attorney calling the witness will always want to use the narrative answer format. Some witnesses are able to tell a good, clear story in a narrative. Others will merely ramble, go off on tangents and never put the proper evidence before the jury. In talking with witnesses before trial, attorneys have to decide what question and answer format to use. Once the opposing counsel objects to the narrative format, the trial court has the discretion to decide what is appropriate.

Another purpose stated in the rule is to "avoid needless consumption of time." Fed. R. Evid. 611(a)(2). This allows the trial judge to prevent an attorney and witness from merely repeating the same evidence. It also allows the trial judge to prevent an attorney from calling multiple witnesses to introduce the same evidence. This rule is similar to the portion of Fed. R. Evid. 403 which allows the exclusion of evidence that is a waste of time.

A final principle stated is that the trial judge has this discretion to "protect witnesses from harassment or undue embarrassment." Fed. R. Evid. 611(a)(3). This is usually raised during the cross examination of a witness. The attorney that originally called the witness may object that the cross examination is being conducted in a manner that is intended to harass, intimidate or embarrass the witness. It should be remember, of course, that cross examination is designed to show the witness is not worthy of belief. Attorneys conducting cross examination may frequently put witnesses in positions that are uncomfortable.

That alone does not make the questioning improper. The trial judge must decide when the questioning goes beyond the usual scope of cross examination and is designed merely to harass or embarrass.

2. Cross examination

The trial judge is also granted the authority to control the overall scope of cross examination. That authority is limited by the language of Fed. R. Evid. 611(b). It is important to note that there is a conflict in jurisdictions over the general scope of cross examination. That conflict must be understood before seeing the rule that was adopted by the federal rules of evidence. There are two possible rules that can be used in deciding the proper scope of cross examination. The rules may be simply called the "scope of direct" rule and the "wide open rule."

The "scope of direct" rule limits the cross examination to only those matters that were originally raised on the direct examination of the witness or matters which relate solely to the credibility of the witness. This rule is designed to limit the amount of material that can be raised on cross examination. The attorney doing the cross examination may feel that a witness has knowledge of additional matters that are relevant to the case and that were not raised on direct. Under this rule, those matters may not be raised on cross examination. If the attorney conducting the cross examination wishes to pursue those additional matters, that attorney must re-call that witness as his or her own witness during a later stage of the trial.

The "scope of direct" rule has both positive and negative aspects. The primary positive aspect is that it allows attorneys to plan, organize and present their cases in a orderly fashion. Attorneys can call witness and present an organized story from beginning to end. Opposing counsel can contest the validity of that story through cross examination, but cannot raise other stories until the first attorney is finished with his or her side of the case. As a practical matter, prosecutors and plaintiffs lawyers in civil cases prefer the "scope of direct" rule. Prosecutors and plaintiffs lawyers have the burden of proof in cases and present their case in chief first. They like to be able to present their whole case without defense lawyers raising conflicting stories during that period. Of course, the defense lawyers can use cross examination to challenge the story being offered and the credibility of the witness, but they must wait for their own case in chief to offer other ideas.

One of the negative aspects of the "scope of direct" rule is that it can lead to endless objections and arguments. During cross examination, the attorney that originally called the witness may object claiming that a line of questions on cross examination is "outside the scope of direct." The trial judge then has to try to work through what the direct examination covered in order to properly rule on the objection. If the witness has been testifying for an extended period, this can be a difficult problem. If the attorney who originally called the witness decides to make objections on this basis for almost everything, the time spent deciding objections can be lengthy.

The second possible rule for scope of cross examination is called the "wide open" rule. Under the rule, the attorney conducting cross examination may raise any matter that is relevant to the case and matters affecting credibility. This would allow the cross examination to be conducted to cover any matter, whether or not it was raised on direct, so long as it was relevant to the case.

The "wide open" rule also has some positive and negative features. For the trial judge, it simplifies the cross examination process. There is no reason to try to remember exactly what was discussed on direct with a witness. The only issue is whether the matter raised is relevant to the case. Defense attorneys prefer this rule for obvious reasons. It allows them to begin to raise their issues early in the case while the prosecutor or plaintiff's lawyer is trying to present their view of the case.

The negative aspects of the "wide open" rule are twofold. First, of course, prosecutors and plaintiff's lawyers in civil cases see the rule as disruptive to the orderly presentation of the case. It can, therefore, lead to some confusion in the mind of jurors. Secondly, a trial judge may find that a defense lawyer is delaying the presentation of a case by having the same evidence repeated by several witnesses.

The federal rules of evidence adopted something of a hybrid between the two rules. Fed. R. Evid. 611(b) indicates that it is adopting the "scope of direct" rule. "Cross-examination should be limited to the subject matter of the direction examination and matters affecting the credibility of the witness." Fed. R. Evid. 611(b). Had the rule ended at that point, it would have clearly adopted the "scope of direct" rule. The rule, however, has additional language. "The court may, in the exercise of discretion, permit inquiry into additional matters as if on direction examination." Fed. R. Evid. 611(b). This line gives the trial judge discretion to expand the cross examination beyond the scope of direct and allow questions on any matters that are relevant to the case. It could be stated that the federal rules of evidence adopt the "scope of direct" rule with the trial judge discretion to expand the examination to any matter that is relevant. The Advisory Committee notes then provide a full discussion of the background and distinctions between the two forms of the rule. After noting the trial judge discretion, the notes say, "The matter is not one in which involvement at the appellate level is likely to be fruitful."

Advisory Committee notes, Fed. R. Evid. 611(b). This sentence seems to be hinting strongly at an important point. The trial judge has been granted discretion to determine the full scope of cross examination. Once it has been decided by the trial judge, the appellate courts are not going to review that decision. Attorneys will need to object and argue their point of view on this issue before the trial judge with the understanding that the decision of the trial judge is probably final.

3. Leading Questions

Most non-lawyers have heard of "leading" questions and realize that there is something wrong with such questions. The rule that deals with that problem is Fed. R. Evid. 611(c). Such questions are objectionable, but the issue is more complex than non-lawyers comprehend.

It is, of course, important to know what a "leading" question is. Simply stated, a leading question is one that suggests the answer. A question, for example, that asked a witness "Wasn't the traffic light green when you went through it" would be a leading question. The witness was being told what to answer. A proper question would be, "What color was the traffic light?"

The form of the question is not always as obvious as the example shown above. It would seem that any question that allowed a yes or no answer would not be leading. The attorney asking the question, however, may be able to word it in such a way as to suggest the answer. For example, the question "Was the light green when you went through it" may appear leading in some circumstances. Frequently, it will depend on the nature of the question and the circumstances of the whole testimony to decide whether a question is leading.

If the question is leading, the initial rule is that such "leading questions should not be used on the direct examination of a witness except as may be necessary to develop the witness' testimony." Fed. R. Evid. 611(c). This, of course, indicates that leading question "should not" be used. Ordinarily, leading questions are objectionable. The use of the word "should" and the fact that the rule provides that such questions may be used where "necessary" allows broad discretion in the trial judge. Judges will generally allow leading questions to begin the testimony, go through generally uncontested matters, and get the witness to the point of the testimony that is critical. The witness, for example, is usually asked to state his or her name and address for the record. Such a question is leading because it assumes that the witness has a name and address. An objection to that question would be absurd. In a case where all the parties agree that a traffic accident happened on January 1, 2005, the attorney on direct may get to a point where he or she says, "Let me now direct your attention to the traffic problem that occurred on January 1, 2005." Obviously, that is leading the witness. If the material is uncontested, there would be no reason to force the attorney to go through the long process of asking non-leading questions to reach the same point.

When an attorney begins to ask questions on direct about critical matters that are in dispute, the opposing counsel will probably object if the question is leading. This will force the attorney asking questions to allow the witness to testify rather than supplying the answers. The response by the trial judge is frequently to force the question to be re-phrased.

The above discussion noted that the prohibition on leading questions was for direct examination. "Ordinarily leading questions should be permitted on cross-examination." Fed. R. Evid. 611(c). On cross examination, for example, an attorney could ask, "Isn't it a fact that you ran the red light?" That is a leading question; it suggests the answer. The question would probably be allowed. The only real objection would be that, at some point, such questions were merely designed to harass or embarrass the witness.

The rule also allows leading questions in another area. "When a party calls a hostile witness, an adverse party, or a witness identified with an adverse party, interrogation may be by leading question." Fed. R. Evid. 611(c). Since attorneys may call anyone as a witness and be free to impeach any witness, see Fed. R. Evid. 607, an attorney may frequently call witnesses that are clearly more inclined to be helpful to the other side. In such circumstances, the examination may be "as on direct" and, therefore, include leading questions.

4. Judge Called Witnesses (614)

At common law, an attorney that called a witness was held to "vouch" for the credibility of the witness. As such, the attorney could not impeach a witness that he or she called. That principle, among others, gave rise to a practice allowing the judge to call witnesses. There could be witnesses that neither side wanted to call, but one or the other would like to ask a few questions of that witness. The trial judge could call the witness and then either attorney could question, cross examine and impeach.

Today, the need for the power of the judge to call witnesses is not as great. Under Fed. R. Evid. 607, any lawyer can impeach any witness. That includes witnesses the lawyer calls. In addition, a lawyer may conduct the examination as if on cross if the witness is hostile or identified with the opposing party. With those two ideas in place, attorneys are less hesitant to call witness identified with the other side.

Although the need for the power of the judge to call witnesses is not as great as it once was, that authority is still there. The judge can call a witness and either side may cross examine. Fed. R. Evid., 614(a).

Fed. R. Evid. 614 includes additional authority that adds to the power to call witnesses. In addition to the authority to call witnesses, the trial judge has the authority to ask any witness questions whether the judge called the witness or one of the attorneys called the witness. The assumption is that the judge has this authority in order to make sure the testimony is clear. This authority by a trial judge may, of course, lead to abuse. A trial judge must be careful not to leave the proper role of judge as neutral party and appear to be an advocate for one side. The Advisory Committee notes make it clear that abuse in this area is a proper place for a court of appeal to reverse. Advisory Committee notes, Fed. R. Evid. 614(b).

Since there is the possibility of abuse by the trial judge in calling witnesses or asking questions, an attorney may feel the need to object to the judge's conduct. That would be a difficult thing to do in the presence of the jury. The jury will look upon the judge as the central power figure in the courtroom and not like attorneys challenging that authority. Recognizing this problem, the rules provide an alternative method of objection. The objection may be made "at the time or at the next available opportunity when the jury is not present." Fed. R. Evid. 614(c). This allows the objecting attorney to raise the matter out of the presence of the jury.

F. Sequestration of Witnesses — The Rule (615)

The exclusion of witnesses from the courtroom until it is time for each of them to take the witness stand is a well known and recognized rule. Many jurisdictions refer to it as The Rule of Sequestration of Witnesses. It has been so well recognized that it is sometimes merely referred to as "The Rule." In some jurisdiction, attorneys invoke this process by asking the trial judge to "Invoke The Rule."

In Fed. R. Evid. 615, the rule is called "Exclusion of Witnesses." Upon request of any party, the "court shall order witnesses excluded so that they cannot hear the testimony of other witnesses." Fed. R. Evid. 615. There are several important features of the rule that are apparent from the language. It is clear that this rule is not vested in the discretion of the trial judge. The rule is mandatory. When a party makes a request for exclusion of witnesses, the court "shall" grant it. It is also clear that the purpose of the rule is to avoid having witnesses listen to other testimony in order to tailor their own to fit what they have heard. It is hoped that witnesses will be offering their own testimony and not that they heard in the courtroom. Although not specifically stated in the rule, the judge will frequently instruct witnesses that they are not to discuss their testimony with other witnesses in the case.

The rule itself does not state a specific procedure or time for making the request for exclusion. It appears that the request could be made at any time. It is usually made at the very beginning of the trial.

The rule does provide for some specific exemptions to those who are to be excluded. Clearly, people who are parties to the litigation should not be excluded. Fed. R. Evid. 615(1). Plaintiffs and defendants in civil cases and defendants in criminal cases have the right to be present in the courtroom throughout the trial even if they intend to testify at some point. In addition, many times companies, corporations, partnerships or other entities are parties to litigation. When that occurs, a person designated, by the attorney, as the representative of that party is entitled to remain in the courtroom throughout the trial. Fed. R. Evid 615(2). At times, a person who meets neither of those categories but "whose presence is essential to the presentation" of the case is entitled to stay. Fed. R. Evid. 615(3). Such persons may include an agent who handled a matter before trial or a critical expert that will assist the litigating attorney. Finally, anyone authorized by other law to be in the courtroom may not be excluded. Fed. R. Evid. 615(4).

The rule of exclusion is well known and used in most trials. It is so commonly done that it usually requires little discussion. It can, however, provide a serious problem when it is violated. If a witness has remained in the courtroom in violation of the rule of exclusion, the trial judge may refuse to allow that witness to testify. Attorneys would not knowingly allow a witness to remain in violation of the exclusion, but mistakes can occur. In a trial that is intended to last for several days, witnesses may be schedule to come to the court house several days after the trial has started. Being unfamiliar with court proceedings, a witness could casually walk in to the courtroom and be seated. Court rooms are open for the general public. It could be some period of time before either attorney realized that an important witness had been sitting through other testimony in violation of the rule of exclusion. As a practical matter, it is important for attorneys to remind every witness to stay out of the courtroom until called. Attorneys will frequently instruct witness on the appropriate place to go while waiting for their turn on the witness stand.

Checkpoints

- The federal rules of evidence generally recognize all witnesses as competent to testify.

- All witnesses must be able to understand the importance of telling the truth and affirm that they will do so.

- Ordinarily, law witnesses must be able to testify to facts from first hand knowledge.

- Holding a witness incompetent to testify will prevent the witness from giving any testimony. Impeaching a witness is a method of allowing the witness to testify but offering further evidence to the jury that will encourage the jury to disregard that testimony.

- Routine methods of impeaching a witness include evidence of bias or interest in the outcome of the litigation.

- Impeachment by prior inconsistent statements is allowed. The attorney using the impeachment technique must make sure that the witness has the opportunity to explain the inconsistency.

- A witness may be impeached by character evidence that relates to character for truthfulness. The character evidence may be in the form of reputation or opinion.

- A witness may be impeached by evidence of prior convictions of crimes. If the witness is an accused in a criminal case, then evidence of a prior conviction of a crime punishable by death or imprisonment in excess of one year is admissible if the probative value of the evidence outweighs the danger of unfair prejudice.

- A witness who is not the accused in a criminal case may be impeached by evidence of a crime punishable by death or imprisonment unless the probative value of the evidence is substantially outweighed by the danger of unfair prejudice.

- Any witness may be impeached by any crime that relates to dishonesty.

- Crimes that are occurred more than 10 years ago since the date of conviction or date of release cannot be used unless the probative value of the evidence substantially outweighs the danger of unfair prejudice.

- If a witness's character for truthfulness has been attacked, it may be rehabilitated by evidence of good character for truthfulness.

- The trial judge exercises discretion over the manner of introduction of evidence.

- The scope of cross examination in federal court is limited to the scope of direct. The trial judge, however, has discretion to expand the scope of cross examination.

Chapter 7

Opinion Evidence and Expert Witnesses

Opinion Evidence and Expert Witnesses Roadmap

- Understand the condition under which a lay witness can testify to an opinion.
- Completely analyze the issues that arise when an expert witness testifies.
- How is an expert qualified?
- What is the current trend in the law on validity of the underlying science for expert testimony?

A. Introduction

It is assumed that most of the evidence that is to be offered into the trial of a law suit will be fact testimony. The witnesses are to relate to the jury what happened and the jury will reach conclusions based on those facts. As pointed out in the chapter on Witnesses, it is assumed that witnesses will testify to facts from first-hand knowledge. Fed R. Evid. 602. Not all evidence offered in a trial, however, is "fact" evidence. Frequently it is important for attorneys to offer evidence in the form of opinion. The easiest example of opinion evidence is to be found in a medical malpractice case. In such cases, it is important for the plaintiff to prove that the defendant doctor failed to use the care and skill of a qualified professional. Ordinary jurors will not know what the appropriate skill level is. In fact, if a doctor appears in the panel as a possible juror in a medical malpractice case, the plaintiff's lawyer will strike the doctor from the jury. The lawyers do not want anyone on the jury that is actually knowledgeable about the details of the case. It is necessary, therefore, for the attorneys to offer expert testimony to tell the jurors what is usually expect of physicians in a particular field and then to offer an opinion as to whether the defendant met that standard. Article VII and the 700s rules in the Federal Rules of Evidence regulate the introduction of expert and opinion evidence.

B. Opinions by Lay Witnesses and First-Hand Knowledge Recap (701)

In the discussion of Fed. R. Evid. 602, it was explained that lay witnesses are limited to testifying about facts that they know from first-hand knowledge. Ordinarily, that is the purpose of a non-expert witness. Trials routinely have witnesses testify about descriptions of the scene of an incident or the chronological series of events that occurred. The only necessary foundation to that evidence is something to indicate that the witness has learned that information from first-hand observation. This has led, in the past, to it sometimes being stated that non-experts cannot testify to opinions. They can only testify to facts from first-hand knowledge. This is not, however, true.

Lay witnesses are allowed and, in fact, need to testify to opinions on a regular basis. What may appear to be a simple question, may also require the statement of some opinion. If a witness was asked to identify a person in a photograph, it could be argued that is asking for an opinion. Recognition of the facial features and characteristics is based upon many little facts observed over a period of time. The witness is able to identify the person in the photograph because the witness has learned to observe the lines and structure of the face and then is willing to give the opinion as to who it is. If the law required lay witnesses to only testify to facts, the witness would have to explain the recognition of certain lines, features and coloring on the face. That is not required. The law does, therefore, allow lay witnesses to express opinions on some matters.

Fed. R. Evid. 701 allows the expression of some opinions by lay witnesses. It states what has become the general rule in this area. The first requirement for allowing the testimony in the form of opinion is that it must be "rationally based on the perception of the witness." Fed. R. Evid. 701(a). This requirement picks up the concept that the witness must have first-hand knowledge of the events that formed the opinion. The lay witness is not allowed to testify to opinions based upon facts gained from other people. The lay witness, for example, cannot base an opinion on hearsay. The lay witness must have gained the underlying facts from his or her own observation.

The requirement of "rationally based on perception" also suggests something more. The witness must not only gain the underlying facts from first-hand observation, but must have been able to "rationally" form the opinion. It must be the type of opinion that lay witnesses are able to form. As such, it is the type of opinion that does not require an expert witness. Some jurisdictions have actually stated this whole requirement as something like a two part test. It is recognized that the witness had to have he opportunity to observe the event and the ability to form an opinion.

Applying this requirement to a series of facts, it is easy to see some examples. The above discussion already noted that lay witnesses can give testimony concerning the identity of other people. In addition, lay witnesses have generally been allowed to testify to what emotions they believed other people were feeling. A witness would be allowed to testify that someone was anger, mad, upset, happy, or in love. This type of testimony has, at time, been referred to as the "collective facts" rule. It is recognized that such testimony would be difficult to break down into individual facts. At the same time, most adults have had sufficient experience with a wide range of emotions and are able to identify those feelings in others. Courts, therefore, routinely allow lay witnesses to give such testimony.

Although it would seem that the mental stability of a person could be best described by a witness with expert training in mental illness, courts have routinely allowed lay witnesses to testify about a persons sanity or insanity. Again, it is assumed that a lay witness that has had the opportunity to observe another person, and could form an opinion as to whether that person was sane.

There are also a wide range of examples that allow lay witnesses to give opinions on physical conditions. Witnesses may testify to speed, color, size, heat, cold and other such details. A typical example would be in an automobile accident case. A lay witness that observed the events leading up to the accident could be allowed to testify to the approximately speed of the automobiles before that accident.

The first requirement is, therefore, easy to state. The opinion of a lay witness is admissible if it is rationally based upon the perception of that witness. It is a little more difficult to apply. The courts have viewed many different situations where such testimony has been allowed.

The second problem with lay opinion testimony is also specifically regulated by Fed. R. Evid. 701. As the common law of evidence began to allow the introduction of some lay opinion, a rigid rule developed concerning the types of cases or examples where such evidence could be admitted. The law limited such testimony to those examples where the introduction of lay opinion was "necessary." The lay opinion would not be admissible unless there was no other way to get the evidence into the trial and the lay witness was unable to provide the evidence without resorting to language that seemed to suggest opinion or speculation. Such a rule would be limiting. Such a rule would also lead to some argument and confusion. Trial judges would have to make a ruling on whether the evidence was "necessary" before it could be admitted. The federal rules of evidence have adopted a broader rule.

Fed. R. Evid. 701 states that the opinion of the lay witness is admissible if it is "helpful to a clear understanding of the witness' testimony or the determination of a fact in issue." Fed. R. Evid. 701(b). This rule of "helpfulness" makes it much easier to admit lay opinion then the older rule of "necessity." This rule of "helpfulness" seems to also be partially explained by the "collective facts" rule. As noted earlier, witnesses are allowed to testify to such things as the emotions of someone else. A witness could testify, for example, that the defendant in a criminal case seemed "angry." In a jurisdiction that followed a rule of "necessity" that evidence would only be admitted if it was not possible for the witness to reduce that opinion to the facts observed. The facts observed would be that the defendant's face was red, the defendant was speaking in a loud voice and such other additional facts. The courts have determined that it makes more sense to allow the witness to just reduce those facts to the opinion. This "collective facts" testimony is helpful to the jury and less likely to cause confusion.

One final feature of Fed. R. Evid. 701 must be noted. The rule makes it clear that the opinion testimony of law witnesses is not to be based on any specialized knowledge, training or skill. Fed. R. Evid. 701(c). The opinions of lay witnesses are limited to those that the usual lay witness is able to form. If the witness is only able to form the opinion due to some specialized knowledge, training, or skill, then the witness is to be treated like an expert under Fed. R. Evid. 702.

C. Opinions by Experts (702)

Expert witnesses are allowed to give opinions during trials. This use of experts is a practice that has a long and well recognized history. It is, in fact, a fairly routine practice. The easiest examples to note for the use of expert witnesses would be medical malpractice cases. As noted earlier, in such cases, it is necessary to prove that the defendant failed to use the care and skill of a qualified professional. Only another medical professional would be able to give testimony as to what was the appropriate course of conduct under particular circumstances. The use of experts, however, is not limited to that type of case. Modern traffic accident cases see the use of experts in "accident reconstruction." Products liability cases routinely use engineering experts to offer opinions on manufacturing and design. In criminal cases, a wide range of forensic experts are used to help explain and to offer opinions on basic facts in the case. It may be rare today to find a case where an expert would not be used.

With the broad use of experts, it is necessary to note one issue. As with lay opinion, the law once assumed that expert opinion would only be admissible where it was necessary. The attorney proposing the expert opinion would have to show that the evidence could not be produced in any other manner. That rule has been broadened. Fed. R. Evid. 702 states that the opinion of an expert will be admissible where it will "assist the trier of fact to understand the evidence or to determine a fact in issue." Fed. R. Evid. 702. Much like the rule of lay opinion, this allows the trial judge to permit the use of expert opinion where it is deemed helpful.

One of the limiting features on the use of experts has more to do with practical considerations then legal problems. Expert testimony, and the background work the expert must do before being ready to testify, can be very expensive. In cases that appear to be able to generate low sums of money, it may not be possible to hire the expert. The party to the litigation will ultimately have to pay for the expert hired to prepare and testify in his or her behalf. Once it is determined that an expert would be helpful to the case, and the case is of sufficient size to justify the expense, there are then the legal issue concerning expert witnesses that must be confronted. The law concerning the use of experts had become well settled prior to the 1990's. In the 1990's, however, the United States Supreme Court handed down a few decisions that caused substantial upheaval in the law. Those issues, along with the other legal problems of experts, are discussed below.

1. Qualifications

The use of an expert witness to give an opinion assumes that the expert has specialized knowledge, training or skill. In order to ask the expert for the opinion, therefore, it is necessary to first ask questions to lay a sufficient foundation to show that the witness has that specialized knowledge, training or skill. Fed. R. Evid. 702 assumes that only a witness with such background can give that opinion.

The foundation to show the appropriate background is routinely referred to as "qualifying the expert." This is just a practice of asking the expert witness a series of questions that allows the expert to go over all of his or her education, training, work, and experience. Obviously these questions will focus on the training and education that relate most directly to the issues being tried. It is necessary for these qualifications to be in the record prior to the expert expressing an opinion.

Once the qualifications have been stated, the method of challenging those qualifications can arise in, at least, two different ways. The opposing attorney can challenge the witness's qualifications immediately. In fact, that opposing attorney can ask to be allowed, at that point, to cross examine the witness on the qualifications. If the trial judge is convinced that the witness lacks sufficient qualifications to state and opinion, then the witness may be excused from the witness stand. A second approach is to merely wait until the attorney who called the witness gets to the opinion question. Once the opinion question is asked, then the opposing attorney may object to the witness being allowed to state that opinion.

In laying the qualification foundation, there is an interesting practical issue that should be noted. The presentation of the witness' qualifications actually serves two purposes. The first, obvious, purpose is to show a sufficiently qualified expert in order to have the trial judge, and maybe a latter appellate court, rule that the expert should be allowed to state an opinion. That is the "legal" reason for "qualifying the expert." A second reason has to do with the jury. Ultimately the jury in the case will have to decide the outcome of the case. The attorney presenting the expert will want the jury to believe that the expert is well qualified before giving an opinion. The better the expert looks in the minds of the jurors, the more likely the jurors are to believe the witness.

The importance of the jury's sense of the expert may lead to an interesting procedural step. There are times when an attorney will begin the questions to "qualify the expert," and the opposing attorney will announce that he or she is willing to stipulate that the witness is qualified to give an opinion. The trial judge will be anxious to accept this stipulation and have the attorney asking the questions to move on to the substance of the testimony. The reason that the opposing attorney may offer to stipulate is that the opposing attorney realizes how qualified the expert really is. By offering to stipulate that the expert is qualified, the opposing attorney is trying to keep the jury from hearing all of the qualifications. The attorney offering the expert witness may want to try to refuse to accept the stipulation and convince the trial judge that the jury needs to heard the qualifications.

Once the trial court is convinced that the witness is sufficiently qualified to give an opinion, additional legal issues must be addressed. The major issue that arises in such cases is whether the underlying science or technology is sufficiently valid in order to allow the jury to hear opinions based upon it.

2. *Frye* and *Daubert*

Before the trial judge will allow an expert to give an opinion based upon some science or technology, there must be some foundation evidence presented to convince the judge that the science of technology is valid. The law will not allow witnesses to speculate based upon some false or fantasy theories. Courts and text writers have, at times, referred to the fear of allowing such evidence as the introduction of "junk science." This is one area of expert testimony law that has seen substantial change over the years.

Prior to the 1990s, the law in this area was relatively stable. Based upon the case of *Frye v. United States*, 293 F. 1013 (D.C. Cir. 1923), the courts had developed the "*Frye* test." The *Frye* test held that the expert opinion could be admissible if the underlying science that was used to produce the opinion was "generally accepted in the scientific community." The theory behind this rule was that trial judges were not really able to reach the scientific conclusion as to whether science was valid. The test would require the trial judge to rely on the "scientific community" to decide the validity of the science. If the evidence indicated that the "scientific community" believed the science to be valid, then it could be used in trials. The decision would usually be left to the trial judge with little opportunity for reversal on appeal. Using that test, such "science" as "lie detectors" was excluded from trials, while finger print identification was admitted. The law in this area, however, saw major change in the 1990s.

In 1993, the United States Supreme Court decided a case by the name of *Daubert v. Merrell Dow Pharmaceuticals,* 509 U.S. 579 (1993). The opinion of the Supreme Court noted that the federal rules of evidence had been adopted in 1975, which was some 50 years after the decision in *Frye*. The opinion further noted that the *Frye* decision was not cited anywhere in the federal rules or the Advisory Committee notes. Using this logic, the Court decided that the federal rules of evidence had overruled the *Frye* decision and that the federal rules must be interpreted to determine when science would be held valid. The Court used Fed. R. Evid. 702 to find language that could be used to justify when science was valid. (Fed. R. Evid. 702 received minor amendments in 2000 to ensure that the language of that rule was consistent with the opinions of the Supreme Court.)

The *Daubert* decision abandoned the *Frye* test as a strict rule to use to determine the validity of scientific evidence. In its place, the Court adopted a series of flexible factors. The trial judge would act as a "gatekeeper" to keep invalid science out of the case. The judge would apply the factors to determine what was valid.

The factors that the Court noted in *Daubert* were:

1. Whether the theory can be or has been tested;
2. Whether the theory has been subject to peer review;
3. Whether there is a known rate of error when the theory has been applied:
4. Whether there are standards and controls over the theory;
5. Whether the theory is generally accepted in the scientific community.

After the decision in *Daubert,* there remained several questions. The Supreme Court returned to the issues in the opinion in *Kumho Tire Co. v.*

Carmichael, 119 S. Ct. 1167 (1999). The court in that opinion added further explanation. First, the question arose as to whether the *Daubert* decision only applied to scientific evidence or did it also apply to technical and other specialized knowledge areas. The Court held that the basic concepts in *Daubert* applied to all of those. It would apply when the expert was being asked to state opinions based on scientific, technical or other specialized knowledge. The Court was also faced with deciding whether the factors specified in *Daubert* were the only factors or, in fact, where they each mandatory factors. The Court held that the factors stated in *Daubert* were flexible. The trial court could use those factors, some of those factors, or other factors. Flexibility in approach was the key. The trial judge was to be the gatekeeper for the introduction of evidence and would not be bound by any one set of specified factors.

Over the 10 year period following *Daubert* and the addition of *Kumho Tire*, the lower courts had to work with the new principles. The opinions by the United States Supreme Court were so broad as to make it difficult for the trial judges to feel comfortable with making rulings. During that 10 year period some underlying principles seem to emerge.

The basic underlying principles seem to be consistently followed. The trial judge acts as gatekeeper to determine the validity of scientific evidence being presented. The judge should use the basic factors stated in *Daubert* but is not bound by them. The judge may use some, all, or even other factors to make the determination on admissibility.

3. Bases of Opinions (703, 705)

Once the trial judge has determined that the expert is qualified to state an opinion and that the underlying science is sufficiently valid to justify the admission of that opinion, an additional problem remains. The federal rules of evidence refer to this problem as the "Bases of Opinion Testimony by Experts." Fed. R. Evid. 703. Another way of looking at the issue is to consider how does the attorney seeking to offer the opinion into evidence ask the questions to get to that opinion.

The traditional method of presenting the expert opinion was to ask the "hypothetical question." This method of presenting the opinion required that the attorney seeking to introduce the opinion first make sure that all underlying facts had been offered into evidence. Those underlying facts could be offered by either that attorney's expert, that attorney's other witnesses, or even witnesses called by the opposing side. Once all of the underlying facts had been admitted into evidence, it was then possible to ask the hypothetical question. The attorney asking the question had to state all of the important facts making sure not to leave out any such facts. In addition, the attorney had to make sure that no facts were added to the hypothetical which had not been admitted into evidence. After stating all of those important facts, the attorney could then ask, "Based on those facts, what is your opinion?"

As a practical matter, the hypothetical question would routinely draw an objection from opposing counsel. The objection would either be for "stating facts not in the record" or "leaving out facts that are a part of the record." This format also seemed to ignore the realities of preparation of experts. Expert witnesses did not wait until they had arrived at the courtroom before considering the evidence. The expert was expected to do substantial work prior to arriving for testimony. Additional methods for presenting the opinion testimony needed to be added. The federal rules of evidence provide those methods.

Fed. R. Evid. 703 states the methods that may be used to introduce opinion testimony. The opening line of that rule is, "The facts or data in the particular case upon which an expert bases an opinion or inference may be those perceived by or made known to the expert at or before the hearing." Fed. R. Evid. 703. The issue is how is the expert supposed to learn of the underlying facts before stating the opinion? Although the sentence seems a little unclear, it actually provides for three different methods of providing the underlying facts and then introducing the opinion.

First, the attorney may still use the traditional hypothetical question. This is assumed where rule states that the facts may be "made know to the expert at ... the hearing." Fed. R. Evid. 703. Under that part of the rule, the attorney may state the facts to the expert while that witness is on the witness stand and then have the witness give an opinion.

A second method of presenting the opinion may be the easiest. Some experts may have gained knowledge of the underlying facts by way of firsthand knowledge. Several examples of those may be imagined. The Advisory Committee notes mention the obvious example of a treating physician. Where a physician had been treating a patient and that patient is then involved in litigation seeking damages for those injuries, the treating physician may be called to testify. If the physician is offering an opinion about the possibility of future, permanent losses, the underlying facts would have been gained through firsthand knowledge. The rule allows such a procedure when it says that the opinion may be based on underlying facts "perceived by ... an expert ... before the hearing." Fed. R. Evid. 703.

The third method of informing the expert of the underlying facts is also simple. As the rule states, the underlying facts may be "made known to the expert ... before the hearing." Fed. R. Evid. 703. This procedure assumes that the expert will review files, talk to witness, run tests, and gather such other facts as necessary before the actual trial. At the trial, the attorney, after confirming that the witness has done this, will then ask for the opinion. As suggested in the Advisory Committee notes, this practice is consistent with the way experts perform their job outside of the trial setting. When experts are working together, they do not each gather information and perform every test independently. Experts will rely on the reports, documents and tests of others in order to reach an opinion. This even occurs in the medical profession. When a patient has a serious illness, that patient may ask to seek a "second opinion." That is a request to bring in another physician for an opinion. It would be rare for that second physician to begin anew to run all tests that had already been performed. Instead, the second physician would review all of the tests, documents and lab work, and then express an opinion based on that material. This portion of Fed. R. Evid. 703 allows experts testifying in court to use the same practice. The expert witness can review all available data before trial, then just express the opinion at trial.

The portion of the rule that allows the expert to consider underlying facts outside of the courtroom and then base an opinion on those facts gives rise to yet another problem. There is the possibility that the expert might be basing an opinion on facts that would not, themselves, be admissible. When the law required the use of the traditional hypothetical question, this issue did not arise. The hypothetical question procedure required that facts be presented in the trial. The expert would then base the opinion on all the facts, but only the facts, presented and admitted into the trial. Under the new procedure that allows the expert to consider facts outside the trial, the problem of basing the opinion on otherwise inadmissible evidence arises.

The federal rules of evidence address this problem of basing opinions on fact evidence that might not be admissible. The rules states that, "If of a type reasonably relied upon by experts in the particular field in forming opinions or inferences upon the subject, the facts or data need not be admissible in evidence in order for the opinion or inference to be admitted." Fed. R. Evid. 703. In short, the rule allows the expert to consider facts which may not be admissible in the trial, if those facts are the type of facts that are reasonably relied upon by such experts when they ordinarily do their work. Using the example of a patient seeking a second opinion from another physician, this example can be understood. In the field of medicine, when a patient seeks a second opinion, the second physician does not run new lab tests. The second physician will consider the lab tests, results, documents and reports prepared by the first physician. The second physician will then express an opinion to the patient based on those documents. If, therefore, a physician is called to testify in a trial, the testifying physician does not need to run all new tests and lab work. The testifying physician can consider the lab work, tests, and documents prepared by other physicians in preparing the testimony. This is because that is the way that physicians usually conduct their work when litigation is not the issue.

Since experts can use otherwise inadmissible evidence to form an opinion, there may be times when one party would like to use that opinion as an excuse to admit that inadmissible evidence. The federal rules of evidence address that issue. "Facts or data that are otherwise inadmissible shall not be disclosed to the jury by the proponent of the opinion or inference unless the court determines that their probative value in assisting the jury to evaluate the expert's opinion substantially outweighs their prejudicial effect." Fed. R. Evid. 703. As should be obvious, this rule is designed to keep the proponent of the opinion from using the opinion as an excuse to then admit otherwise inadmissible evidence. Just because the rule allows the expert to consider those facts in reaching the opinion, that does not allow that party to introduce those facts. The rule will allow the proponent of the opinion to introduce those otherwise inadmissible facts only after satisfying the balancing test that the probative value of those facts substantially outweighs the prejudicial effect.

Notice that the rule does not prohibit the opposing party to the opinion from offering the evidence upon with the expert based the opinion. Although the underlying facts may not have been otherwise admissible, if one side uses those facts to form an opinion, the opposing side can then present those facts into evidence.

Since a major portion of the problem with expert opinions deals with the issue of the underlying facts that support those opinions, one additional problem remains. The rules of evidence discuss when and if those underlying facts need to be presented to the jury. The rules make it clear that the expert may give the opinion without being first required to state the underlying facts. Fed. R. Evid. 705. Again, it is important to note how this differs from the traditional hypothetical question practices. The traditional practice required the introduction of all underlying facts prior to the introduction of the opinion. Under the federal rules of evidence, the expert may state an opinion before any underlying facts are introduced. The rules do state, however, that the expert may be required to disclose the facts and data considered in reaching the opinion during the cross examination by the opposing party.

4. The Ultimate Facts (704)

With the use of opinions offered by expert or lay witnesses, one additional, complex issue arises. It is usually identified as limiting the use of opinions on "ultimate issues." The problems with ultimate issues seem to raise arguments and be difficult to resolve. The federal rules of evidence regulate this issue in Fed. R. Evid. 704.

The initial problem with ultimate issues is that the law assumes that witnesses should not give opinions on issues that are reserved for decision to the jury. The basic concept is that the witness should tell the facts while allowing the jury to reach conclusions that decide the case. Witnesses should not be telling the jury how to decide the case. This has led to a traditional rule that prohibited witnesses giving opinions on ultimate issues. As should be obvious, trying to decide what is exactly the ultimate issue to be determined leads to argument.

The federal rules of evidence begin the approach by abolishing the traditional rule excluding evidence on the ultimate issue. Advisory Committee notes, Fed. R. Evid. 704. The rule, however, institutes a limitation on the type of opinion that an expert can give when it relates to matters that are contained in the ultimate issue. The rule, for example, says, "testimony in the form of an opinion or inference otherwise admissible is not objectionable because it embraces an ultimate issue to be decided by the trier of fact." Fed. R. Evid. 704(a).

That language, however, does not allow the introduction of any opinion. Certain opinions are still excluded. The jury is to decide questions of fact based upon the evidence that has been admitted. The witnesses may give opinions on those facts. Questions of law, however, are to be instructed by the trial judge and not open to decision by the jury. In addition, witnesses may not give opinions on law. This is the limitation that is a part of this rule.

The basic limitation, therefore, is that the witness may not express an opinion that mixes law and fact. The Advisory Committee notes give one classic example of this distinction. It is pointed out that a mental health professional testifying in a will contest based upon lack of mental capacity to make the will could testify that "the deceased knew the nature and extent of the property and the natural objects of his or her bounty." The same witness could not testify that the deceased "had the mental capacity to make the will." Advisory Committee notes, Fed. R. Evid. 704(a). Those questions appear almost identical. It is the usual rule that the test for whether a deceased had mental capacity is whether the deceased knew the nature of the property and the natural objects of his or her bounty. The difference in the two questions is that asking for an opinion about understanding property and objects of bounty focuses the opinion on the facts. When the witness is asked if the deceased had the capacity to make the will, that forces the witness to go the extra step to reach the legal conclusion. That is the ultimate issue that the jury will decide.

Other examples may be seen in seeking to understand the difference. In a medical malpractice case, an expert witness may be asked if the treating physician followed the usual practices of physicians in good standing. The witness could not be asked if the treating physician committed malpractice. In an automobile accident case, a witness could be asked his or her opinion about the speed of an automobile. That witness could not be asked if the driver was negligent.

Fed. R. Evid. 704(b) provides a special section to deal with testimony in criminal cases dealing with the mental capacity of the defendant to commit the crime. This provision indicates that the witness may not state an opinion "as to whether the defendant did or did not have the mental state or condition constituting an element of the crime charged or a defense thereto." Fed. R. Evid. 704(b). The purpose of this rule appears to prohibit the witness from testifying as to whether the defendant "appreciated the natural and quality of his or her acts." In addition, the rule should prohibit the witness from testifying that the defendant did or did not "appreciate the wrongfulness of the act." Those are, of course, the legal definitions of the mental state that concerns the defense of mental defect in criminal cases. The witness, however, should be able to testify about any mental illnesses or defects and the nature of such illnesses or defects. It has even been suggested that the witness can testify as to whether the conduct was a product of such illnesses or defects.

Fed. R. Evid. 704(b) was added to the rules in 1984 as an apparent reaction against the use of mental health professionals in criminal trials and the conflicting evidence they would tend to offer. The use and interpretation of this addition is still in some debate by the courts.

D. Court Appointed Experts (706)

Just as a trial judge may call lay witnesses and question such witnesses, the federal rules of evidence specifically provide that the judge may call expert witnesses. The details of this authority is contained in Fed. R. Evid. 706. The judge may select such a witness on his or her own motion or allow the attorneys for the parties to participate in that decision.

Since expert witnesses are expected to perform tests and research prior to giving opinions, the issue of compensation for such witnesses is important. The federal rules of evidence specifically provide for such compensation. Fed. R. Evid. 706(b).

The fact that the trial judge appoints an expert, does not limit or hinder the right of either or both of the parties to the litigation from obtaining their own experts to testify. Fed. R. Evid. 706(d).

Checkpoints

- Lay witnesses can testify to opinions under limited conditions. It must be the type of the opinion that a lay witness can form, and the witness must have had the opportunity to observe and form and opinion.

- Lay opinion can be given when it will aid the jury.

- Experts can testify to opinions if they court determines that the witness is sufficiently qualified to discuss the issues.

- In order to determine if the underlying science is valid, the trial court must act as gatekeeper and apply flexible factors to the circumstances offered.

- The factors to determine if the science is valid include, but are not limited to:

  - Whether the theory can be or has been tested;

  - Whether the theory has been subject to peer review;

  - Whether there is a known rate of error when the theory has been applied:

  - Whether there are standards and controls over the theory;

  - Whether the theory is generally accepted in the scientific community.

- Expert opinion may be admitted into evidence if it is an aid to the jury.

- Opinion evidence may touch upon ultimate issues in the case, but may not include opinions as to law.

Chapter 8

Hearsay and Exceptions

Hearsay and Exceptions Roadmap

- What is a good organization to analyze a hearsay problem?
- Learn the basic "hearsay rule."
- Closely study the definitions associated with "what is hearsay?"
- Divide the hearsay exceptions into two distinct groupings. Those groupings are "availability of declarant immaterial" and "declarant unavailable."
- Carefully learn the elements of the exceptions for "availability of the declarant immaterial." The most important exceptions in this group are found in the first 10.
- Carefully learn the element of the exceptions for "declarant unavailable."
- Analyze the issues concerning the confrontation clause and the hearsay exceptions.

A. Introduction

As noted in other sections, the hearsay rule is one that can arise in numerous cases. When a party to litigation seeks to introduce a document, there are, at least, three possible evidence issues that can arise. Those three issues are: Authentication, Hearsay, and the Best Evidence Rule. It is important to consider each of those when confronted with a document to determine whether document meets or violates those rules.

The hearsay issue may be one of the more difficult for students to understand in their first study of evidence. The most difficult issue in hearsay is the question: "What is hearsay?" That topic is discussed in part C below and deserves close attention.

In reviewing the hearsay material, it is easiest to approach if there is an organization to the analysis. It is recommended that every hearsay problem be approached in the same way. (1) Begin the analysis by asking, "Is the evidence hearsay?" If the evidence is hearsay, then it should be excluded. If the evidence is not hearsay, then the problem is solved and the evidence is admissible. (2)

If the evidence is hearsay, then next step to the analysis is, "Is there an exception for the evidence?" If there is an exception, then the evidence is admissible.

The material that follows is presented according to that analysis organization. The material will first cover, "What is hearsay?" It will then cover the exceptions. Before getting to that analysis, however, there is an initial problem. It is necessary to clearly state the "Hearsay Rule."

B. The Hearsay Rule and Underlying Purpose (802)

As complicated as the issues surrounding hearsay appear to be, the basic rule is simple to state. Hearsay evidence is not admissible unless there is some other rule that allows it to be introduced. The Federal Rules of Evidence state the rule as, "Hearsay is not admissible except as provided by these rules or by other rules prescribed by the Supreme Court pursuant to statutory authority of by Act of Congress." Fed. R. Evid. 802.

This simple rule raises numerous issues. First, of course, it indicates that "hearsay" is not admissible. As such, it is necessary to determine "What is hearsay?" The next section of this material fully discusses that issue. Second, the basic rule indicates that hearsay may be admissible if other rules or statutes allow it to be admitted. Obviously, all of the hearsay exceptions listed in the Federal Rules of Evidence would allow admission.

With the difficulty experienced by many with understanding the hearsay rule, the question is frequently asked as to why the rule continues to exist. The hearsay rule is seen by some as merely one of those legal "technicalities" used to exclude evidence. The hearsay rule has a long and important history. Its purpose is basic to litigation.

Rules of evidence are designed to make sure that juries hear credible evidence. The rules make sure that most of the evidence has some basis in truth and then provide additional methods to test that truth. Witnesses are required to take an oath to tell the truth and then be subject to cross examination on any evidence that has been offered. In addition, jurors can watch witnesses while they testify and decide whether the witnesses' demeanor seems to suggest truth telling or falsifying. The oath, cross examination and observation of demeanor are important tools to reach the truth by the conclusion of a trial.

If attorneys were allowed to introduce hearsay evidence, all of those important safeguards to seeking the truth would be lost. The person who made the statement would not be in the courtroom. That person would not take an oath. That person could not be cross examined. The jury could not watch that person while the story was told. The techniques for checking the credibility of the witness would be lost.

Hearsay evidence is just not deemed to be as credible. A witness who takes the stand to testify can be checked for many things. Whether the witness was actually in a position to observe the facts and then able to remember those facts can be challenged. If the evidence is introduced by hearsay, the opportunity to challenge the ability to observe and remember is lost. In addition, it is possible that the original witness to the event saw it correctly, but the person offering the hearsay statement did not hear it correctly when told about it. Hearsay evidence just lacks credibility and the opportunity to challenge that credibility. For those reasons, hearsay is excluded.

With the importance of hearsay being excluded, it raises further questions about why the law should allow hearsay exceptions. If hearsay is so lacking in credibility, the exceptions should not exist. When the exceptions are studied, there is one recurring feature with all of the exceptions. Something about the circumstances that produce each of the exceptions has convinced the courts that there is a ring of trustworthiness with that evidence. The circumstances that must be proven to meet the exceptions provide the credibility test that is lost by offering the evidence as hearsay. When studying the exceptions, it is important to note the trustworthiness features of each of those exceptions.

C. What Is Hearsay? (801)

1. The Definition

The definition of "hearsay" is contained in the Federal Rules of Evidence. "Hearsay is a statement, other than one made by the declarant while testifying at the trial or hearing, offered in evidence to prove the truth of the matter asserted." Fed. R. Evid. 801(c). This definition has also been stated as, "An out of court statement being offered for the truth of the matter asserted."

The definition has several key parts. It can be broken down into at least four different elements. Another way to express the definition of hearsay is to list those elements. If that were to be done, the definition would be:

1. A statement,
2. Made by a declarant,
3. While not at the trial or hearing (out of court statement),
4. Being offered to prove the truth of the matter asserted in the statement.

Each of those four parts must be understood since they each have an impact on the operation of rule concerning hearsay.

A statement is defined as "(1) an oral or written assertion or (2) nonverbal conduct of a person, if it is intended by the person as an assertion." Fed. R. Evid. 801(a). Although some issues will be discussed further below, several items should be obvious. A statement would include particular assertions that people make. In a case involving a traffic accident, a comment by a witness that, "The traffic light was red," would be a statement. Clearly that would be an "oral" assertion. As the definition points out, the words may be oral or written. Words, however, are not needed. If, for example, while at the scene of the accident someone said, "Who ran the red light?" and another person pointed to a Ford on the side of the road that would be an assertion. That would be "non-verbal conduct" that was intended to assert something. Oral, written, or non-verbal conduct intended as an assertion would all be statements.

The definition also identifies who made the statement. The "declarant" is the person who made the statement. Since the problem is hearsay, the declarant is usually not at the trial.

In order for it to be a hearsay problem, the statement was made "out of court." That means that the statement was not made during the course of the trial or hearing where the evidence is sought to be introduced.

Finally, in order for the statement to be considered hearsay, it must be offered to prove the truth of the matter asserted in the statement. This is one of the difficult concepts in hearsay. More about this topic will be covered in the following section, but a few examples will help with understanding at this point. Imagine the example of the person at the scene of the accident saying, "The traffic light was red." If a witness wants to testify that the person said that at the scene of the accident and the reason for offering the evidence is to prove the light was red, then the statement is hearsay. It is being offered to prove the truth of the matter asserted. The declarant said the light was red, and the parties are trying to prove the light was red. If, however, the witness is testifying about the person making the statement in order to prove that the person who made it was at the scene of the accident at the time it occurred, that would not be hearsay. The statement is not being offered to prove the truth of the statement, it is, instead, being offered for some other reason. Here it would be offered to prove the identity or location of a person.

In short, the basic rule of hearsay is simple. If the evidence is hearsay, it is not admissible unless some other rule makes it admissible. In order for the evidence to be hearsay, it must be a statement made by a declarant at some time other than the trial or hearing and offered in the trial or hearing to prove the truth of the matter asserted in the statement.

2. Common Examples of What is Not Hearsay?

Since all of the above discussion helps to illustrate "what is hearsay," it is important to view some common examples that do not meet that definition. A few simple examples were given above, but the following will provide a discussion of the traditional problem areas.

a. To Prove Notice

A good first example of a type of evidence that looks like hearsay but is not, is evidence of a statement that is offered to prove the effect it had on the mind or thoughts of the listener. These statements are not offered to prove the statement is true. They are offered into evidence to prove that someone else heard the statement being made. In many cases, the evidence is being offered because there is some "notice" requirement in the case. By proving a party heard a statement, it proves that the party was on "notice."

Imagine, for example, that a person wants to sue for breach of warranty under the Uniform Commercial Code. The U.C.C. requires that notice of the claim be given. The plaintiff sends a letter notifying the defendant that a product was defective. Before trial, the defendant claims a variety of defenses including no notice and no defect in the product. If the plaintiff tries to introduce the letter that was mailed to the defendant into evidence, the defendant will claim it is hearsay. The defendant will claim that the letter speaks of a defect in the product and that is the purpose of the trial. The plaintiff, however, will point out that there will be other evidence of the defect. The only reason the letter is being introduced into the trial is to prove that the defendant was on notice of the claim. The letter should be admissible as not being hearsay. Since the letter addresses the nature of the defect, it is not being introduced to show the truth of the matter asserted in the letter. It is merely being introduced to prove the defendant was on notice of a claim.

Another good example is where someone is told that the tires on their automobile are worn and slick. That person subsequently has an accident due to a tire failure. The statement that they were told the tires were worn and slick should be admissible. They would not be used to prove that the tires were worn and slick; other evidence could be produced for that. The statement would be offered to prove that the owner of the car knew the tires were worn and slick. This knowledge, along with evidence of failure to repair the tires, would prove negligence. Again, the statement is not being offered to prove the truth of the matter asserted, but is, instead, offered to prove notice to the automobile owner.

When an employer hires a driver, the employer must usually do a background check. If the employer of a driver was told that the driver had a terrible driving record, that evidence might be important. If the driver had an accident while in the scope of employment, the employer would be sued for two basis. The employer would be sued for vicarious liability and negligent entrustment. On the claim of vicarious liability, the evidence of the prior statements about the driver's driving record would not be admissible. The only reason to introduce that evidence for the vicarious liability claim would be to prove that the driver had a bad driving record. It would be hearsay. (It would probably also be inappropriate evidence of character.) The prior statement about the driving record would, however, be admissible in the negligent entrustment claim. The evidence would be used not to show the bad record, but to prove that the employer knew about the bad record. This knowledge, or notice, would be evidence of negligence in hiring and allowing the driver to continue to drive for the employer. As such, the evidence would not be used to prove the truth of the matter asserted in the statement, but to show the effect it hand on the mind of the listener.

There are, of course, numerous examples of how an out of court statement could be used to prove notice. The key to understanding this problem is looking at the purpose of the use of the evidence. If the evidence is being offered to prove, as true, a fact stated in the statement, then the evidence is hearsay and not admissible. If the evidence is offered to prove the effect it had on the mind of the listener, then it is not hearsay and is admissible.

b. "Verbal Acts"

A common, traditional type of statement that was not considered to be hearsay was called "Verbal Acts." The term is not sufficiently descriptive to be helpful, but it is one that continues to be used. The Advisory Committee notes to the Federal Rules of Evidence even mention this example by noting that the definition of hearsay is such as "to exclude from hearsay the entire category of 'verbal acts' and 'verbal parts of an act,' in which the statement itself affects the legal rights of the parties or is a circumstance bearing on conducting affecting their rights." Fed. R. Evid. 801(c), Advisory Committee notes.

The quoted material above mentions that the "verbal acts" issue is one where the words spoken or written create or effect legal rights. Although it seems to be confusing, numerous examples may be seen where the words spoken or written effect legal rights.

Imagine, for example, that someone hands you a ball point pen. Until they speak, you do not know the nature of the transaction. By handing you the pen, it could be a gift, an offer of sale, or a loan. The spoken words that follow create the legal obligations. The person may say, "Here, accept this pen as a gift from me to you." They might say, "I am offering to sell you this pen for $1.00." They might say, "You may use this pen until tomorrow, but I expect it to be returned at 10:00 a.m." If a challenge arose as to the ownership of the pen, the spoken words would be admissible. The words would not be admitted to prove the truth of the matter asserted, but they would be admitted because they created the legal obligations that arose after the transfer.

In the example above, it is frequently argued that the words are introduced to prove the truth of the matter asserted. They are being introduced to prove a contract was created, a gift was given or a loan was given. That argument, however, is not accurate. The truth of the words is not at issue. It could be a case where the person handing over the pen had no legal right to the pen. That person may have stolen the pen. As a thief, the person handing over the pen could not sell, give or lend it away. The words spoken would be untrue. Even though the words are untrue, they do define the legal rights as between the two people to the transaction. The words, therefore, are being offered to show the legal effect and not the truth of the matter asserted.

It should be obvious that all forms of contracts, both written and oral, are verbal acts or verbal parts of acts. In any contract action, even one based on a written contract, it is necessary to introduce the contract to show the terms of the agreement. A challenge could be made that the contract is hearsay. That challenge would be overruled. The contract language is offered not to prove the truth of the matter asserted, but in order to show the legal obligations that were created.

(Just as a reminder, it was noted several times in this work that the introduction of most documents can raise three issues. The party challenging the document may raise authentication, best evidence rule and hearsay. If the document being introduced is a contract, the "verbal acts" rules solve the hearsay problem. Authentication and best evidence rule would still have to be confronted.)

Contract law is not the only place that "verbal acts" occur. Defamation cases can give rise to the issue. When someone makes a defamatory statement that may give rise to a civil action. Obviously it would be necessary to introduce the defamatory words. This would be necessary whether the words were oral in a slander case or written in a libel case. In some ways, this is even an easier example then the contract example. As is well known in tort law, it is necessary to show that the defamatory statement is false in order for the plaintiff to win the action. The defamatory words are clearly admissible. The words are being introduce to show that a legal effect occurred and not to prove the truth of the matter asserted. In fact, the plaintiff will introduce the words and then prove they were false.

Misrepresentation cases are another good example of "verbal acts." If someone sues another for misrepresentation, it is necessary to introduce the words spoken or written. That evidence will be admitted to prove the legal effect of the misrepresentation. Again, the words are not offered to prove the truth of the matter asserted but only to prove the legal effect of those words.

The use of "verbal acts" is not limited to civil cases. Many crimes are committed by the words spoken. As with the civil cases, many fraud crimes rely upon words that have been written or spoken. The defendant has made claims that others have relied upon. In order for the prosecution to prove the crime, the words spoken or written must be introduced. The words are admitted to prove the crime and not to prove the truth of the matter asserted in the fraud. In fact, the prosecution will have to prove that the words were false.

There are crimes that are similar to contract cases. Offering to sell illegal drugs and prostitution are crimes where words and negotiations for sales often arise. The words create the crime.

Certain crimes of violence also use "verbal acts." Statutes create crimes for making threats of violence against some people. Federal law, for example, makes it a crime to make a threat against certain high ranking federal officials. In a case involving such a crime, the words spoken or written would have to be admissible. The words would be introduced in order to show the threat was made. Those words would not be admitted to prove the truth of the matter asserted. It would be hoped that the threat could not have been carried out and that the defendant arrested on the basis of the threat alone.

c. State of Mind

There are times when a person makes as statement where the statement is operative on several bases. The statement may be seeking to assert a point, but it may also reflect, indirectly, the speaker's state of mind about the topic. It should now be obvious how this analysis will work. If the statement is offered to prove the truth of what the person asserted then it is hearsay and inadmissible. If it is offered to show the indirect thoughts or feelings the person had, then it is admissible as not being hearsay.

Imagine a statement by a wife that her husband was, "Mean and cruel. He never treated me well. He beat me." The wife has died and not available to testify. If the case is a criminal case against the husband for beating his wife, then the statements should not be admissible. They would be introduced to prove the truth of the matter asserted as to the beatings. If, however, the husband had sued someone else for loss of companionship or consortium of the wife, then the statements would be admissible. They are not being introduced to show that the husband beat his wife. They have another purpose. The extent of love, affection and mutual services would be relevant to the measure of damages. The statements would be admissible because they indirectly show that the wife "believed" there was no love, affection and mutual services between her and her husband.

In a child custody dispute, a child might testify that, "Daddy tried to kill me." That would be admissible. It would not come in to prove that "Daddy tried to kill" the child. It would be admitted to show that the child had great fear of the father. That would be relevant to making decision "in the best interest of the child."

One of the classic examples of this problem arose in a trademark dispute.(*Zippo Mfg. Co. v. Rogers Imports, Inc.* 216 F. Supp. 670 (S.D. N.Y. 1963). Zippo Lighter Company had (and continues to have) a very distinctively designed cigarette lighter. They believed that another company had intentionally used a similar design to manufacture a cheaper lighter and to try to create confusion in the market place. Zippo believed that this other company was using this confusion to take customers away from Zippo. Zippo did a market study to try to prove this confusion in the mind of buyers. They sent out a team of experts to do the study. The experts got a scientifically significant random sample of people and showed them one of the other manufacturer's lighters. The experts would then ask, "Whose lighter is this?" The subjects of the experiment would routinely say, "It's a Zippo." During the trial, the experts wanted to testify to the large numbers of people who looked at the opposing manufacturer's lighters and said, "It's a Zippo." The opposing party objected and claimed the out of court statements were hearsay and inadmissible.

The Zippo attorneys argued that the evidence was not being introduced to prove the truth of the matter asserted. In fact, when people said, "It's a Zippo," usually they were wrong. It was, in fact, the opponent's lighter. Since it was not being introduced to prove the truth of the matter asserted, the statements should be admissible. They were merely being offered to prove the speaker's state of mind at the time the statements were made. When they said, "It's a Zippo," the evidence was being offered to prove that the speakers believed it was a Zippo.

The counter argument was very good. The opponents claimed that when the speakers said, "It's a Zippo," they knew they were being questioned in a poll. What the speakers were really saying was, "I believe it's a Zippo." Since the speakers were really saying, "I believe it's a Zippo," and Zippo was introducing the statement to prove that the speakers believed it was a Zippo, the statements should not be admissible. They were, in fact, being offered to prove the truth of the matter asserted. It is possible, for example, that during the poll, some speakers being questioned may have actually said, "I believe it's a Zippo."

The judge writing the opinion was left with this apparent insolvable problem. Depending on how the statement, "It's a Zippo," was interpreted, it could be hearsay or not hearsay. They judge felt the statements reflected state of mind and should be admissible as not being hearsay. There was an alternative basis. Most jurisdictions, and now the Federal Courts under Fed. R. Evid. 803(3), recognize an exception to the hearsay rule for state of mind evidence. Such problems could now be interpreted to be not hearsay and admissible. If the parties thought the evidence looked too much like hearsay, it would still be admissible under the exception in Fed. R. Evid. 803(3). (That exception will be discussed in more detail below.)

As for opinion polls of the type used in Zippo, the Federal Rules of Evidence have also provided an even easier way to admit such evidence. In the discussion on expert witness in Chapter VII, the material discussed the bases of expert testimony. It was noted that the underlying information used to form an opinion need not be admissible. "If of a type reasonably relied upon by experts in the particular field in forming opinions or inferences upon the subject, the facts or data need not be admissible in evidenced in order for the opinion or inference to be admitted." Fed. R. Evid. 703. Opinion polls are based upon asking numerous people the same questions. In any such example, the same problems would arise that arose in Zippo. The statements by the participants in the poll may or may not be hearsay depending on how the statements were made and how the judge interpreted the statements. This rule allows the expert to give an opinion based upon the poll without regard to whether the underlying answers should be admissible. As long as the expert followed scientifically valid polling techniques and the underlying data was the type reasonably relied upon by other experts, then the opinion is admissible. The Advisory Committee notes recognized this as an improvement. "The rule also offers a more satisfactory basis for ruling upon the admissibility of public opinion poll evidence. Attention is directed to the validity of the techniques employed rather than to relatively fruitless inquiries whether hearsay is involved." Fed. R. Evid. 703, Advisory Committee notes, citing the Zippo case.

d. Non-Verbal Conduct and Implied Assertions

As noted above, non-verbal conduct which is intended as an assertion may be hearsay. If, for example, the police say, "Who robbed you?" and the victim points to suspect number 2, that is an intended assertion by non-verbal conduct. The problem with evidence about conduct, and some statements, is that in order for it to be hearsay, it must have intended to be an assertion. Obviously, the example of pointing out the person who robbed you after being asked who robbed you was intended to be an assertion. There are many examples of conduct, however, that the actor did not intended to assert anything, but may have indicated, indirectly, something important.

An easy example to use would involve people walking around outside with their umbrellas raised. If an action arose concerning a traffic accident and the parties were in dispute as to whether it was raining, one of the parties might want to testify that everyone had their umbrellas raised. The opposing party might object by claiming that is hearsay. The argument would be that the raising of the umbrellas was an assertion that it was raining. The evidence ought to be admissible. Raising the umbrellas does indicate that it was probably raining. When the people began to raise the umbrellas, however, they did not INTEND to assert it was raining. They merely raised their umbrellas to keep from getting wet. The evidence could be admitted since it was merely an unintended assertion that it was raining.

Another example could arise if someone claimed that the building temperature was kept at too low a point. The other side might offer evidence that no other tenants complained about the cold. The theory would be that if it was that cold, others would complain. Since they did not complain, it was probably warm enough. Although this appears to be an assertion that the temperature is adequate, it is merely an unintended assertion. The tenants did not intend to state that it was warm enough. They just failed to complain about the cold.

Another good example is where the police are asking a husband and wife about a possible crime. During the discussion, the police officer describes a unique leather jacket that the alleged criminal had worn. Just as the jacket is described, the wife faints. The fainting is an unintended assertion that the husband had a jacket just as had been described. The wife did not intend to assert anything. In fact, she would have liked to avoid asserting anything. Unfortunately, her conduct implied the idea for her.

A classic example of unintended assertions can arise when people exchange letters. Assume there is a will contest and those contesting the will claim that the deceased was not competent to make the will. The proponents of the will want to introduce letters that had been written to the deceased in a short period of time before the death. The letters do not discuss the person's competency, but they discuss usual and ordinary things. They might, for example, discuss family members, recent activities, or even request business advice. The proponents of the will would want to introduce these letters to prove that the people writing the letters assumed that the deceased was sufficiently competent to read and respond to such letters. Since the letters do not say, "I intend to assert that he is competent," but only imply competency by the nature of the letters, they should be admissible.

Another classic example of non-verbal conduct which may be considered hearsay, is the fact of remaining silent in the face of serious accusations. Imagine that person A approaches person B in front of several other people. Person A says to person B in a loud voice, "You owe me $1,000. When are you going to pay it?" Person B remains silent and does not respond. If person A sues person B for the $1,000, the evidence of remaining silent while being accused of owing the money would be admissible. The theory is that people accused of something serious would object or complain if it were not true. The fact of remaining silent is an admission that it is probably true. It would, of course, have to be shown that person B heard the accusation. Since the law assumes that someone would respond to such an accusation, the fact of remaining silent is an "intended" assertion that it is true. Since it is an intended assertion, then it is hearsay. At this point in the analysis, the statement should be excluded from evidence. As the material will point out below, however, admissions of a party are admissible under other rules. That issue will be discussed below. This problem is frequently referred to as he tacit admission rule.

The fact that the admissions by a party can be admitted under other rules, does not solve all of the hearsay issues. Using the example above, assume that person A subsequently sues person C for the $1000. Person C would like to introduce evidence of the accusation and the silence of person B to prove that B probably owed the money and that C did not. Since B is not a party to that action, the silence is probably hearsay and not admissible.

It should be noted that special problems arise when this issue arises in a criminal case. Since defendants in a criminal case have the right to remain silent and their silence can not be used against them, the constitutional rules will, ordinarily, exclude evidence of their silence.

3. Defined as Not Being Hearsay

The Federal Rules of Evidence specifically define several types of out of court statements as not being hearsay. These are contained in Fed. R. Evid. 801(d). The traditional common law referred to most of these examples as exceptions to the hearsay rule. The general policy behind defining these as not being hearsay rather than calling them exceptions seems to be based on the nature of litigation itself. The following examples all involve out of court statements where the person who made the statement, the declarant, is in the court room. If the statement is used in the trial, the person who made it is available to explain or be cross examined on it. In speaking about one such example, it was said, "Admissions by a party opponent are excluded from the category of hearsay on the theory that their admissibility in evidence is the result of the adversary system rather than satisfaction of the conditions of the hearsay rule." Fed. R. Evid. 801(d)(2), Advisory Committee notes. Whether the law of the jurisdiction defines the evidence as not being hearsay or declares it to be hearsay and then creates an exception for it, the evidence is admissible. When using the Federal Rules of Evidence, however, it should be remembered that these examples are not hearsay because the rules specifically declare them not being hearsay. It would be technically incorrect to refer to these as exceptions to the hearsay rule. The following material explains the circumstances that must be shown in order to have these types of statements admitted.

a. Statements of Witnesses

Certain statements that were made prior to the trial by a person who will testify at trial will be admitted to prove the truth of the matter asserted in the prior statement. Since the prior statement was made before the trial, and it being admitted into the trial to prove the truth of the matter asserted, the statement appears to be hearsay. As noted above, the Federal Rules of Evidence define some of these statements as not being hearsay. Fed. R. Evid. 801(d)(1). It must be noted, however, that if the prior statement does not meet the exact terms of this portion of the federal rule, it is likely to be declared to be hearsay and excluded from the trial.

There are three types of prior statements by a witness that may be introduced in the trial used to prove the truth of the matter asserted. Each of these three has its own particular requirements, but they all start with the same general requirement. In order to use the prior statement of a declarant, that person must testify "at the trial or hearing and [be] subject to cross-examination concerning the statement." Fed. R. Evid. 801(d)(1). This allows the parties to question the witness concerning the statement that was made.

The first type of statement that may be introduced is a prior statement of the witness that is "inconsistent with the declarant's testimony, and was given under oath subject to the penalty of perjury at a trial, hearing, or other proceeding, or in a deposition." Fed. R. Evid. 801(d)(1)(A). This allows the introduction of a prior inconsistent statement made by the witness who is testifying at trial.

It is important to recall that these prior inconsistent statements were previously discussed in the Chapter VI material dealing with the impeachment of a witness. In that material, when witnesses take the stand, if they have made prior statements that are inconsistent with their trial testimony, those prior statements may be entered into evidence for the limited purpose of attaching he witnesses' credibility. Fed. R. Evid. 613. Under those circumstances, the prior statement cannot be used to prove the truth of the matter asserted in the statement and the jury should be instructed accordingly.

Fed. R. Evid. 801(d)(1)(A) expands the use of the prior inconsistent statement. Under this rule, the statement may be offered into evidence, not only to attack the credibility of the witness, but also to prove the truth of the matter asserted in the prior statement. The prior statement, therefore, actually comes in to the trial as substantive evidence in the case.

Using the prior inconsistent statement is, however, limited by the terms of this rule. The prior inconsistent evidence can only be used to prove the truth of the matter asserted when the prior statement was made "under oath subject to the penalty of perjury." Fed. R. Evid. 801(d)(1)(A).

This rule is commonly used and is easy to understand in its application. Imagine that a witness to an event gives a deposition. During the deposition, that witness answers a series of questions. Later, during the trial of the case, the same witness is called to testify and answers the same questions. At the trial, however, the witness gives answers that are inconsistent with the answers given during the deposition. At this point, either attorney can question the witness about the deposition and introduce those answers into the trial. The inconsistent answers do come in as impeachment to the credibility of the witness under Fed. R. Evid. 613, but they also come into the trial as substantive evidence that tends to prove the truth of the matter asserted in the prior statement.

This rule may be used in civil or criminal cases. The key to using the prior statements to prove the truth of the matter asserted is that the prior statements must have been made under oath. If the prior statements were not made under oath, they may still be used for impeachment under Fed. R. Evid. 613, but may not be used to prove the truth of the matter asserted under Fed. R. Evid. 801(d)(1)(A).

The second type of prior statement by a witness is a more complicated and less likely to be used. It does not arise as commonly as the prior inconsistent statement example. A prior statement of a witness may be introduced into evidence to prove the truth of the matter asserted when that statement is "consistent with the declarant's testimony and is offered to rebut an express or implied charge against the declarant of recent fabrication or improper influence or motive." Fed. R. Evid. 801(d)(1)(B).

Unlike the first example above, this example assumes that the prior statement that is being offered into evidence is consistent with the testimony being given at trial. It is not every prior consistent statement, however, that is allowed to be introduced. They may only be admitted if they are being used to rebut a claim that the testimony being given at trial was the result of "recent fabrication or improper influence." Fed. R. Evid. 801(d)(1)(B). Imagine that a witness gave statements to investigators during the early stages of fact gathering for a civil or criminal case. When that witness is called to testify at trial, the opposing counsel, during cross examination, suggests that the testimony is based upon some recent decision to lie or some influence that led the witness to personally dislike one of the parties. At that point, the prior consistent statement could be introduced in order to show that the witness had been given the same statement throughout the investigation and trial. The evidence would rebut the allegations by opposing counsel and be admitted to prove the truth of the matter asserted. Notice also, that unlike the prior inconsistent statement, the prior consistent statement does not need to have been made under oath in order to be admitted.

The third type of prior statement by a witness is used most commonly in criminal cases, but could be used in civil cases. This portion of the rule allows the introduction of prior statements by a witness where the prior statement is "one of identification of a person made after perceiving the person." Fed. R. Evid. 801(d)(1)(C). This admission of prior identification evidence is easy to understand. A victim of a crime may be asked to identify the person who committed the crime. This could occur near the scene of the crime or at a police line up after the crime. During the course of the identification process, the victim clearly identifies the person he or she believes committed the crime. Later the case will go to trial and the victim will be called as a witness. It has occurred that, at the trial, the victim/witness has been unable to identify the alleged criminal. It is possible that a substantial period of time has passed and that the criminal defendant has substantially changed his or her appearance during the interim. If the victim/witness fails to identify the alleged criminal or identifies the wrong person in the court room as the alleged criminal, then the prosecution can introduce evidence of the prior identification as substantive evidence of the truth of the matter asserted. As such, that prior identification is admitted to identify the defendant as the one who committed the crime.

b. Admission by Party Opponent

The next types of evidence that appear to be hearsay but are defined as not being hearsay are admissions by a party opponent. Fed. R. Evid. 801(d)(2). The very name of this evidence hints as several important elements. Although there are five different sets of circumstances that will allow admission of this evidence and each of those five have its own requirements, they all have several general requirements that must be met.

There are two important general requirements that must be met before the specific types of statements can be considered. Fed. R. Evid. 801(d)(2) states that it must be a "statement ... offered against a party." This calls to attention first that the statement is one that comes from a party to the litigation. In civil cases it may be the plaintiff's or defendant's statement. In criminal cases it may be the defendant's statement. By assuring that it was a statement of a party, the rule assures that the person who made the statement is available and could take the witness stand to explain or be cross examined on the statement. The second important part of that general requirement is that the statement may only be offered "against" the party. This means that the party who made the statement may not offer it into evidence in order to support his or her own case. The statement may only be offered to attack the case of the person who made the statement.

There are several things that should be noted about those general requirements. By limiting the use of the statement to being introduced against the party that made the statement, that increases the likelihood that the statement is true. Since the statement is such that it is now possible to use it against the party, it is unlikely the party would have said something damaging unless it was true. Notice also, there is no requirement that the prior statement by the party was made under oath. Any statement made by a party may be used as an admission against that party

Since the statement will be used against the party, it is likely that the party knew the statement was damaging when it was made. Because of this, care must be used to distinguish the "party admission" rule from another and quite different hearsay exception. There is an exception to the hearsay rule that allows the introduction of statements by people when those statements are against the interest of the person making the statement. Those are called Statements against interest. Fed. R. Evid. 804(b)(3). Those, however, require that the declarant knew it was against interest when the statement was made and it must be shown that the declarant is not available to testify at the trial. The admissions by a party opponent require that they be made by a party. In addition, although it is likely that the party knew it was against his or her own interest when the statement was made, there is no requirement in the rule that the party knew it was against his or her own interest when made. In order to avoid this commonly made mistake, care should be taken to always use the correct names of the two different rules. The rule under discussion at this point concerns "admission of party-opponent." The other rule which will be discussed later is "statement against interest."

Once it is determined that the statement is being used against a party, there are the five different types of circumstances that must be understood as coming within the rule. The first is when the statement is "the party's own statement, in either an individual or a representative capacity." Fed. R. Evid. 801(d)(2)(A). This example is the simplest to understand. These are statements that the party made him or herself. As an example, there may have been a traffic accident. One of the drivers of a car gets out of the car and says, "I'm so sorry. I ran that stop sign and did not even see you coming." If that driver is sued for the injuries that resulted from the accident, that statement could be introduce and used against the party at trial. Since it is defined as not being hearsay, it would be introduced to prove the truth of the matter asserted. In a criminal case, confessions are admissible because that are admissions of a party. Although there may be constitutional issues to be addressed with such confessions, the admission of a party rule takes care of any hearsay problem

The second type of admission is a "statement of which the party has manifested an adoption of belief in its truth." Fed. R. Evid. 801(d)(2)(B). It is not necessary for the party to have actually vocalized the statement that is being used against him or her. If the party "manifested an adoption" of the statement, it becomes admissible against them. There may be formal methods of adopting a position, but the most troubling one for this rule is the "tacit admission" rule. When a person is confronted with an allegation that a reasonable person would immediately and openly rebut, remaining silent may be viewed as adopting the statement as true. Imagine, for example, that a person approaches another and says, "You owe me $1000. Pay me now." The listener does not speak. Later, when the speaker sues the listener for $1000, the events, including the silence of the listener could be offered into evidence to show that the listener probably owed the $1000. The remaining silent is viewed as an admission by manifestation of adoption.

The use of silence as an admission in civil cases does not cause other legal problems. In criminal cases, however, substantial constitutional problems arise. Imagine, for example, that a person is arrested and taken to the police station. The person is charged with a crime of robbery. When the person is told by the police officer, "You committed the crime of robbery and we're going to send you to jail," the person who had been arrested remains silent. The prosecution would like to use that silence as evidence of an admission by manifestation of adoption. The courts would probably exclude that evidence. Criminal defendants have the right to remain silent. In addition, the defendant was probably told he or she had the right to remain silent when he or she was given Miranda warnings. In criminal cases, the use of silence as evidence is usually not allowed.

The third type of evidence that may be used as an admission by a party is "a statement by a person authorized by the party to make a statement concerning the subject." Fed. R. Evid. 801(d)(2)(C). Traditionally, this was a called a speaking agent. This would be a person who was employed in the capacity to make statements for others. If those statements were later offered in evidence against a party for whom the agent spoke, they would be admissible. Examples of agents speaking for a principal are numerous. Some companies or celebrities employ press agents for the very purpose of making statements. Attorneys, for example, are hired to speak for their clients. Real estate agents, stock brokers, purchasing agents or any of a number of other types of agents may be recognized as someone who can make an admission for their principal.

The fourth type of evidence that may be used as an admission by a party is "a statement by the party's agent or servant concerning a matter within the scope of the agency or employment, made during the existence of the relationship." Fed. R. Evid. 801(d)(2)(D). This is a broader rule then the traditional "speaking agent" rule that is noted above. In this rule, the agent does not have to be employed specifically for the purpose of speaking for principal. This rule allows statements made by agents and employees that concern matters within the scope of employment. This type of example could arise much more often then the one immediately preceding it.

In a typical traffic accident case, the driver may be employed as the driver of a truck for a delivery company. While making deliveries, the driver of the truck runs a stop sign and causes and injury. The driver gets out of the truck and says, "I am sorry. I ran that stop sign and did not even see you." The injured parties sue the driver and the company for whom the driver works. The statements that the driver made would be admissible in the case. They would first be admissible against the driver as a party because the statements were the "party's own statement." Fed. R. Evid. 801(d)(2)(A). The statements would also be admissible against the employer since they were statements "by the party's ... servant concerning a matter within the scope of the ... employment, made during he existence of the relationship." Fed. R. Evid. 801(d)(2)(D).

This portion of the rule allows a much broader use of admission evidence in agency relationships. The tradition rules that required a speaking agent frequently left the courts saying that speaking was not a part of the agent's job description. This rule allows the evidence to be admitted if the statement merely concerns a matter that is within the agent's job description.

The fifth type of evidence that may be used under this rule is usually a part of a criminal action. It allows use of statement made concerning a conspiracy and then allows that statement to be used against all co-conspirators. The Federal Rules of Evidence provide that it is admissible if it is "a statement by a coconspirator of a party during the course of an in furtherance of the conspiracy." Fed. R. Evid. 801(d)(2)(E).

The importance of the coconspirator rule is that it allows evidence of statements made by one conspirator to be used as an admission against all defendants in the conspiracy. The elements to use the statement, however, must be noted. Obviously, the statement could be used against the person who said it. That would be a statement that is "a party's own statement." Fed. R. Evid. 801(d)(2)(A). To use it against the other coconspirators, however, it must have been made in the course of and in further of the conspiracy. This means that it must include discussion of putting together and carrying out the conspiracy while the conspiracy is in progress. It does not include mere idle chatter or discussions that do not further the conspiracy.

It is important to note that three of the above examples assume that some type of relationship exists between or among a group of people before the out of court statements can be used. Two of the examples assume there is an agency relationship while the third example discusses the existence of a conspiracy. If those relationships do not exist, then the statements made would not be admissible. For a party to the trial, one way of trying to get the statement excluded from evidence would be to deny that the relationship existed. The rules proceed with a method to help the court to determine if the relationships exist.

Frequently, the statement that is offered into evidence may, itself, mention the existence of the relationship. A truck driver who has just had an accident, for example, may say, "My employer, ABC, Corporation, is going to be really upset that I ran the stop sign and caused this accident." The statement is then used against ABC, Corporation in a trial for damages. In a conspiracy trial, the speaker of the statement may have said, "John, you, Bill and Fred, get the guns for the robbery, while Sam and I will get the car." The statement is used against Bill in a trial for conspiracy. In both of those examples the defendants may claim that the relationship did not exist. The party seeking to introduce the evidence may claim that the statement itself shows the relationship existed. The question for the trial court would be whether the statement alone is enough to prove the existence of the relationship.

The Federal Rules of Evidence state that, "The contents of the statement shall be considered but are not alone sufficient to establish the declarant's authority under subdivision (C), the agency or employment relationship and scope thereof under subdivision (D), or the existence of the conspiracy and the participation therein of he declarant and the party against whom the statement is offered under subdivision (E)." Fed. R. Evid. 801(d)(2). This would allow the trial judge to consider the evidence of the relationship that is found in the statement, but some additional evidence would be needed of that relationship before the statement would be found to be admissible.

In the traffic accident example noted above, the statement of the driver would not alone be enough to establish the employment relationship. If, however, additional witnesses could testify that the truck had the distinctive markings of the ABC, Corporation and that the accident happened during the normal working hours of the day, that should be sufficient additional evidence that the employment relationship existed. In the conspiracy example, the statement alone would not be sufficient to use the statement in a trial against Bill. If, however, some of the other members of the conspiracy would testify that Bill was involved in the conspiracy, that should be sufficient to allow the evidence to be admitted.

A problem that may arise with offers of admissions by a party is that the statements that were made were not in the proper form or format. A party may wish to object, for example, that the statement that was made was in the form of an opinion. The party may also claim that the statement was not made from his or her own first hand knowledge but was, instead, gained from others. As discussed in earlier material, there are strict requirements about opinion evidence and witnesses can only testify from first hand knowledge. The courts are likely, however, to allow the introduction of statements as admission against a party even though the statements contain opinions or were not based on first hand knowledge. The law assumes that a party would not have made a damaging statement if he or she did not believe it was true. The party's own belief in the truth of the statement is enough of an assurance of credibility to allow the statement to be admitted.

The discussion of admissions also raises one additional issue. Courts frequently distinguish between "judicial admissions" and "evidentiary admissions." Judicial admissions are held to be conclusive in a case. Once the judicial admission is made, the issue is not open to decision by the jury. It is decided. Evidentiary admissions, however, are just what the name implies. Evidentiary admissions are mere evidence in the case and may be subject to cross examination, challenge, dispute, rebuttal, and ultimately are a question of fact for the jury. It is important, therefore, to understand the difference between the two.

Judicial admissions are admissions that are usually made as a matter of formal pleading in a case. They may be admissions made in the complaint, answer or in stipulations. They may also be made by formal pleading in criminal cases. The admissions of a party that have been discussed in this section of the book are considered evidentiary admissions. They are used as evidence against one of the parties, but are not conclusive. The party against who they were used, can challenge them.

D. Exceptions

Now that the definitions of the important elements of hearsay are understood, the next step is to consider the exceptions to the hearsay rule. The importance of the exceptions is that they allow the introduction of evidence that would otherwise be excluded. There are two major classifications of types of exceptions. The first type of exception includes those for which it is not important whether the declarant is available to testify or not. Those are covered in Fed. R. Evid. 803 and shall be discussed first. The second major classification includes those exception for which the declarant must be unavailable. In fact, the party seeking to introduce the statement must be able to show that the declarant is unavailable. Those exceptions are covered in Fed. R. Evid. 804 and shall be covered later.

1. Availability of Declarant Immaterial (803)

As noted in the earlier discussion, the exceptions found in this section of the Federal Rules of Evidence consider the "availability of the declarant immaterial." To state that more directly, it does not matter whether the declarant of the statement that is being sought to be introduced is available to be called as a witness. The statement can be offered without any foundation being offered as to this issue.

Each of the following exceptions has specific elements that must be met in order for the evidence to be admissible. The evidence is hearsay and would not be admissible in the absence of these exceptions.

a. Present Sense Impression and Excited Utterance — Time (1, 2)

The first two exceptions that are to be discussed are similar. The time element is the key difference that must be noted in these. These exceptions are contained in Fed. R. Evid. 803(1) and 803(2). Both of the exceptions concern statements made during or immediately after the event that is being described. Imagine, for example, that an automobile wreck has just occurred. A bystander on the corner says, "Oh my!! That Ford just ran a red light." Under all of the definitions we have seen in this chapter, that would be hearsay and not admissible. Under these exceptions, that statement would probably be admissible.

The theory for allowing these statements to be admissible is that they are usually thought to be trustworthy. A person who speaks while viewing an event is probably telling the truth. That person has not had time to think about the event, maybe forget some of the details, or just change the story as he or she learns who was actually involved. The immediacy of speaking during the event gives the statement a strong sense of trustworthiness.

These exceptions are well recognized and have been developed through the common law. These exceptions were routinely said, at common law, to be part of the "res gestae." The phrase, "res gestae," can be roughly translated as "things done." It is used to describe the circumstances and events surrounding any particular occurrence. When statements were made during or immediately after such an event, they were referred to as being a part of the res gestae.

The Federal Rules of Evidence have avoided using the phrase, res gestae. Over years of development, courts have used that phrase to cover many different types of exceptions. The word has become somewhat confusing. The Federal Rules of Evidence opted to avoid that word and describe the individual exceptions by terms that were more precise.

The first exception, Present Sense Impression, is found in Fed. R. Evid.803(1) and allows admission of a "statement describing or explaining an event or condition made while the declarant was perceiving the event or condition, or immediately thereafter." Several things should be noted with this exception. This exception assumes that the statement is made while the event is occurring. The time between the event and the statement must be extremely short. It is also important that there is nothing in the rule about the nature of the event. It may be any type of event. (The next exception requires a "startling event.") This exception, therefore, allows the introduction of a statement that is made during the event.

The theory behind allowing this exception is the unlikely possibility that the declarant would have taken the time to falsify the statement. Since the statement is made during or immediately after observing the event, there is not the time for the declarant to think about the facts. It has been suggested that this is admissible because it is "the event speaking" and not the declarant.

The second exception, Excited Utterance, is found in Fed. R. Evid. 803(2) and is similar to the first. This exception allows the introduction of a statement that concerns a "startling event" while the declarant is under the "stress of the excitement." Notice how this exception is both similar to, but differs from the one immediately proceeding. This exception assumes that the declarant is describing an event. This event, however, must be "startling." That means that something about the event must increase the tension or stress of the moment. The theory behind this exception is that the stress or excitement of the moment will further delay the opportunity the declarant has to falsify the event. Since the exception is based upon the startling nature of the event, the time period between the event and the statement may be extended. Where the "Present Sense Impression" must be made at or immediately after the event, the "Excited Utterance" may be made for so long as the declarant is under the stress of the event.

It is possible to see examples to distinguish these two exceptions. The "presence sense impression" may be made while a person is just speaking about events that are occurring. A declarant may be outside of a bank when he or she notices an interesting looking automobile parked outside. The declarant may say, "Isn't that an interesting color of purple on an automobile." The statement is overheard by several other people. Later, when it is discovered that the bank was being robbed and there are allegations of a purple car used in the robbery, the statement could be introduced to help show the car was there.

An example of an "excited utterance" may be seen in most automobile accidents. After an accident, witnesses may speak out about what happened. Imagine, for example, a person saying, "Oh my!! That was a horrible accident. That Ford ran that red light." The accident would provide the startling event. As long as the witness was under the stress of the event, the statement would be admissible by those that heard it made.

Several problems may arise with these two exceptions. It has been questioned as to whether the declarant needs to have been a participant in the events that occurred. That is, of course, not necessary. The declarant just needs to be someone who observed the event and commented on it.

There is some question as to whether the declarant needs to be able to be identified in order to introduce the statement that was made. This has caused more difficulty for the courts. The problem is that there needs to be some foundation that the declarant actually observed the event that was being described. If the witness can testify that they observed the declarant and the declarant did observe the event, then the foundation should be met. If the only evidence is that some unidentified person seemed to have shouted out the statement, the courts are hesitant to allow admission of the statement.

For the excited utterance, the existence of a startling event can also be a problem. Ordinarily, several witnesses will be available to testify that a startling event occurred. The witnesses can then also testify as to what the declarant said about the event. There are times, however, where the only evidence of the startling event is the statement itself. Imagine, for example, a night security guard that watches over a factory. While on a walk alone through the factory, the guard sees some metal that begins to fall. The guard tries to stop it, but feels something pull in his or her back. When the guard gets back to the guard station, he or she tells the other guards, "Wow!! Some metal sheeting was falling back in building 12. When I tried to stop it, I think

I hurt my back. It feels pretty tight." If the guard wanted to use that statement in a Worker's Compensation claim, the only evidence of the startling event is the statement itself. Courts appear to be dealing with these on a case by case basis. The trend seems to be to allow the introduction of the evidence.

Finally, the nature of the statement itself must be concerning the event that gave rise to the statement. A declarant, for example, could not see a car accident and say, "Wow!! That was a horrible accident. That reminds me of how my brother-in-law mistreats his wife." A family court dealing with issues between the brother-in-law and the aggrieved wife should not let that statement in evidence. Although it was made while under the stress of a startling event, it does not concern the event.

b. Mental State (3)

The next broad exception to the hearsay rule allows statements that reflect the declarant's state of mind. Recall that the earlier discussion noted that some courts have found that statements concerning the declarant's state of mind may not be hearsay at all. If they are not hearsay, they would, of course, be admissible. Because of the confusion noted in that earlier discussion, it is easier to recognize the evidence as being admissible under an established exception.

Fed. R. Evid. 803(3) allows the introduction of statements of a person's "existing state of mind, emotion, or physical condition." The statement needs to reflect what the declarant is currently thinking about the topic being stated. The statement may reflect current feelings about ideas, emotions, or physical condition. The easy examples can be quickly noted. A declarant may say, "I feel very angry with John." Such a statement might be used in an action where the declarant was subsequently found to have injured John. Another example is that the declarant may say, "My back feels very good today." That statement might be used when the declarant is seeking recovery for a back injury and the witness is offering evidence the declarant had no pain on that day. Each of those examples are statements of the then existing state of mind about present emotions or physical conditions. Those statements would be admissible. The rule is more difficult, however. The courts must consider statements of "then existing" states of mind about possible past, present or future events. Each of those need separate discussion.

1. Past

It is possible to imagine a statement of a then existing state of mind where the declarant currently remembers something that happened in the past. When questioned, the declarant might say, "I seem to remember that when I saw that traffic accident two weeks ago that the Ford ran the red light." That statement reflects the declarant's then existing state of mind about facts remembered from the past. Fed. R. Evid. 803(3) states that although state of mind statements are admissible, that does not include "a statement of memory or belief to prove the fact remembered or believed." The reason for such exclusion is clear. If the law allowed the introduction of then existing state of mind about things remembered from the past, then all hearsay statements would be admissible. Every statement is, in fact, a then existing statement of what the person remembers. Such a broad allowance of evidence would fail to have the indicators of trustworthiness that the traditional exceptions have. The Advisory Committee notes to the Federal Rules of Evidence note that this exclusion "is necessary to avoid the virtual destruction of the hearsay rule." Fed. R. Evid. 803(3), Advisory Committee notes.

The rule does allow one type of statement of memory or belief to be admitted. Where that statement of memory or belief "relates to the execution, revocation, identification, or terms of declarant's will" then it is admissible. Fed. R. Evid. 803(3). This narrow rule will usually come into play once the declarant is dead and there is a probate matter concerning the declarant's estate. This allowance of the evidence is seen as something of a necessity in order to get what little evidence that is available before the court. Fed. R. Evid. 803(3), Advisory Committee notes.

2. Present

Currently existing state of mind about currently existing emotions, ideas or physical condition are clearly admissible under this exception. Fed. R. Evid. 803(3). Examples of this exception are easily found. A declarant's statement about currently felt love, anger, hate, aches, pains, illness, or well being includes just some examples. As long as the statement is concerning the then existing state of mind about a present condition, it is admissible.

3. Future

One of the more interesting uses of Fed. R. Evid. 803(3) is allowing statements of what the declarant intends to do in the future to be used to prove what that person probably did. In the classic case of *Mutual Life Insurance Co. v. Hillman*, 145 U.S. 285 (1892), the United States Supreme Court was faced with the statement by the declarant that he intended to go into the mountains. The statement was admitted for the purpose of proving that the declarant probably went on the trip. This rule allows the continuation of that theory.

The difficulty with this use of the rule arises when the statement of future intent also mentions other people. Imagine, for example, that the declarant says, "I am going to the corner of Main and Third Street at mid-night to meet John." Later, the declarant is found dead on the corner of Main and Third Street. The police want to arrest John for the murder of the declarant. The question arises as to whether the statement can be used to place John at the scene of the crime. The drafters of the Federal Rule of Evidence did not intent for the rule to go so far. "Rule 803(3) was approved in the form submitted by the Court to Congress. However, the Committee intends that the Rule be construed to limit the doctrine of *Mutual Life Insurance Co. v. Hillmon*, 145 U.S. 285, 295–300 (1892), so as to render statements of intent by a declarant admissible only to prove his future conduct, not the future conduct of another person." Fed. R. Evid. 803(3), Advisory Committee notes.

Although the drafters of the rule intended to limit Fed. R. Evid. 803(3), the appellate courts have been less than clear on the topic. Although some have allowed the use of such statements to prove something about the conduct of other parties, the approach is limited. Those that allow the use of such evidence appear to look for some additional evidence in support of such statements.

c. Medical Diagnosis and Treatment (4)

Statements that are made concerning medical history, physical condition, and ailments are admitted into evidence as an exception to the hearsay rule. Fed. R. Evid. 803(4). In some ways, this rule appears similar to the one immediately preceding it. Fed. R. Evid. 803(3) allows the admission of statements of currently existing state of mind concerning, among other things, physical condition. This rule, however, allows the admission of not only statements of current physical condition, but also past physical condition. For example, a declarant's statement that he or she is suffering pain and it all started "two weeks ago" would be admissible under Fed. R. Evid. 803(4), but not Fed. R. Evid. 803(3).

The key to Fed. R. Evid. 803(4), however, is that the statement must be made for the purposes of "medical diagnosis or treatment." This portion of the rule distinguishes it from the other rules. When the statements about physical conditions are made for the purposes of "medical diagnosis or treatment" they may contain statements of present or past physical condition. In addition, the rule goes on to say that the statements must be "reasonably pertinent to diagnosis or treatment." Fed. R Evid. 803(4).

There are, of course, several issues that can arise due to the language of the rule. First, there is the question of whether the person testifying to the statement that was made must have been an actual treating physician or could that witness be a physician especially hired to testify at trial. The difference is sometimes stated as being between a treating physician and a testifying physician. The rule indicates that the statement may be admitted if it was for purposes of diagnosis or treatment. Obviously, the treating physician can testify to any statements made in the course of taking medical history. The treating physician listened to the statements for purposes of "treatment." The courts have ruled, however, that testifying physicians can also testify to statements they heard while taking a medical history. A physician that is hired to prepare and testify at trial, is taking the medical history from the declarant in order to prepare a diagnosis. Since the rule allows statements offered for purposes of diagnosis or treatment, the statements made to a testifying physician are also admissible.

As the above discussion indicates, the statements are usually ones made to a physician. The rule does not, however, require that the statement be made to a physician. During the course of treatment, a patient may give statements to technicians, nurses, emergency room intake people, or others in a hospital. The rule provides that statements are admissible if they are for the purpose of diagnosis or treatment. The courts have ruled that statements offered to these other people for the purpose of diagnosis or treatment are also admissible.

The usual case sees the injured party as the one who makes the statement. The rule, however, does not require that. There are times when family members or friends may make statements to the health care professionals about the nature of the injury. Since the rule only requires that the statements be for the purposes of diagnosis or treatment, those statements would also be admissible.

It is important to note that the statements must be reasonably pertinent to diagnosis or treatment. Statements that merely cast blame or fault and do not relate to diagnosis or treatment are not admissible. Examples of the differences between those can be easily seen. Imagine a traffic accident where a pedestrian crossing the street is hit by a car. When the injured party is taken to an emergency room, the patient may say, "I was hit by a car." That would be pertinent to diagnosis or treatment. The type of accident would give the medical staff some idea as to the type of trauma suffered. That statement would be admissible. On the other hand, if the patient added, "And, when I was hit, it was because the Ford ran the red light," that addition line would not be admissible. The fact that a car ran a red light is not pertinent to treatment. The medical staff may need to know that the patient was hit by a car, but they do not need to know that the car ran the red light. A similar example can be seen in a criminal case. When a patient is brought into the emergency room, the statement that, "I was stabbed by a knife," would be admissible in a trial. If the patient added, "I was stabbed by a knife and John did the stabbing," the portion about John doing the stabbing would not be admissible. Knowing the type of injury would be pertinent to diagnosis or treatment, but knowing who did it would not.

The rule is consistent with the purposes that support it. The reasons courts have traditionally allowed these types of statements is that they appear to be very trustworthy. The law assumes that when a patient makes statements for the purposes of diagnosis or treatment, the patient tries very hard to be accurate. People going to the doctor want the doctor to arrive at the correct diagnosis. This indication of trustworthiness makes the statements admissible. Since it is the seeking of diagnosis or treatment that gives the statements the indication of trustworthiness, statements that do not relate to diagnosis or treatment are not considered trustworthy. That is the reason that the portion of statements offered for diagnosis or treatment are admissible, but portions of the statements that only relate to fault or blame are not.

d. Past Recollection Recorded (5)

The exception to the hearsay rule known as Recorded Recollection, Fed. R. Evid. 803(5), sometimes referred to as "Past Recollection Recorded," is similar to another concept and often confused with it. The other concept is the using of notes to refresh memory while a witness is testifying. This is covered in Fed. R. Evid. 612 and in Chapter VI of this book. Although the Federal Rules of Evidence refer to that as "Writing Used to Refresh Memory," it has been called "Present Recollection Refreshed." That name is probably what leads to the confusion with the hearsay exception, Past Recollection Recorded. In the context of "Writing Used to Refresh Memory," the witness is allowed to use anything to refresh his or her memory. The law assumes that the witness actually remembers the events and is merely using some notes to refresh that memory. There are no formal requirements for the notes that may be used.

The hearsay exception, Recorded Recollection, has a series of formal requirements. The reason that this appears as a hearsay exception is because in this context the witness has no present memory of the facts that are being brought out. The witness is not testifying from memory but, instead, wants to read the notes or document that he or she has. Since the witness is reading a statement that was prepared out of court, that is hearsay. It may only be admitted if there is an exception for it. In order to allow the reading of the document into trial, the elements of Fed. R. Evid. 803(5) must be met. The rule requires these elements:

1. The witness once had knowledge of the facts.
2. The witness currently does not have knowledge sufficient to testify about the matter.

3. The witness prepared or adopted the recording document at a time when the witness did have knowledge of the facts.
4. The witness can testify that the document was correct when made.

Each of those above elements must be met in order to allow the witness to read the document. The attorney seeking to have the witness read the document would ask questions to lay that foundation. An example of this exception can be easily seen. A witness to a tort or crime may have written down an automobile license number as the automobile was leaving the scene of the event. The witness saves the piece of paper on which the license number was written. Three years later when the civil or criminal action goes to trial, the witness is called. That witness will testify that they were at the scene of the event and knew the license number of the vehicle that left the scene. He or she will also testify that in the intervening three years, that number has been forgotten. The witness will be able to say, however, that he or she wrote the number down immediately after seeing it on the vehicle and that it was correct at that time. Upon laying that foundation, the trial judge should allow the witness to read the number from the piece of paper.

This rule has one additional issue. Where this exception is use, the document may be read into evidence, but the document is usually not admitted into evidence as an exhibit. It may be admitted as an exhibit if offered by the opposing party. This requires the witness that is offering the statement to read it, but not give the document to the jury. If the opposing side wants the document to go to the jury as an exhibit, then that side may so request.

e. Business Records (6, 7)

Frequent civil litigation occurs between major companies. Such litigation may usually involve breach of contract actions. In the modern business world of today, it would be impossible for individuals in the companies to know and remember everything that occurs each day in the business. Imagine, for example, that a company wants to sue a supplier for breach of contract in consistently being late with the monthly delivery of goods. The way the plaintiff company will want to prove the late deliveries, will be with the records from the warehouse that show the dates of delivery of those goods. In fact, in actually running the businesses, the individuals rely on the records kept for the business to make major decisions. The business owners themselves assume the business records are accurate. The law also assumes that accuracy and allows the introduction of business records as an exception to the hearsay rule as "Records of Regularly Conducted Activity," Fed. R. Evid. 803(6) and "Absence of Entry in Records Kept in Accordance with the Provisions of Paragraph (6)," Fed. R. Evid. 803(7). Generally, these rules allow the admission of business records that have been kept in compliance with the elements of the rules.

Before looking at the modern rules for business records, it is important to look briefly at the more traditional hearsay exception. This area of hearsay law has a long history. The original concept of the Business Records Rules was known as the "Shop Book Rule." Before modern technology, business would keep all of their records in simple "Shop Books." The custodian of the book would write down all transactions that occurred. A lender of money, for example, might have a clerk that watched the transactions and wrote down the details in a single book. The book would list the name of the borrower, the amount of the loan and terms of the loan. When payments were made, that same clerk would enter those payments in the book. If litigation was necessary, the clerk would testify to identify the record book and the book would be entered into evidence. Although the book was made out of court, it would be allowed into evidence as an exception to the hearsay rule as the "Shop Book." (For those who know the Charles Dickens story, *A Christmas Carol*, Bob Cratchit would serve in the role as clerk and custodian of the Shop Book.)

Modern businesses no longer keep all of their records in one book with one clerk doing the recording. Modern businesses operate on a global scale. Records are kept in computers and entered by employees from around the world. Imagine a large company making and selling goods worldwide. The manufacturing plant will prepare the goods and ship them to the company warehouse. Salespeople will get orders from all over the world. When orders are sent to the warehouse, the goods will be shipped out. Payments will be sent to the accounting office. All of that information would be entered into company computers by employees working in each of those different areas. If someone did not pay for the goods they ordered, the company would sue. Since no one individual participated in the entire chain, the records would have to be used to prove that the goods had been shipped, received, and not paid for. The modern "Business Records" Rule allows that evidence to be admitted.

Fed. R. Evid. 803(6), Records of Regularly Conducted Activities is the modern Business Records rule. In order to introduce the records into evidence, the following elements must be met:

1. The records may be in any form.
2. The records must have been made at or near the time the event occurred that is being recorded.
3. The information must have been recorded by a person with knowledge of the events or from a person with such knowledge.

4. The information being recorded must be the type of information regularly kept in the course of business of the business keeping it.

5. The form that the information was recorded into must be of the type the business keeps in the regular course of business.

6. All of the elements of this exception must be shown by a custodian of the records, other qualified person or by certification found in Fed. R. Evid. 902(11).

Laying the foundation of showing those elements will allow the records to be admitted into evidence unless the "source of information or method or circumstances of preparation indicate lack of trustworthiness." Fed. R. Evid. 803(6).

As these elements illustrate, the possible circumstances that may allow the introduction of business records is very broad. Since business may keep a variety of records in a variety of different formats, the rule allows the introduction of most of the regularly kept records.

Imagine again our example of the global corporation that manufactures and sells goods worldwide. One of the customers has paid an amount less than agreed upon for goods that were shipped. In an action for the purchase price of the goods, the manufacturing company, as plaintiff, will need to prove that the goods were shipped and that the buyer paid less then the amount agreed. First, of course, the plaintiff would have to introduce a copy of the contract showing the agreed upon price of the goods. (Just for a little review, the contract would be admissible. The contract would be a "verbal act" and not hearsay. In addition, the plaintiff would have to authenticate the signatures on the contract in order to meet the authentication requirement. Finally, the plaintiff would have to produce the original of the contract to meet the Best Evidence Rule.) The plaintiff would then want to introduce the records from the warehouse to show that the goods were shipped, and the records of the accounting office to show that less than full price was received. In a modern business, all of these records would be on computers.

The computer printouts from the warehouse would be admissible. The plaintiff would probably call the custodian of the shipping records to testify that as items are shipped, they are entered into the computer program. Each month, a print out is produced to keep track of all shipments. The custodian would then show a copy of the print out showing the shipments. Clearly this record is one that is made at or near the time of shipment. The information for the record is entered by people with knowledge or gained from people actually working in the warehouse. Both the shipping information and the computer printouts are regularly kept in the course of business. The custodian is the one that can authenticate that record. It could, of course, be self-authenticated by a certification under Fed. R. Evid. 902(11). (For another quick review since a document is being introduced, the Best Evidence Rule must also be met. For data stored in a computer, any printout is included in the definition of original. Fed. R. Evid. 1001(3).) The plaintiff would also want to introduce the records of the accounting office. It would follow the same process as above. A custodian of the records of the accounting office could show that as money is received it is entered into the computer program. Obviously, both the type of information and the format of the record are both kept in the regular course of business. The only thing that would keep these two records from being admitted would be if the defendant could show there was something about the record keeping that displayed a lack of trustworthiness. Since showing that would be difficult, the evidence would probably be admitted.

An important feature of this exception is the type of businesses that may use it to introduce records. It is important to note that the Federal Rules of Evidence do not call this the Business Record Rule. The Rules name this exception the "Records of Regularly Conducted Activity" rule. This rule is intended to cover a broad range of activities. "The term business as used in this paragraph includes business, institution, association, profession, occupation, and calling of every kind whether or not conducted for profit." Fed. R. Evid. 803(6). Obviously, the rule applies to manufacturing companies that are engaged in global sales. Since the rules also say professions, it also apples to "businesses" like law firms, accounting firms, engineering firms and doctor's offices. The rule also makes it clear that it can be used by non-profit organization. Such non-profit organizations might include schools, hospitals, churches and charitable clubs. Where some activity has the regular practice of keeping information, that activity will probably be found to be able to use this rule.

An additional issue has arisen with the use of the Business Records Rule. At times, businesses have sought to use there records to prove that certain information in not in the records and, therefore, probably did not happen. A good example of this type of problem could be imagined using our prior example of the manufacturing company that sells to a global market. In this example, however, the buyer does not merely underpay on the contract, but does not pay anything at all. The plaintiff/manufacturing company would like to introduce the accounting records to show that there is no entry for payments by the buyer. The Federal Rules of Evidence allow this type of evidence to be admitted. "Evidence that a matter is not included" may be admitted if the records are sufficient to be admissible under the previous rule. Fed. R. Evid. 803(7). In our example, the plaintiff keeps the accounting records in compliance with Fed. R. Evid. 803(6). Those records could then be admitted under Fed. R. Evid. 803(7) in order to prove there is no entry for payments by the defendant. That would tend to show that the defendant did not pay for the goods that were shipped.

f. Public Records (8, 9, 10)

The previous exception assumed that the business records were records of private companies. The Federal Rules of Evidence have a similar series of rules that allow the admission into evidence of public records. Such public records are frequently sought to be introduced and the law allows that admission. As with other exceptions to the hearsay rule, there are specific elements that must be met before the evidence can be introduced.

The general "Public Records" Rule is contained in Fed. R. Evid. 803(8). This rule is broader then the Business Records rule, but does have some limiting issues.

First, the Public Records rule allows admission of records of a public office or agency when those records set forth "the activities of the office or agency." Fed. R. Evid. 803(8). This rule would cover the records of any activity normally carried on by an agency. Certain agencies, for example, are responsible for contract procurement and assuring that contracts are paid. Records reflecting such payments or disbursements would be admissible as an activity of the agency. Agencies also have the responsibility of paying their own employees. Obviously, such payment records would meet this definition.

The second type of record is more complicated. Records that show "matters observed pursuant to duty imposed by law as to which matters there was a duty to report" are also admissible. Fed. R. Evid. 803(8). Those examples may also be seen. Agencies are responsible for observing and reporting everything from weather conditions to environmental problems. All of that information is reported and recorded. Such information would be admissible. The difficulty arises with an exception that is contained in this portion of the rule. Although matters observed are ordinarily admissible, the rule excludes "in criminal cases matters observed by police officers and other law enforcement personnel." Fed. R. Evid. 803(8). This exclusion was obviously a policy decision to opt for having the law enforcement person testify on the witness stand rather than merely introducing a report made by the officer. The rule does not allow reports of observation made by law enforcement officers to be admitted in criminal cases as an exception to the hearsay rule. The officer, however, could clearly testify on the witness stand to matters observed and known from first hand knowledge.

The final portion of the general rule is still more complex. The first two portions of the rule assumed that agency personnel were merely observing and recording facts. The final portion of the rule recognizes that there are times when government agents do investigations and write reports which evaluate the information in order to reach conclusions. This is the most troubling type of evidence and there is a strong desire to force such agents to appear on the witness stand. If the agent testifies, that agent is subject to cross examination. If the evaluative report is merely read into the record, there is no cross examination. The rule states that such reports are admissible "in civil actions and proceeds and against the Government in criminal cases." Fed. R. Evid. 803(7). Reading the rule it is clear that such evaluative reports can be introduced by either side in a civil case. In a criminal case, however, the prosecution cannot use such reports against the defendant. The defendant, however, may use such a report against the government. Even though the rule allows use of such reports, there is another limitation. They may be used, "unless the sources of information or other circumstances indicate a lack of trustworthiness." Fed. R. Evid. 803(8). As can be seen, these evaluative reports are the least well accepted of any of the public records.

With the limitations that appear on using public records as admissible evidence, some parties have sought to introduce such public records under the rule allowing introduction of "Records of Regularly Conducted Activities," Fed. R. Evid. 803(6). As was noted when that exception was discussed above, the definitions are so broad as to include almost any activity. Clearly government agencies are regularly conducted activities. Courts have not been inclined to allow this use of the Business Records Rule. Since there is a specific public records rule, then that rule is controlling. Parties cannot use the broader Fed. R. Evid. 803(6) when public records would be excluded under the narrow, specific public records rule.

There are a couple of additional public records rules. As a routine matter, government agencies keep records of births, deaths, and marriages. Such records are admissible. Fed. R. Evid. 803(9).

There may be times when a party would like to introduce a public record to show that certain information is not contained in the record. If the record keeps an accurate list of certain types of events, the absence of a record would tend to prove the event did not occur. Fed. R. Evid 803(10) allows the introduction of public records to prove the absence of the record of an event in question.

g. *Other Records (11, 12, 13, 14, 15, 17)*

The traditional common law and the Federal Rules of Evidence have recognized that there are a variety of different kinds of records that have an indication of trustworthiness. As such, there are hearsay exceptions for many of these types of records. Although these exceptions are not used as commonly as the ones already discussed, they do need to be mentioned.

Religious organizations routinely keep records. The Federal Rules of Evidence recognize an exception to the hearsay rule for these records where they show "births, marriages, divorces, deaths, legitimacy, ancestry, relationship by blood or marriage, or other similar facts of personal or family history." Fed. R. Evid. 803(11).

Basic family information is frequently contained on certified documents. Such documents are admissible where they show marriages, baptisms, or other similar sacraments. Fed. R. Evid. 803(12).

Traditionally, families kept important family information in family Bibles or other important locations. The Federal Rules of Evidence provide an exception to the hearsay rule for "Statements of fact concerning personal or family history contained in family Bibles, genealogies, charts, engravings on rings, inscriptions on family portraits, engravings on urns, crypts, or tombstones, or the like." Fed. R. Evid. 803(13).

Records of property titles are also admissible. The rules provide an exception to the hearsay rule for "documents purporting to establish or affect an interest in property." Fed. R. Evid. 803(14). Similarly, statements contained in such documents are also admissible. Fed. R. Evid. 803(15).

The public routinely uses market quotations or directory listings for a variety of matters. Recognizing the trustworthiness of such documents, the Federal Rules of Evidence provides an exception to the hearsay rule for them. Fed. R. Evid. 803(17).

h. Ancient Documents Rule (16)

The use of an Ancient Documents Rule as an exception to the hearsay rule is consistent with the use of that concept to authenticate documents. The exception to the hearsay rule is simply stated as, "Statements in a document in existence twenty years or more the authenticity of which is established." Fed. R. Evid. 803(16). This would allow the introduction of statements in a document that was twenty years old or older. Notice the language about authenticity. As noted several times, every document must be authenticated. This hearsay rule refers back to that requirement because of the traditional connection between using the Ancient Documents Rule to authenticate the document and provide an exception to the hearsay rule. When the authentication rules are discussed in Chapter IX, Fed. R. Evid. 901(b)(8) allows for the authentication of a document by showing it to be 20 years old or older, found in the place where it would be expected to be found and having no suspicion on its face. This authentication rule and the hearsay exception work together.

Once a document is authenticated under the Ancient Document Rule, it is also held to have met the exception to the hearsay rule.

i. Learned Treatises (18)

The issue of the introduction of learned treatises raises a complex point. Ordinarily the issue only arises in cases where expert testimony is needed. The traditional use of learned treatises was in the cross examination of an expert. A party would call an expert witness to testify and conduct the direct examination. The opposing party would want to question that expert on cross examination and use a "learned treatise" to question that witness. The purpose would be to illustrate to the jury that the witness's testimony was inconsistent with writings in a recognized text. Using the text as mere cross examination to attack the credibility of the witness would not raise a hearsay problem. If the text was being read to attack credibility and not being introduced to prove the truth of the matter asserted in the text, it was not hearsay. The text could be read and the judge would instruct the jury on the proper use of the text. In addition, the most restrictive view of the use of such texts was that they could not be used unless the witness on the stand testified that he or she had actually used the text in preparing testimony.

The Federal Rules of Evidence take a much broader view of the use of learned treatises. It is clear that since the rules provide for a hearsay exception for the use of learned treatises, the reading of the text comes in as substantive proof of the truth of the matter asserted. The text is not only coming in to impeach a witness but is being used as actual evidence in the case. The only difficulty is the foundation that must be laid in order to convince the trial judge to allow the learned treatise to be admitted.

Fed. R. Evid. 803(18) provides for several methods of laying the foundation. It is important to note, that the text must be called to the attention of the witness during cross examination unless the witness has already noted that he or she relied upon the text during the direct examination. As such, the initial use of the text is in the nature of the traditional attack on credibility. By continuing to make it a hearsay exception, completing the requirements of the rule allows the introduction as substantive evidence. Once it is clear that the witness has been confronted with the text, there are four methods that may be used to lay the proper foundation. They are:

1. The witness may testify that he or she relied upon the text. This is the traditional method of laying the foundation and may occur during the witness's direct or cross examination.
2. The witness may deny relying upon the text but admits that the text is an authority.

3. Another expert may testify that the text is an authority.

4. The trial judge may take judicial notice that the text is an authority.

It is clear, therefore, that the Federal Rules of Evidence have substantially broadened the common law rule dealing with learned treatises.

One additional feature of the rule deals with the proper use of the text. The rule provides that the text may be read into evidence, but the actual book may not be received as an exhibit. Fed. R. Evid. 803(18).

j. Character Issues (19, 20, 21, 22, 23)

In the chapter on Relevance (Chapter IV) and the chapter on witnesses (Chapter VI) there was substantial discussion about character evidence. There are times when character evidence is admissible. In addition to the items mentioned in those two chapters, there are additional times when the reputation concerning events or property may be relevant to a case. In all of those examples, character evidence presents a hearsay problem. When a witness wants to testify about the reputation of someone in the community, that reputation evidence is really the collective thoughts, statements, and ideas of numerous people. Clearly all of those thoughts, statements and ideas were expressed out of court. It could be argued that the testimony about reputation is hearsay. The Federal Rules of Evidence resolve that problem by making certain types of reputation evidence an exception to the hearsay rule.

The rules provide that reputation concerning personal or family history, Fed. R. Evid. 803(19), reputation concerning boundaries or general history, Fed. R. Evid. 803(20), and reputation of character of a person, Fed. R. Evid. 803(21) are all exceptions to the hearsay rule.

There are also times when it becomes necessary to enter into evidence the judgment from a prior case. It could be argued that the judgment was not made in this court during this trial and would, therefore, be hearsay. The Federal Rules of Evidence provide hearsay exceptions for such judgments. Fed. R. Evid. 803(22) & (23).

2. Declarant Unavailable (804)

All of the above hearsay exceptions begin with the assumption that the availability of the declarant is immaterial. When seeking to use those exceptions, there is no necessity of first accounting for the presence or absence of the declarant. There is a second list of exceptions, however, where the availability of the declarant is an issue. For this shorter list of exceptions it is first necessary to show that the declarant is unavailable. The following exceptions cannot be used unless there was foundation evidence showing the unavailability of the declarant.

In order to understand how the following exceptions are used, it is necessary to take a two step approach to the analysis. It is first necessary to determine what is meant by the concept of "Declarant Unavailable" and then determine the nature of the exceptions that can be used when that declarant is unavailable. The following discussion will follow that organization.

a. Unavailable defined (a)

As noted above, in order to use these exceptions, there must be proof that the declarant of the statement is unavailable. The Federal Rules of Evidence provide for five definitions of unavailable. In order to use the following exceptions, the declarant must be contained in one of those definitions.

The first definition of unavailable is that the declarant is exempt from testifying by ruling of the court that the declarant has a valid privilege. Fed. R. Evid. 804(a)(1). The way this example would arise would be that the witness would be called to the stand. The witness would be asked a couple of questions and would then refuse to testify on the basis of a privilege. If the trial court is willing to rule that the privilege is valid, the witness is allowed not to testify. At that point, however, the witness is "unavailable" for purposes of these exceptions. If one of the exceptions found in this rule can be found to apply, prior statements of the witness may be admitted in the trial.

The second definition of unavailable frequently arises in cases where the first definition is also challenged. The second definition provides that a witness in unavailable when that witness refuses to testify even though that witness has been ordered by the court to testify. Fed. R. Evid. 804(a)(2). It can be easily seen how this example and the privilege example could work together. The witness is on the stand and refuses to testify. The witness claims a privilege. If the court rules that the testimony is privileged then the witness is "unavailable" under the first definition. If the court rejects the claim of privilege and orders the witness to testify, but the witness continues to refuse to testify, then the witness is "unavailable" under this second definition of privilege.

Notice that the language of the rules requires a ruling of the court. If a party wants to use an out of court statement under one of the exceptions found in this general rule but believes the witness may be privileged, it may be still be necessary to call the witness to the stand. It is necessary to force the witness to claim the privilege and let the trial judge rule.

The third definition of unavailable may also require that the witness be called to testify. This definition provides that a declarant is unavailable when the declarant "testifies to a lack of memory of the subject matter of the declarant's statement." Fed. R. Evid. 804(a)(3). This definition, therefore, assumes that the declarant will be called to testify. During the testimony, the witness would testify that he or she does not remember the events. The witness would probably be confronted with prior statements and asked if those prior statements helped refresh the memory. Only after continuing to claim a lack of memory should the trial court decide that the declarant is unavailable.

The fourth definition provides that a declarant is unavailable due to "death or then existing physical or mental illness or infirmity." Fed. R. Evid. 804(a)(4). Clearly a dead declarant is unavailable as a witness. Some evidence of that death should convince the trial court that the witness cannot be called to testify. Unavailability duty to physical or mental illness, however, is more difficult. Live testimony is always preferred over reading prior out of court statements. The trial judge has some discretion to determine whether the declarant is truly unavailable, or whether the live testimony can be gained in some other way. The testimony could be sought at a later date or at some other location.

The fifth definition of unavailable is the most complex. The exact limits on this definition depend upon which of the hearsay exceptions are sought to be used. The basic elements of this definition will be discussed here, but also reviewed in the discussion of the exceptions themselves.

The fifth definition provides that the declarant is absent from the hearing and could not be procured by the party seeking to introduce the statement. This initial provision assumes that the party wanting to use the out of court statement has sought to get the declarant to the trial. This means that the attorney should have subpoenaed the declarant or sought other legal measure to force that attendance. If the attorney has used the subpoena and other reasonable means to get the declarant to the trial, then the declarant is, at least initially, unavailable. For the hearsay exception listed below that is called "Former Testimony," that is all that is needed in order to show that the declarant is unavailable. For the hearsay exceptions "impending death," "against interest," and "personal or family history" there is another feature to the rule of unavailability. The attorney seeking to use those exceptions to introduce a prior out of court statements, must show the declarant is not at the trial and that there is no other available testimony of that declarant. This would mean that in seeking to use one of those three listed exceptions the attorney would have to show that the attendance of the witness was sought and the testimony of the witness was sought by deposition or otherwise and that neither of those attempts was successful.

The following discussion will focus on the nature of the specific exceptions to the hearsay rule that are included in Fed. R. Evid. 804. Keep in mind that each of the following exceptions assumes that the first element of the exception is that the declarant is unavailable as defined by one of the five examples just discussed.

b. Former Testimony (b1)

Fed. R. Evid. 804(b)(1) provides a hearsay exception for "former testimony." This exception has two broad requirements. The first is that the statement that is sought to be introduced must have been given as testimony at another hearing or in a deposition. It may have been given in conjunction with the trial in which it is offered or another proceeding. This element is, therefore, broad. It allows the use of statements made in a wide variety of settings as long as the testimony given was subject to penalties for perjury.

The second element of the exception is more difficult. When the party is seeking to introduce the "former testimony," the party against whom it is offered must have had an "opportunity and similar motive to develop the testimony by direct, cross, or redirect examination." Fed. R. Evid. 804(b)(1). This language is different from and broader than the traditional common law rule. A brief review of the common law rule, however, will offer some insight into the meaning of the new rule. At common law, the rule would say that the former testimony had to have an identity of parties and identify of issues. By that, the rule meant that the former testimony had to be given in an action where the same parties were litigating the same issues. That lead to endless debate on whether the parties and issues were sufficiently similar. The modern Federal Rule of Evidence seeks to simplify that rule and reach a more satisfactory result. The issue that gives the former testimony the indication of trustworthiness is whether there was sufficient opportunity to cross examine the declarant on the statements made. The modern federal rule just goes directly to that point. If the party against whom the statement is now offered had sufficient opportunity and motive to cross examine the witness, the statement can be offered.

An easy example of the use of this hearsay statement can be seen. Imagine litigation is proceeding and a witness answers questions during a deposition. Before the date of the trial, the witness dies. At trial, one of the parties wants to introduce the testimony given in the deposition. The statements would be admissible. The declarant is unavailable due to death. The deposition was given under oath in the same proceeding. Both parties had the opportunity to develop the testimony either through direct or cross examination.

The rule does provide for one additional problem when used in civil actions. When offered in a civil action it is sufficient if the opportunity to develop the testimony was not actually by the party against whom it is now offered. It is sufficient was in the hands of a "predecessor in interest." That can arise, for example, where an initial party sells or transfers an interest to someone else. A party may own a claim against an opposing party. During earlier litigation, depositions or testimony is taken. After earlier decisions and appeals, it will be necessary to retry the case. During the interval, one of the parties transfers his or her interest to someone else. If the earlier testimony is offered against the new party, there must be a determination that the "predecessor in interest" had the similar opportunity and motive to develop that testimony.

c. Dying Declaration (b2)

The traditional common law name for this exception was the Dying Declaration. It is an exception that seems to be frequently discussed, but rarely used in trials. The modern Federal Rules of Evidence have renamed it a Statement under belief of impending belief. In addition to a name change, the Federal Rules of Evidence have made substantial changes in the rule. It is instructive to view the elements of the common law rule in order to understand the modern rule.

At common law, the rule was simple. There was an exception to the hearsay rule for statements made:

1. While the declarant was under the belief of impending death, and
2. The declarant had to die, and
3. The statement was concerning the cause of that death, and
4. The statement could only be used in a criminal action of homicide for the death of the declarant.

This common law rule was easy to apply. A person would have been the victim of a brutal assault and believe that he or she was about to die. Believing death to be coming, the victim might identify the attacker. When the victim dies and a criminal action for homicide brought, the victim's "dying declaration" could be introduced into evidence as an exception to the hearsay rule.

Fed. R. Evid. 804(b)(2) made substantial changes in the rule. The current elements are:

1. The declarant was under the belief of impending death, and
2. The declarant does not have to die, but must be unavailable to testify as defined in Fed. R. Evid. 804(a), and
3. The statement was concerning the cause or circumstances of what the declarant believed was his or her impending death, and
4. The statement can only be use in a criminal action of homicide for the death of the declarant or any civil action that may have arisen out of the circumstances that the declarant believed was his or her impending death.

The first element is, of course, the same. The declarant is under the belief of impending death. This usually occurs when something has happened and the victim believes he or she is about to die. The second element, however, is substantially different from the common law rule. There is no requirement that the declarant actually die. It is enough that the declarant be "unavailable." An easy example of this could occur if the victim was brutally beaten, but survives the beating. By the time a trial occurs, the victim is still physically unable to attend and testify. The third element is the same as the common law rule. The only portion of the statement that may be admitted is that portion that concerns the circumstances or the cause of the events that led the declarant to believe that he or she was about to die. The fourth element is, again, substantially different from the common law. If the declarant does die, the statement can, of course, be used in the homicide action. The rule indicates, however, that it may also be used in civil actions. This would allow, for example, the family of the declarant to use the statements in a wrongful death action brought to recover damages for the death of the declarant. There is, however, another use. Imagine, for example, that the declarant receives a brutal beating. While injured and believing that he or she is about to die, the victim identifies who did the beating. The victim does not die, and later sues for the injuries. By the time of trial, the victim is still too physically injured to attend. The statement could be introduced into the trial.

One of the difficult points of this exception is that the declarant must be under the belief of impending death. That means that hope of recovery needs to have been lost. If they declarant believes there is some possibility of recovery, the statement is not admissible. The declarant, however, does not need to speak any particular words to indicate the belief in impending death. Obviously, if the declarant said, "Believing that I'm about to die…, " that would be sufficient. It would also be sufficient if the declarant was in the process of saying goodbye to family and friends and dispersing belongs.

The reason for allowing this type of statement to be an exception to the hearsay rule is that there is a feeling that it has a strong indication of trustworthiness. It has always been felt that if someone felt he or she was about to die, they would try to be truthful in everything that was said. This was especially true of important and serious matters concerning who had been responsible for the impending death. It is the belief in impending death, therefore, that gives the exception the indication of trustworthiness. For this reason, evidence of that belief in impending death may be closely reviewed before allowing the statement to be introduced.

d. Statement Against Interest (b 3)

The Statement Against Interest, Fed. R. Evid. 804(b)(3), is one that may be confused with Admissions by a Party. In order to avoid that confusion, a review of Admissions by a Party should be conducted with close scrutiny applied to the details of that type of statement. The easiest difference to notice is that Admissions by a Party are statements that have been made by a party to the litigation. In addition, there is no requirement that the party knew the statement was against his or her interest when the statement was made. Statements Against Interest were made by other witnesses who now must be unavailable in order to use the exception. In addition, the declarant must have realized that the statement was against his or her interest when the statement was made. With that distinction, it is important to more closely view the elements of the exception.

The elements of this exception require that the statement be one that was so against the interest of the declarant at the time it was made that a person in the declarant's position would not have made the statement unless it was true. This is what gives this exception its indication of trustworthiness. The law has just assumed that people do not make serious statements against their own interest unless they believe the statement was true. It important that the declarant know the statement is against his or her own interest in order to give it that indication of trustworthiness.

The rule also indicates what types of statements may be considered statements against interest. They include:

1. Statements against the declarant's pecuniary interest, or
2. Statements against the declarant's proprietary interest, or
3. Statements tending to subject the declarant to civil liability, or
4. Statements tending to subject the declarant to criminal liability, or
5. Statement that would tend to render a claim invalid that the declarant may have against another.

Each of those types of against interest statement may be easily seen. The following list is merely a collection of some examples. A statement against a pecuniary interest would be one where the declarant admits to owing someone else money. A statement against a proprietary interest would be one where the declarant admits to not owning certain property. A statement that would subject the declarant to civil liability would be one admitting a tort or breach of contract. A statement that would subject the declarant to criminal liability would be one that confessed to a crime. A statement that would render a claim invalid might be one where the declarant admits that he or she has already been paid on a debt. As can be imagine, the variety of possible statements against interest is large. The possible uses of this exception are quite varied.

One further problem is raised by this exception to the hearsay rule. Imagine that person in jail admits to additional crimes. Later, when someone else is being tried for one of those crimes, the defendant would like to use the declarant's statement against interest as a way to exculpate him or herself from the crime. The problem with this type of statement is that the declarant who made it may have had reasons other than trustworthiness for making the statement. There may have been something to gain in jail society by appearing to have committed multiple crimes. In addition, the prisoner may be serving such a long sentence that there are no fears of further criminal actions. In such cases, the statement cannot be introduced to exculpate the defendant unless "corroborating circumstances clearly indicate the trustworthiness of the statement." Fed. R. Evid. 804(b)(3).

e. Personal or Family History (b 4)

It is assumed that when live testimony is not available, prior statements about a persons personal or family history are usually trustworthy. For this reason, Fed. R. Evid. 804(b)(4) provides an exception to the hearsay rule for such statements. The exception would allow admission of those statements from the unavailable witness where they deal with birth, adoption, marriage, divorce, legitimacy, relationships, and death.

f. Forfeiture by Wrongdoing (b 6)

A relatively new addition to the declarant unavailable exceptions to the hearsay rule is the one for Forfeiture by Wrongdoing, Fed. R. Evid. 804(b)(6). It is, in fact, founded on a different basis then the other exceptions. Each of the other exceptions is based on the idea that something about the statement gives it an indication of trustworthiness. This exception is based on the idea of waiver. It can occur where a possible witness has given statements concerning a matter. When it comes time for trial, that declarant is unavailable due to wrongdoing of the person against who the statement would have been offered. Imagine, for example, that witness to a crime has given statements to the police. By the time of trial, the defendant has either killed or had the witness killed. The prior statement of the declarant would be admissible.

3. Residual Exception (807)

When the drafters of the Federal Rules of Evidence were preparing the hearsay rule with exceptions, it was believed that they should not completely limit the future development of the exceptions. It was recognized that new, and presently unanticipated, circumstances could arise where a new exception should be created. In that spirit, the drafters added a "residual" exception. The theory behind this exception is that where the introduction of the statement was necessary and probably not available in other ways, there was something to be gained by allowing its introduction. Furthermore, if the evidence had some indication of trustworthiness that was similar to the trustworthiness found in other hearsay exceptions, then it should be admitted. Fed. R. Evid. 808. Federal Courts continue to expand the exceptions to the hearsay rule using this residual exception.

4. Hearsay Within Hearsay (805)

An interesting problem may arise when a hearsay statement contains additional hearsay statements. Imagine, for example, a hospital record. Ordinarily the records of a hospital record would be admissible under the exception for Records of Regularly Conducted Activity. On the hospital record, however, is a notation that on March 23, 2007, the patient said that he felt fine and had no pain. If that record was offered into evidence, the Records of Regularly Conducted Activity would allow admission of the hospital record generally, but there would be a question about the portion that reports the patient's statement. Patients are not part of the hospital and do not write statements into the record as a regular course of business. The statement, however, would be admissible as a statement of current state of mind or admission by a party. By combining the hearsay exceptions, the record, complete with statement, would be admissible. The Federal Rules of Evidence specifically allow this practice. "Hearsay included within hearsay is not excluded under the hearsay rule if each part of the combined statements conforms with an exception to the hearsay rule provided in these rules." Fed. R. Evid. 805.

5. Credibility of Declarant (806)

An issue that should be confronted with hearsay statements is the ability to attack the credibility of the statement. Although the exceptions to the hearsay rule allow the admission of such statements that does not relieve the statements of the possibility of attack. Once such a statement has been admitted, the credibility of the declarant, even those declarants that are not at the trial, are subject to attack. Fed. R. Evid. 806

E. Constitutional Issues with Hearsay

The constitutional issue that may arise with hearsay is the right of a criminal defendant to confront witnesses used against that defendant. This area of the law has received substantial attention from the United States Supreme Court and may be in a period of change. Attention must be directed to the most recent decisions in order to keep abreast of any ongoing changes.

Before analyzing the details of the current rules, it is probably easier to determine where the problem actually arises. In some ways, it is even easier to first determine where the problem does not exist. Criminal defendants in state court, through the 14th amendment and in federal court, through the 6th amendment, have the right to confront witnesses being used against them. This has been interpreted to include the right to place such witnesses under oath and allow for cross examination. This right applies to criminal defendants. There is not similar right to parties to a civil action. The issue of constitutional rights, the confrontation clause and the hearsay rules does not arise in civil cases. It is only an issue in criminal cases.

The courts have not extended the right to confrontation to the prosecution in a criminal case. The defendant has the right, but the prosecution does not.

The issue of confrontation clause only arises when the statement is hearsay and is being admitted. If the statement is hearsay and being excluded, there is no confrontation clause issue. In addition, if the statement is not hearsay and therefore being admitted, there is not a confrontation clause problem. The statement is not coming in to prove the truth of the matter asserted and is only coming in to show the statement was made. Any cross examination may be of the person who claims to have heard the statement.

The confrontation clause is also not raised when the statement was made by the defendant to the criminal case or by a witness who is there to testify. In both example, the person who made the statement is in the courtroom and can be cross examined about the statement.

With that discussion, it should be clear where the confrontation clause arises. It arises in criminal cases when the evidence is used against the defendant. It then only arises when the evidence is hearsay and being admitted under one of the exceptions. As a general rule, that means that Fed. R. Evid.

803 & 804 raise Constitutional issues when the evidence is used against a defendant in a criminal case.

The major decision in this area is *Crawford v. Washington*, 541 U.S. 36 (2004). In that case, the Supreme Court noted that the confrontation clause was a clear protection against generally using out of court statements against a defendant in a criminal case. The case should be closely read to determine the exact results offered by the Court. Some general comments may be made.

First, if the declarant is available in the trial and subject to cross examination, then there is no confrontation issue. Any statements that would be admissible could be cross examined in the trial. In addition, where the statement is not offered for the truth of the matter asserted, there is no confrontation problem. The statements may be admitted.

The critical distinction was found to be between "testimonial" and "nontestimonial" statements. If an out of court statement was "testimonial" in nature, it could not be admitted unless the criminal defendant had the opportunity at trial or at some early time to cross examine the declarant on the statement. Since the key element in this opinion is the meaning of the term "testimonial" it is important to try to figure out what that term means. Unfortunately, the Supreme Court did not give a clear definition. The Court did suggest some examples and ideas as to what was meant by "testimonial." It appears to include in court testimony, affidavits, custodial statements, depositions or the equivalent that would give the declarant the impression that the statements were being preserved for use at trial. Some specific examples of "testimonial" statements were also given. These examples included affidavits, testimony at preliminary hearings, testimony at former trials, testimony at grand juries, and statements to police in testimonial form.

It does appear that if the out of court statement is "non-testimonial" then a broader rule would apply. Using older cases, the Court would allow the admission of such statements as long as they continued to have some indication of trustworthiness. Typically, traditional and long recognized exceptions are thought to have this indication of trustworthiness.

One addition exception may require special note. It was suggested that due to a special history, the "dying declaration" exception may not raise confrontation clause issues.

It should be recognized that this area of the law of evidence is in a period of transition. The Most recent Supreme Court case was in 2004 and the law continues to change. Reviewing the most recent decisions will be necessary to determine the exact nature of the law.

Checkpoints

- To analyze a hearsay problem first determine whether the evidence is hearsay and, if it is, then look to see if there is an exception for it.

- The basic hearsay rule is that hearsay is not admissible unless there is some other rule that allows it to be introduced. Evidence that is not hearsay is admissible unless there is some other rule that excludes it.

- "Hearsay" is an out of court statement being offered into evidence in court that is being offered to prove the truth of the matter stated in the evidence.

- Statements offered to prove notice, state of mind, or verbal acts are not hearsay.

- Admissions of a party are not hearsay.

- Certain prior statements by a witness are not hearsay.

- Hearsay statements are admissible and the availability of the declarant is unavailable when the statement meets one of the listed exceptions.

- Hearsay statements are admissible when the declarant is unavailable when the statements meet the elements found under that provision of the hearsay rule.

- The confrontation clause of the United States constitution excludes hearsay statements from criminal trials, even when they meet an exception; if they are testimonial statements used against a criminal defendant and the defendant did not have the opportunity to cross examine the declarant on the statement either at the trial or at a prior time.

Chapter 9

Authentication and Proper Foundations

Authentication and Proper Foundations Roadmap

- Distinguish between real and demonstrative evidence.
- Determine the proper foundation that is necessary for evidence that is real and evidence that is demonstrative.
- Understand the importance of what is meant by "authenticating" evidence.
- Learn the basic techniques for authenticating the usual types of evidence that are offered in a trial.
- Learn the basic types of evidence that may be self-authenticating.

A. Introduction

As noted in other sections, the Authentication requirement is one that can arise in numerous cases. When a party to litigation seeks to introduce a document, there are, at least, three possible evidence issues that can arise. Those three issues are: Authentication, Hearsay, and the Best Evidence Rule. It is important to consider each of those when confronted with a document to determine whether document meets or violates those rules.

The Federal Rules of Evidence have a series of rules that assist with the problem of authentication and proper foundation. Some of the issues that arise with this problem, however, are not specifically covered in the rule. Attorneys will frequently speak of a distinction between "real" and "demonstrative" evidence. Those terms are not defined in the federal rules. In addition, the foundation requirement differs between those two types of evidence and those differences are not clearly identified in the rules. The background for this distinction is a part of the common law of evidence. The distinction must also be noted and understood before proceeding to the details of authentication that are covered in Fed. R. Evid. 901 and 902.

B. Real and Demonstrative Evidence

Most trials will have several types of evidence offered. Obviously, there will be testimonial evidence. Testimonial evidence is when a witness is seated on the witness stand and tells what they believe happened. In addition to testimony, the attorneys will want to introduce "things" into evidence. Those "things" may be documents, weapons used in crimes, drugs, photographs, maps, etc. Any "thing" that may be imagined may also be offered into evidence. It is important to first make the distinction between what "things" are "real" evidence and what "things" are "demonstrative" evidence.

Real evidence is an item that was actually a part of the events or circumstances that gave rise to the trial. Examples of such "real" evidence are easy to imagine. The gun or other weapon used in a crime is real evidence. Drugs that were part of a drug crime are real evidence. In civil cases, the product that is claimed to be defective is real evidence. Blood or other tissue samples in any type of case would also be real evidence. In each of these examples the basic requirement of offering a foundation to admit the evidence is the same. The party offering the evidence must prove a chain of custody. That means that the party offering the evidence must prove where the item has been and under what conditions it was kept from the time of the events that gave rise to the trial until the time it is offered into evidence. The purpose of such evidence is to show that the item is in a condition similar to the one it was in when the events originally occurred.

In criminal cases, it is the responsibility of the law enforcement agencies to make sure that real evidence collected at the crime scene is properly marked, stored and preserved until the date of trial. If there is any lapse in the "chain of custody" foundation, the evidence may be excluded from the trial. The attorney offering the evidence can be required to carefully examine a witness on exactly where and how the evidence was stored during the whole period.

In civil cases, the same problem exists. For injured plaintiffs, however, the reality of the situation is that frequently the real evidence is not properly preserved. A plaintiff injured by a product may find that the product was thrown away before anyone realized that litigation might be in the future. Even if the product was not thrown away, it may not have been stored and preserved in a manner that kept it in a condition similar to the one that caused the injury. In other civil cases, the parties just may not have collected physical evidence from an accident location. If there were serious injuries, the primary concern would have been to seek medical treatment. Real evidence of the events leading up to the accident may have been left unattended for months. Of course, evidence collected during medical treatment is usually preserved in a proper manner.

Again, once it is determined that the evidence sought to be offered is "real" evidence, the attorney offering the evidence must prove that "chain of custody." This is usually done by calling a witness that was the custodian of the evidence and having that witness slowly explain each step of the collection and storage process.

Demonstrative evidence is a different type of evidence. Demonstrative evidence was not part of the original event. This type of evidence is usually evidence prepared in preparation of trial that is intended to assist the trier of fact in understanding the events that occurred. Since demonstrative evidence was not part of the original events that gave rise to the litigation, there is not a chain of custody requirement. Instead, demonstrative evidence is merely intended to aid the jury in understanding the case. As such, the pieces of evidence being offered must be such that they accurately represent the issues they are intended to demonstrate.

An easy example of demonstrative evidence would be a model of an intersection being offered in a case that involves a traffic accident. The model is obviously not the actual scene where the accident took place. It is, therefore, demonstrative and not real evidence. The model, however, needs to be a fair and accurate representation of the actual scene of the accident. The witness that is on the stand when the model is introduced will be required to lay the proper foundation. Ordinarily this would begin by having the witness testify to some familiarity with the intersection that is the subject of the litigation. The witness would then be asked to look at the model and tell whether it was a fair and accurate representation of the intersection it was intended to depict.

Using such an example, it can be seen how the court would have to rule. If the model left out several important stop signs, then the model would not be admissible. It could not be an accurate representation of the scene.

Photographs can also be demonstrative evidence. Parties to litigation may return to a scene of an event and take photographs. Again, the basic foundation is that the photograph should be a fair and accurate representation of the scene it is intended to depict. If, for example, one of the parties claimed an intersection was overgrown with shrubs and the photograph was taken after the shrubs were cut down, the photo should probably be inadmissible.

Video tapes may also be made as re-enactments of events. These are also demonstrative evidence. They are not the real event taking place, but merely a representation of the facts as seen by one of the parties. The witness would need to testify that the video is an accurate representation of the testimony.

Photographs, however, are a difficult issue. A photograph or a video may also be real evidence. Most banks have security cameras that take a constant video tape of the area around the tellers. When a bank robbery occurs, the tape is pulled from the machine and used to identify the robbery. That video tape becomes an actual eye-witness to the crime. Such a photograph or video is treated more like real evidence. The party seeking to introduce the photograph or video should offer evidence of chain of custody. This would require showing how the cameras were set up, the tapes run and collected and then any development of the tape or photograph that was necessary. There is a further discussion of photographs below.

X-rays also create a similar problem. Courts are uncertain whether x-rays are real or demonstrative. X-rays are not the actual broken bones themselves, and, therefore, appear to be demonstrative evidence. X-rays, however, look very similar to the actual eye-witness security camera. In addition, because of the use by health care professionals courts frequently require expert testimony to lay a foundation for x-rays regardless of how they are treated. As such, x-rays look more like real evidence then demonstrative evidence. Expert testimony may be required to explain how the x-ray was taken and developed.

A modern type of demonstrative evidence is the computer generated video. With modern technology, parties can have computer experts generate movies to illustrate the events that are alleged to have occurred. This evidence will, in the first instance, require testimony that the scenes shown are accurate representations of the facts from the testimony. It may also be necessary to introduce some expert testimony as to how the scenes were generated.

As can be seen, demonstrative evidence may be limited only by the imagination of the attorney preparing the case. Attorneys may use photographs, documents, models, computer generated scenes or anything else that is available. The only foundation is that the demonstrative evidence is a fair and accurate representation of the facts.

There is, of course, one specific limit to demonstrative evidence. As discussed throughout this work, Fed. R. Evid. 403 provides that relevant evidence may be excluded if the probative value is substantially outweighed by the danger of undue prejudice. This provision allows courts to exclude demonstrative evidence if it is confusing, overly prejudicial or cumulative and a waste of time. Photographs frequently draw an objection based upon this provision. Opposing counsel will claim that photographs are cumulative or prejudicial. A good example of the issue can arise when particularly gruesome photographs showing the victim of a violent crime are offered into evidence in a criminal case where the defendant is charged with that crime. The defense attorney may object to the photographs as being overly prejudicial. Courts view this issue on a case by case basis. Fed. R. Evid. 403 only excludes the evidence if it is "unfairly" prejudicial. Evidence which accurately shows just how violent the crime was may harm the defendant, but that does not mean it is "unfairly" prejudicial. Such evidence may be admissible. Multiple similar photographs, however, may be excluded as being cumulative. Substantial discretion is vested in the trial judge to make this decision.

C. General Requirements of Authentication

The rule that demonstrative evidence must be shown to be an accurate depiction of the scene is part of the general rule of authentication. The law requires that all "things" being introduced into evidence first be identified with a proper foundation. That foundation is that the "thing" is what the party claim it is. Where a party seeks to show a photograph of an intersection, the law requires some evidence that the photograph is actually an accurate photograph of that particular intersection.

The chain of custody requirement for real evidence is also part of the general authentication rule. When a party seeks to offer a part of the actual event into a trial, there must be evidence that the "thing" was at the event and still in the same condition. This is exactly what the chain of custody evidence is designed to show.

By looking at those two examples, the basic rule for authentication becomes clear. In order to offer something into evidence, there must first be foundation evidence that the "thing" is what the party claims it is. The federal rules of evidence adopt this general rule in Fed. R. Evid. 901. "The requirement of authentication or identification as a condition precedent to admissibility is satisfied by evidence sufficient to support a finding that the matter in question is what its proponent claims."

Since the possible variety of "things" that may be offered into to evidence is quite large, the rule is stated in the broad general language. It allows the court to accept any type of evidence, tailored to the particular "thing" being offered, to allow the parties to lay a foundation.

The Federal Rules of Evidence, however, recognize that there are some items that are so routinely offered into evidence that some particular rules can be stated. The federal rules, therefore, provide some specific rules for authenticating the most common examples of "things" that are offered into evidence. The rules break these specifics down into two types. There are certain items that require the proof of foundation evidence to provide the foundation. Those are found in Fed. R. Evid. 901. Other types of evidence are held to be self-authenticating. Those are found in Fed. R. Evid. 902.

D. Most Common Examples (901)

In providing specific examples for authenticating certain types of evidence, the rules are not intended to be limited. The rules make it clear that the illustrations are "by way of illustration only, and not by way of limitation." Fed. R. Evid. 901(b). These examples and illustrations are merely types of evidence that are so common as to be subject to specific rules.

The first common example relates back to the broad general rule. Since the law requires that a foundation be provided that indicates that the "thing" being offered into evidence is what the parties claim it to be, the rules provide that a witness may give "testimony that a matter is what it is claimed to be." Fed. R. Evid. 901(b)(1). This may be the most common form of authentication. Before any item is offered into evidence a witness is asked to describe it. That would satisfy Fed. R. Evid. 901(b)(1). Other common examples receive a more detailed explanation.

1. Handwriting

It is a common issue in trials where one of the parties needs to authenticate handwriting. It may be raised by having to identify a signature or complicated by having to authenticate several written pages. The Federal Rules of Evidence provide several methods of authenticating handwriting.

Handwriting authentication is one of the areas where experts and non-experts may be called to testify. Non-experts may authenticate handwriting when that non-expert is able to state that he or she is sufficiently familiar with the handwriting as to have gained knowledge as to who wrote it. The only limitation on that testimony is that the non-expert must have gained the familiarity with the handwriting at a time other then in preparation for trial. Fed. R. Evid. 901(b)(2). Examples of this type of gaining familiarity can be easily seen. A non-expert may have seen the handwriting of a particular persons on numerous occasions. The non-expert may have seen the person sign documents or even exchanged letters over a period of time. If that has been the case, the non-expert has gained familiarity with the handwriting before the preparation for litigation began. That non-expert may review a challenged document and offer evidence as to who the writer of the document is.

Experts may also offer evidence as to the authenticity of handwriting. Fed. R. Evid.901(b)(3). In using an expert, the expert will be shown examples of handwriting which are clearly identified as to who wrote them. The expert will then be offered the challenged document and be allowed to offer an opinion as to the identity of the writer. Since the rule assumes that an expert will be used, it is, of course, necessary to "qualify" the expert. The attorney offering the expert opinion will have to have the witness go over the background of the expertise in handwriting identification that has been gain.

The Federal Rules of Evidence also assume that the trier of fact may make some comparisons as to the authenticity of handwriting. Fed. R. Evid. 901(b)(3) allows "Comparison by the trier of fact ... with specimens which have been authenticated." Much like the use of experts, the attorney wanting to identify the writer of handwriting will first introduce samples the authenticity of which have already been found. The challenged handwriting will then be introduced into evidence. The trier of fact, usually the jury, will then be allowed to compare the challenged handwriting with those that have already been authenticated and reach their own conclusions as to whether the challenged handwriting is authentic.

Another method of authenticating a letter, whether it is handwritten or not, comes from the common law. This method is called the Reply Letter Doctrine and it is recognized as permissible under Fed. R. Evid. 901(b)(4). It will arise when a party has received a letter through the mail and wants to authenticate it during a trial. The party against whom it is offered denies having sent the letter. In order to use the Reply Letter Doctrine, the party wishing to use it must start by authenticating an original letter that was sent to the opposing party. Imagine, for example, that the party offering the letters mailed a letter to the opposing party that made an offer to create a contract. The party that sent this letter will offer a copy of it into evidence as the offer letter. Several weeks after sending the offer letter, the party received a letter in "reply" that mentions the details of the offer and accepts it. This is the letter that the opposing party challenges. The "Reply Letter Doctrine" will allow the introduction of this challenged letter. As noted in the Advisory Committee notes, "a letter may be authenticated by content and circumstances indicating it was in reply to a duly authenticated one." Fed. R. Evid. 901(b)(4), Advisory Committee notes.

2. Voice

Voice identification and authentication may also frequently arise in trials. A party may need to authenticate a voice that was heard. Much like the handwriting, the Federal Rules of Evidence allow authentication of a voice by non-experts. Fed. R. Evid. 901(b)(5). The rules only require that the witness gained knowledge of the voice "upon hearing the voice at any time under circumstances connecting it with the alleged speaker." Fed. R. Evid. 901(b)(5).

It is important to note that the rules provide that voice authentication can be based upon hearing the voice firsthand or through electronic means. That issue can arise in trials in numerous ways. The voice being authenticated may have been heard firsthand, on a recording, or through a telephone. If the witness is able to identify the speaker, then this method of authentication will be allowed.

There are obviously times, however, when voices over a telephone cannot be authenticated by voice recognition. The party seeking to authenticate a voice heard over the telephone may not have spoken to the person before or may not have recognized the voice due to the shortcomings of the telephonic transmission. One simple method of telephone voice authentication cannot be used alone. The party wanting to authenticate the voice on a telephone cannot base the authentication on the single fact that the person on the other end of the line identified himself or herself. Imagine, for example, that a party wants to testify that he or she received a phone call. Upon picking up the phone, the voice on the other end identified himself as the President of the United States and offered the listener an important job in Washington, D.C. More than likely, that was a practical joke. Mere self identification is not enough evidence for authentication of a voice on a telephone call. "The cases are in agreement that a mere assertion of his identity by a person talking on the telephone is not sufficient evidence of the authenticity of the conversation and that additional evidence of his identity is required." Fed. R. Evid. 901(b)(6), Advisory Committee notes. The rules do provide, however, other means of authentication of telephone calls.

A party may authenticate a telephone call by showing that the call was made to a number that had been assigned to a person and when the other person answered the circumstances of the conversation indicate that the person was the one called. Fed. R. Evid. 901(b)(6)(A). This allows some degree of discretion. The circumstances could be that the conversation was about matters that the person on the other end of the line would have known about. The rule also allows self identification to be a circumstance that may be used under this rule. To see an example, consider these facts. A party notices an ad in the paper by an individual named John seeking to sell a used car. The party calls the number assigned to John and when the phone is answered, the person says, "John here." The party making the call then asks about the used car. The person on the other end of the line describes the car and quotes a price. The party making the call then accepts the offer. Later when John is sued for failing to deliver the car and also claims that he never offered to sell it, the circumstances of the call can be used to authenticate John's voice. The call was made to the number assigned to John. John "self identified" himself. The call discussed matters that John would be familiar with.

Another method of telephone authentication arises when a party makes a call to a business and uses the phone number that is assigned to that business. Once the phone is answered, the call may be authenticated if the conversation is "related to business reasonably transacted over the telephone." Fed. R. Evid. 901(b)(6)(B). This example can also be easily seen. A party calls a number assigned to an Automobile Oil Change business. When the phone is answered, the party asks about the prices of oil changes. The person on the other end of the line says, "We are running a special. All oil changes are only $10.99 today." When the party goes to the Automobile Oil Change business that day and the phone call is denied, the party can use this rule to authenticate the call. The call was made to the number assigned to the business and the conversation concerned matters that would reasonably be discussed by that business.

Notice that the special telephone authentication rules under Fed. R. Evid. 901(b)(6) can only be used when the party seeking to authenticate the call is the one who initiated the call. If the party seeking to authenticate the call was the one who received the call, this rule may not be used to authenticate it. In order to authenticate a call that was received, ordinarily the party will have to rely on being able to recognize the voice.

There is one additional way of authenticating a telephone call other then those described. Under Fed R. Evid. 901(b)(4), the party seeking to authenticate a telephone call, whether one made or received, may do so by showing distinctive characteristics. The Advisory Committee notes use the example of a "telephone conversation may be shown to have emanated fro a particular person by virtue of its disclosing knowledge of facts known peculiarly to him." Fed. R. Evid. 901(b)(4), Advisory Committee notes.

3. Photos and Videos

As discussed in the earlier parts of this chapter on real and demonstrative evidence, photograph and videos must be authenticated. The discussion earlier covers the basic problems with those types of evidence. The Federal Rules of Evidence do not supply a specific rule for photos and videos. They would fall under the general requirement that evidence must be authenticated and that testimony that the item is what it is claimed to be is sufficient. Fed. R. Evid. 901(b)(1). It is not, for example, necessary to bring in the photographer to authenticate a photo or video. The photographer would obviously be able to authenticate such evidence but his or her testimony is not necessary. Anyone that can testify that the photo or video accurately reflects the scene it is intended to depict can authenticate the evidence.

4. Other Examples

The types of evidence discussed above are the most common examples found in litigation. The Federal Rules of Evidence, however, provide specific rules for four additional types of evidence.

When a party seeks to introduce a copy of the public record, evidence that the record was found to be filed in the place where such records are stored is sufficient authentication. Fed. R. Evid. 901(b)(7). Interestingly enough, this method of proving public documents is not ordinarily used. In the material discussed below in this chapter, it is clear that many public documents are "self authenticating."

At common law, there was a special authentication rule known as the "Ancient Documents" rule. This rule has been adopted by the Federal Rules of Evidence. If a document is free from suspicion on its face, was found stored in a place where such documents would be found, and the document has been in existence for over twenty years, then it is declared to be authenticated. Fed. R. Evid. 901(b)(8). It is interesting to note that the traditional common law rule required the document to be 30 years old or older. The drafter of the Federal Rules of Evidence just chose the shorter period. It is also interesting that by meeting the Ancient Documents Rule for authentication, statements in the document will be held to be an exception to the hearsay rule. Fed. R. Evid. 803(16).

With the advent of modern technology, the Federal Rules of Evidence have added a special authentication method. Where data is produced by a "process or system," evidence showing that the process or system will produce accurate data is sufficient to authenticate the evidence.

The Federal Rules of Evidence also supply a "catch-all" authentication rule to allow authentication by "any method ... provided by Act of Congress or by other rules prescribed by the Supreme Court." Fed. R. Evid. 901(b)(10). It is interesting that the drafters of the rules thought that this "catch-all" was necessary. The beginning of the Illustrations in Fed. R. Evid. 901(b) make it clear that the illustrations are examples only and not a limitation on the available methods of authentication. Any other methods of authentication, even those not stated in Fed. R. Evid. 901(b), should be allowed. The Advisory Committee notes indicate that the reason for this "catch-all" was to make sure that it was clear that other forms of authentication enacted Congress or prescribed by the Supreme Court would not be held to be superseded. Fed. R. Evid. 901(b)(10), Advisory Committee notes.

E. Self Authentication (902)

Some evidence is held to be "self authenticating." This evidence is general the type found in public records or certified documents. The underlying theory is that the certification found on the document was placed on the document by one with knowledge and under responsibility of law to assure accuracy. Fed. R. Evid. 902 provides the rules that deal with the Self Authenticating documents.

The most commonly used self authenticating document is the certified copy of the public record. When a party needs to introduce a copy of the public record, the rules allow the certification on the document to authenticate it. Fed. R. Evid.902(4). The reason for such a rule is obvious. If the courts required testimony to authenticate such a document, the custodians of public records would be spending a substantial amount of time testifying in trials merely for the purpose of authenticating documents. In addition, the custodians of public records are required by law to maintain some degree of accuracy of the records. The formal certification of such documents is sufficient for authentication.

Similar authentication is allowed for Domestic documents under seal, Fed. R. Evid. 902(1), Domestic documents not under seal, Fed. R. Evid, 902(2), and Foreign documents under seal, Fed. R. Evid. 902(3). The formalities of maintaining those documents and producing them are considered sufficient for authentication.

The rules also allow self authentication for business and professional documents. Official publications, Fed. R. Evid. 902(5), Newspapers and periodicals, Fed. R. Evid, 902(6), Trade Inscriptions, Fed. R. Evid. 902(7), Acknowledged documents, Fed. R. Evid. 902(8), Commercial paper, Fed. R. Evid. 902(9), Certified domestic business records, Fed. R. Evid 902(11), and Certified foreign business records, Fed. R. Evid. 902(12) are considered self authenticating

Finally, the rules of self authentication also have a "catch-all" provision. "Any signature, document, or other matter declared by Act of Congress to be presumptively or primae facie genuine or authentic" is considered self authenticating. Fed. R. Evid. 902(10).

Checkpoints

- Real evidence is that evidence that was actually a part of the events leading up to the trial. Demonstrative evidence are those items prepared for the trial that help explain the facts being presented.

- Real evidence requires the proof of the "chain of custody."

- Demonstrative evidence requires some evidence that the item being presented accurately reflects the information it is suppose to support.

- Authentication of evidence may be by evidence to show it is what it is claimed to be, or it may be self authenticating.

- Handwriting may be authenticated by a lay person with knowledge not gained in preparation for litigation, by distinctive characteristics, by an expert, or by the trier of fact in comparison with a known sample.

- A voice may be identified by anyone who claims knowledge of the voice.

- Telephone conversations may be identified in several ways: a. through voice identification; b. a call was made to the number assigned to a person or business and the circumstances, including self identification, indicate it was that person or business; c. a call was made to a number assigned to a business and the conversation was related to that business.

- Public records may be authenticated by showing they were found in the office where such public records were kept.

- Old documents may be authenticated by showing that there is nothing on the face to cast suspicion on the document; it was found in a place that such documents would be found; and it was 20 years or more old.

- Evidence generated by a process or system may be authenticated by showing that such a process or system generates accurate information.

- Other items may be authenticated as prescribed by acts of congress or rules of the Supreme Court.

- Certain documents may be held to be self-authenticated. These include: a. documents under seal; b. foreign public documents; c. certified copies of . public records and other similar documents.

Chapter 10

Best Evidence Rule

Best Evidence Rule Roadmap

- Understand the limited application of the best evidence rule.
- Analyze the definitions of original and duplicate.
- Learn the exceptions to the best evidence rule.

A. Introduction

The "Best Evidence Rule" is a traditional, common law rule that continues to be recognized in the law of evidence. It would have been easier to apply in the distant past, and would have been of greater importance. With the modern explosion of technology, the rule is much more difficulty to use. This is one area of evidence law that may be subject to change in the future. As noted in other sections, the Best Evidence Rule is one that can arise in numerous cases. When a party to litigation seeks to introduce a document, there are, at least, three possible evidence issues that can arise. Those three issues are: Authentication, Hearsay, and the Best Evidence Rule. It is important to consider each of those when confronted with a document to determine whether document meets or violates those rules.

B. The Best Evidence Rule (1002)

The Best Evidence Rule itself is fairly easy to state. As enacted in Fed. R. Evid. 1002, the rule is, "To prove the content of a writing, recording, or photograph, the original writing, recording, or photograph is required, except as otherwise provided in these rules or by Act of Congress." That simple statement must be closely examined in order to avoid confusion in application.

The most common use of the rule is in proof of the contents of written documents. As indicated, where the contents of that document are the item to be proven, the original of the document is required. Where, for example, the parties to contract litigation disagree over the terms of the contract, the original of that contract should be introduced into evidence to prove that content. One party may claim that the contract allowed three months for completion while the other party claims that the contract only allowed two months. For a written contract that has a specific clause that tells when the contract was to be completed, the original of the contract would have to be introduced.

The reasons stated for this rule have varied over the years. Some suggested that the rule was designed to avoid fraud. A fraudulent party may seek to avoid the true content of a contract by offering false testimony as to what was agreed. Others have suggested that problems arise even in the absence of fraud. Where there is a writing that expresses some agreement, oral testimony based on memory may just be in error. The writing would provide the "Best Evidence." Regardless of the reason for the rule, where the content of the document is the issue in the case, the original is required by the rule.

The scope of the rule appears broad. It mentions that the original is required when proving the content of a writing, recording or photograph. The rule is most commonly used with writings. A routine part of every civil and criminal trial is the presentation of documentary evidence. Usually the content of that written document is the issue. This may occur whether the trial is a civil trial contesting the terms of a written contract or a white collar criminal trial concerning some type of corporate fraud. Where the content of the document is important, the original must be produced.

The rule also states that the original of a recording or photograph must be produced where the content of the recording or photograph is at issue. It is true that photographs and recordings are presented as evidence in many trials. Frequently, however, the use of recordings and photographs does not concern the content of the item being introduced. Photographs, for example, are frequently introduced as mere demonstrative evidence to aid the understanding of the jury. The actual content of the photograph is not at issue. A good example might be a civil trial for a traffic accident. The parties testify as to what the accident location looked like on the day of the accident. During the testimony of one of the witnesses, an attorney seeks to introduce a photograph taken of the accident location some time later. The evidence is not being offered to prove the content of the photograph. The photograph is merely being offered as an aid. Rather than having to introduce an original, the foundation is merely some evidence that the photograph accurately represents the scene it is intended to depict. In addition, the mere fact that photographs of the scene happen to exist, does not prevent witnesses from giving oral testimony of what they saw. Again, it is important to note that the Best Evidence Rule only applies when the content of the writing, recording, or photograph is at issue.

There are times when the content of a photograph may raise the Best Evidence Rule. Where, for example, the prosecution in a criminal case seeks to use the video of a hidden camera that caught the commission of the crime, the Best Evidence Rule will apply. There are no witnesses to the crime. The video tape provides independent evidence of that crime. It is the content of that video that is at issue in the case. The prosecution would have to produce the original.

With the discussion of the important of identifying when the contents are at issue, it must be realized that the same problem exists with writings. The original of a writing is only required when the contents of that writing are at issue. As noted above, that may frequently be the case when the terms of a contract are disputed. The original of the contract must be introduced. There are times, however, when the content of the writing is not the major issue. A case could arise where a party denies having received notice. Opposing parties wish to introduce a copy of a letter sent giving notice. The content of the letter may not be at issue. The only question to be answered was whether the letter was sent. The original would not be required. In a criminal case, a party may be charged with stealing stock, bonds or negotiable instruments. The prosecution might want to introduce copies of the items that were stolen. There would be no issue as to the content of the documents, only a question as to whether the documents existed.

Another common problem that arises when discussing the "content" issue is when a discussion or event is recorded. A case could arise over a dispute about agreements reached during meetings. Meetings are frequently recorded or result in minutes being kept. If the case revolves around the actual agreements, then the writings or recordings that transcribed those agreements are not required under the Best Evidence Rule. The case is not concerned with the contents of the recording or writing, but the terms of the actual agreement.

It is important to note yet another difficulty. After the above discussion, it is clear that the rule only applies to writings, recordings or photographs. It does not apply to physical objects. Where, for example, the parties to a civil case over an automobile accident are in dispute as to the full extent of the damage to the automobile, some might suggest that producing the original of the damaged automobile in court would be a good idea. That idea is obviously absurd by its very statement. Parties to an automobile accident do not have to introduce the original automobile. The same is true of criminal cases. The parties do not have to introduce the original of items stolen. The rule does not apply to physical objects.

There may be a difficulty, however, with the exclusion of physical objects from the rule. There are times when physical objects are inscribed with information. Where the content of that information is the fact to be proven, having the original of that object would ensure accurate determination of that inscription. A party, for example, may want to identify a police officer by the number on the officer's badge. The badge is a physical object, but the number looks like a writing. Courts are less consistent in dealing with this issue. Jurisdictions are inclined to allow some discretion based upon the need for accuracy, the ability to get the item into court, and the complexity of the inscription. Courts are also likely to refer to such inscriptions as "collateral" to the issues actually before the court.

In short, the initial question that is always posed when thinking about the Best Evidence Rule is a simple one. Is evidence being offered about a writing, recording or photograph that seeks to prove the content of that writing, recording or photograph? If so, then the original of that writing, recording or photograph must be introduced. If some other issue is sought to be proven, then the original is not required.

C. Originals, Duplicates and Copies (1001, 1003)

Since the Best Evidence Rule places importance of submission of an original, questions of definitions arise. Obviously, it is important to know what an "original" is. An original is the item itself or any "counterpart intended to have the same effect by the person executing or issuing it." Fed. R. Evid. 1001(3).

Looking at examples that may arise in a case, it is possible to imagine application of the concept of original. Clearly if someone sent a letter offering to sell a car, the letter that was sent would be the original for purposes of proving the content of the offer. The letter that would be mailed in return to accept the offer would be the original of the acceptance. If two people got together, wrote up a contract and then both parties signed the contract; that contract would be the original for purposes of proving the content of the contract. All of those examples are easy to imagine since they represent the writing itself. Imagine, however, that two people get together to enter into a contract. They make up two identical copies of the contract. Both parties sign both copies of the contract in order for both parties to each have a signed copy. Although they look like "copies," they are, in fact, both "originals." They would both be counterparts "intended to have the same effect" as an original. If, of course, the parties just signed one copy that signed copy would be the original and the unsigned copy would be the "copy."

With the advent of computers and electronic data bases, the definition of original gets more difficult. The definition of original includes the idea that "if data are stored in a computer or similar device, any printout or other output readable by sight, shown to reflect the data accurately, is an 'original.'" Fed. R. Evid. 1001(3). Parties to litigation may have stored substantial data, spreadsheets, or information in a computer program. If the content of such information is at issue, any printout of that information would be recognized as the original.

The rules of evidence recognize another classification for this area of the law. Some items may not be "originals" but may be recognized as "duplicates." The term duplicate is defined by the rules of evidence as "a counterpart produced by the same impression as the original, or from the same matrix, or by means of photography, including enlargements and miniatures, or by mechanical or electronic re-recording, or by chemical reproduction or by other equivalent technique which accurately reproduces the original." Fed. R. Evid. 1001(4).

The concept of "duplicate" arose with some older technology. In a time before computers, legal work would be typed on a manual typewriter. If there was an interest in having multiple copies of a document, the typist would use multiple sheets of paper with carbon paper in between the typing sheets. When the document was finished, there would be one document that appeared to be the original and then multiple documents that were produced by the carbon paper. The "carbon copies" would be identical to and produced by the same keystrokes that produced the original. These "carbon copies" are "duplicates" and not copies.

Looking at the terms "original" and "duplicate," some examples may be studied. Parties to a contract may have a typist produce the original and 4 "carbons" when a contract is being typed. If the parties only sign and execute the original then it is the only original for purposes of the Best Evidence Rule. The "carbons" are considered duplicates. If, however, the parties decide to sign and execute the original and 2 of the "carbons," then the original and the 2 executed "carbons" are all originals. They would be called originals since there were all executed by the parties and intended to have the same effect as originals. The unexecuted "carbons" would be considered duplicates. The same analysis would apply with the modern use of photocopy machines. Imagine that the typist prepares a contract on a computer and prints out one copy of it. They typist then takes the contract and runs 4 additional copies on the photocopy machine. When it is time to sign the contract, the parties sign and execute the contract that was typed and 2 of the photocopies. Under that situation, all of the copies that were signed and executed would be originals and the remaining unsigned documents would be duplicates.

It is important to understand the definition of duplicate because such documents are at an increased priority. When the contents of a document are at issue, the law requires the use of originals. A duplicate, however, may be used as an original "unless (1) a genuine question is raised as to the authenticity of the original or (2) in the circumstances it would be unfair to admit the duplicate in lieu of the original."

The two exceptions to the use of duplicates are designed to make sure that accurate information is received into court. The first exception will exclude the duplicate if a genuine question is raised as to the authenticity of the document. An opposing party, for example, may claim that changes have been made to a document and the duplicate is not accurate. General unfairness, the second exception, allows the court to continue to require the production of the original if the duplicate is considered not appropriate.

It is important to carefully understand the concepts of "original" and "duplicate." Those terms are narrowly defined and must be accurately used. Once the meaning of those two terms is understood, it can be simply stated that all other evidence of the content of a document is considered a "copy." In discussing, using and analyzing the Best Evidence Rule, the terms "original," "duplicate," and "copy" must be accurately used.

D. Exceptions (1004)

There are times when the original is just not available. It may also be true that there are no duplicates. Under those circumstances, the party needing to prove the contents of a writing, recording or photograph would have a substantial deficiency with his or her case. The federal rules of evidence do supply a few exceptions that allow the proof of the contents of such a document without the availability of the original.

If the item was lost or destroyed, that is a sufficient excuse to allow the proof of the contents of the document without the production of the original. Fed. R. Evid. 1004(1). The only limitation on that exception is the loss or destruction cannot have been due to the bad faith of the person who seeks to prove the contents. The person seeking to prove the contents without the original being present would need to offer some foundation as to the absence of bad faith.

Another exception allows the proof of the contents of the item by evidence other than the original if the original cannot be obtained by judicial process, Fed. R. Evid 1004(2). When the proponent of the evidence seeks to use this excuse, some additional foundation is also required. The proponent should offer evidence of trying to trace the original into the hands of some particular person and then seeking to obtain that item through judicial process. As suggested in the Advisory Committee notes, showing the attempt to obtain the original by use of a subpoena duces tecum as a part of taking a deposition in another jurisdiction would be adequate. Advisory Committee notes, Fed. R. Evid. 1004(2).

Another excuse arises when the original was in the hands of an opposing party. "At the time when the original was under the control of the party against whom offered, that party was put on notice by the pleadings or otherwise that the contents would be a subject of proof at the hearing, and that party does not produce the original at the hearing. Fed. R. Evid. 1004(3). This exception assumes that the opposing party once had the original and now is unable or unwilling to produce it. The "notice' requirement is not a formal requirement of attempting to obtain the document as indicated in Fed. R. Evid. 1004(2). This notice requirement assumes that any notice that would have alerted party holding the document to the importance of maintaining it is enough.

Finally, the rule allows the proof of the contents of the document when the document is merely collateral and not closely related to the controlling issue. Fed. R. Evid. 1004(4). Even the Advisory Committee notes admit that this excuse is difficult to clearly define. It will, in many cases, depend on the circumstances. The Advisory Committee notes give two examples. The newspaper in an action for the price of an advertisement. The streetcar transfer in a case where the plaintiff claims to be a passenger. Advisory Committee notes, Fed. R. Evid. 104(4).

Since there are times when the original is not required, the question has arisen as to what is the appropriate form of proof in those instances. Some jurisdictions recognize what could be called the "Next Best Evidence" rule or the "Second Best Evidence" rule. Such a rule would require that, when the original is not available, the party must prove the contents with a written copy. If a written copy is not available, the party must first show one of the specified exceptional circumstances before being allowed to rely on oral testimony. The federal rules of evidence do not adopt the degrees of secondary evidence rules. Once the party is able to show a sufficient foundation to excuse the proof of the original, the party is allowed to prove the contents by any evidence that is available. This can include oral testimony.

E. Summaries and Other Methods of Proof (1005, 1006, 1007, 1008)

There are times when the original is not available or too difficult to produce. To a certain extent, the rapid pace of technological advances may be responsible for some of those difficulties. The rules provide a series of special provisions to deal with difficult circumstances.

Public records are frequently important to the trial of a lawsuit. Where the content of that public record is at issue, a copy of that record in a form that would satisfy the rules of Authentication as specified in Fed. R. Evid. 902, will also satisfy the Best Evidence Rule. In addition, it is permissible to have a witness testify that he or she has compared the copy to the public record and the copy is correct. Fed. R. Evid. 1005.

There are times in modern litigation when the amount documentary evidence is huge. Under those circumstances, the party seeking to show the contents of those documents may offer summaries or charts. When that is allowed, the party offering the summaries or charts must make the originals available to the opposing parties for the purposes of inspection and copying. Fed. R. Evid 1006.

The rules also provide that the contents of such evidence may be proven by the "testimony or deposition of the party against whom offered or by that party's written admission." Fed. R. Evid. 1007. If the opposing party has admitted the contents, then the production of the original is not required.

Finally, there are some important questions of law and fact that must be understood. The federal rules of evidence provide a specific provision to regulate the decision making authority between the judge and jury on the issues surrounding the best evidence. When the admissibility of the contents of originals or copies is in dispute, any factual problems surrounding that admissibility is for the trial judge. Fed. R. Evid. 1008. Examples of that should be easy to imagine. When a party wishes to introduce the contents of a document by oral testimony and claims that the document was lost or destroyed but not in bad faith, that raises an admissibility question. Although there will be factual questions to answer as to why the document was lost, those questions must be answered by the trial judge as would any other questions of admissibility under Fed. R. Evid. 104. There are, however, clear questions of fact for the jury.

When there is a question about whether the original ever existed, that is a question for the jury. Fed. R. Evid. 1008. If there is a claim that two documents, offered by the two parties, are both the originals, then deciding which is the original is a question for the jury. Fed. R. Evid. 1008. When a party has been allowed to introduce evidence of the content in a manner other than using the original and there is a challenge that the evidence correctly reflects the content of the original, that question is to be decided by the jury. Fed. R. Evid. 1008.

Checkpoints

- The best evidence rule only applies when a party seeks to prove the contents of a writing, recording or photograph.

- The best evidence rule requires that the original be produced when the party wishes to prove the contents of that writing, recording or photograph.

- The original is the item itself or any counterpart intended to have the same effect as the original.

- If information is stored in digital form or in a computer, then any print out is an original.

- Duplicates can be admitted like originals unless there is some genuine challenge as to the authenticity.

- Duplicates are counterparts produced by the same impression, matrix, keystroke or photography of the original.

- The production of the original may be excused if the original:

  - was lost or destroyed but not in bad faith;

  - cannot be obtained by legal process;

  - the original is in the hands of the other party;

  - the contents of the original is merely a collateral issue.

Mastering Evidence Checklist

The following reflects the topics covered in each chapter. A good understanding of the overall material would require a detailed knowledge of each of these topics.

Chapter 1 · Roles of the Court, Judge, Jury and Attorneys in Light of Rules of Evidence
❑ The individual stages of a trial
❑ The applicable courts and other forums in which the Federal Rules of Evidence are used
❑ The techniques for making and meeting objections
❑ The role of the judge and attorneys during the course of litigation
❑ Several common objections

Chapter 2 · Judicial Notice
❑ Distinguish legislative from adjudicative facts
❑ The limitations on judicial notice of adjudicative facts
❑ Procedural rules for use in judicial notice
❑ Jury views and jury knowledge

Chapter 3 · Burdens of Proof and Presumptions
❑ Burden of production and the burden of persuasion
❑ Burdens of proof in civil cases
❑ Presumptions and inferences in civil cases
❑ Burdens of proof in criminal cases
❑ Presumptions and inferences in criminal cases

Chapter 4 · Relevance
❑ Basic definitions concerning relevance and the older term materiality
❑ Basic relevance rule
❑ Character evidence used to prove propensity to commit an act
❑ Habit
❑ Subsequent remedial measures
❑ Offers of settlement and compromise in civil and criminal cases

❏ Insurance issues
❏ Rape shield law
❏ Evidence of other sexual crimes

Chapter 5 · Privileges
❏ Federal rules on privileges
❏ Some common privileges that are used

Chapter 6 · Witnesses, Testimony, and Credibility
❏ Issues of competency to testify including the oath and first hand knowledge
❏ Impeachment by bias
❏ Impeachment by capacity
❏ Impeachment by character
❏ Impeachment by prior crimes
❏ Impeachment by prior inconsistent statements
❏ Rehabilitation and refreshing memory
❏ Presentation of evidence and control by the trial judge
❏ Sequestration of witnesses

Chapter 7 · Opinion Evidence and Expert Witnesses
❏ Opinion evidence by law witnesses
❏ Qualifications of experts
❏ Basis of underlying science for expert testimony
❏ Form of questions for introduction of opinion evidence
❏ Ultimate issues

Chapter 8 · Hearsay and Exceptions
❏ Basic rule for hearsay
❏ Basic definitions for "what is hearsay?"
❏ Evidence defined by the rules as not being hearsay
❏ Exceptions where the availability of declarant is immaterial
❏ Exceptions where the declarant must be shown to be unavailable
❏ Constitutional issues, the confrontation clause and hearsay

Chapter 9 · Authentication and Proper Foundation
❏ General rule of authentication
❏ Real and demonstrative evidence
❏ Common examples of foundation for authentication
❏ Rules for self-authenticating

Chapter 10 · Best Evidence Rule
❏ Basic best evidence rule

❏ Definitions required for understanding best evidence rule
❏ Exceptions to best evidence rule

About the Author

Ronald W. Eades received a B.A. in English Literature from Rhodes College, a J.D. from the University of Memphis, and an LL.M. from Harvard Law School. Before joining the University of Louisville law faculty in 1977, he was a staff attorney with the Tennessee Valley Authority. He teaches primarily in the torts and evidence area. Eades received the University's Outstanding Teacher Award in 1991 and was named the inaugural James R. Merritt Fellow in the 1994–95 academic year. His interest in technology combined with the tort law field led to his selection as a CALI Fellow in Tort Law for 2001. That fellowship allowed him to work with other senior tort scholars from around the country to write student materials for use with computers for the Center for Computer Assisted Legal Instruction. Since that time, Eades has been selected to be a member of the CALI Editorial Board and the CALI Board of Directors.

Eades's research interests have tracked his teaching interest. He is the author of a multi-volume set of Jury Instruction books for use on a national level. In addition, he has a series of books on Kentucky law for Kentucky lawyers. His interest in the practical application of the legal theory has led to his appointment, by the Kentucky Supreme Court, to a four-year term to the Kentucky Commission on Rules of Evidence. In recognition of excellence in research, Eades was named a Distinguished University Scholar in 1996.

Eades also has an interest in international issues. He has been a visiting faculty member at the University of Leeds in Leeds, England; the Johannes Gutenberg Universitat in Mainz, Germany; and the University of Turku, in Turku, Finland. In 2001, Eades was named to the Fulbright Senior Specialist list.

Index